THE BIG SMALL STORIES

Contents

Introduction	01	Denise McBay	89 – 94
Foreword by Cecil Linehan MBE	02 – 03	Terry McMackin	96 – 99
THE STORIES OF:		Tony Macaulay	101 – 106
Clare Bailey	05 – 09	Stuart Marriott	108 – 113
Eric Bullick	11 – 16	Roisin Marshall	115 – 123
Aurora Cacharro	18 – 21	Jason Milligan	125 – 128
Noreen Campbell	23 – 28	Denise Morgan	130 – 138
Colm and Anne Cavanagh and Bernie and Tim Webster	29 – 40	Anne Odling-Smee	140 – 144
		Mary Roulston	146 – 155
Norah Connolly	42 – 45	Lawrence Rowan	157 – 162
Grace Doone	47 – 53	Alan Smith	164 – 173
Olwen Griffith	55 – 60	Jane Stewart	175 – 179
Kevin Lambe	62 – 70	Michael Wardlow	181 – 193
Errol Lemon	72 – 79		
Lorna McAlpine	81 – 87	A History in Pictures	194 – 197

L to R – Founder Members of All Children Together (ACT): the late Thelma Sheil; Brian Garrett, ACT Solicitor; Dr. Jonathan Bardon, author of ACT history; Cecil Linehan, Margaret Kennedy & the late Bill Brown, all three Founder Members of ACT. Pictured at the launch of "The Struggle for Shared Schools in Northern Ireland" the story of All Children Together in 2010. This book tells the story of All Children Together, the founders of the first integrated school in Northern Ireland, Lagan College, founded in 1981.

ISBN: 978-1-78926-883-6

Published by the Northern Ireland Council for Integrated Education, 2018

Printed by GPS Colour Graphics Ltd, Belfast

NICIE, 25 College Gardens, Belfast BT9 6BS. Tel.: 028 90972910.
www.nicie.org.uk e: info@nicie.org.uk

NICIE is grateful to The Heritage Lottery Fund, which funded NIICIE's 'Big Small Stories' project and so enabled this book to be created and published.

The Big Small Stories Project began in 2016, to celebrate 35 years since the opening of Northern Ireland's first integrated school, Lagan College in 1981. Since then, another 64 schools have opened, educating over 24,000 children together every day. The Big Small Stories Project aimed to capture part of this journey by recording and archiving the memories and experiences of the people behind the foundation and development of integrated schools.

The Big Small Stories archive can be accessed from 2019 through Public Records Office NI website: www.nidirect.gov.uk/proni

The project also has produced resources for schools which can be downloaded from NICIE's website: www.nicie.org.uk

Acknowledgements

Thank you Cecil for your powerful preface to this book and thank you to this book's story tellers: not just for sharing your stories, but for your contribution to Integrated Education. Northern Ireland is a better place because of your efforts.

We also want to thank the Heritage Lottery Fund, who provided the financial resource that enabled this project.

Thanks also to all the staff team at NICIE who dug deep to help out with events and other activities during the project's duration. Special thanks to Cliodhna Scott-Willis, Senior Development Officer for guidance and supervision throughout the project; to Alex De La Torre, who brought the project to life initially and to Andrea Grimason for a variety of contributions, including this book's name. Also to Declan Roughan Photography for portrait and other images.

The Big Small Stories team
Alexandra De La Torre (Coordinator October 2016 to Jan 2018)
Lynn Johnston (Coordinator Feb 2018 to present, November 2018).

The Big Small Stories Steering Group
Kathryn Glover, Kevin Lambe, Elaine Lennon, Tony Macaulay, Cathy McIver, Bill Rolston.

Introduction

The Big Small Stories project was created to mark 35 years of Integrated Education in Northern Ireland in 2016 and was funded by The Heritage Lottery Fund. It has collected over 3500 items for the Integrated Education Archive, which will be housed in the Public Record Office for NI and will be one of the first wholly digital archives in NI, available in 2019. Each one of the 65 integrated schools across NI has contributed to this and can continue to build the archive with ongoing contributions. If you wish to do this, please contact NICIE or PRONI.

     The project also produced a set of films and learning resources to accompany them and these are available through the NICIE website www.nicie.org.uk

     The above resources and this book of stories are intended to capture some of the history, memories and experiences of the people behind the foundation and development of integrated schools in NI.

A oral history: collecting voices

For this book, interviewees were purposefully selected to represent different perspectives of the heritage, time frame and development of Integrated Education. After some deliberation we selected interviewees who wore more than one hat! Whilst 24 stories cannot represent the depth and breadth of contributions made in the development of Integrated Education, we hope you agree that they provide an interesting collection of perspectives.

     The stories that follow are transcribed from interviews conducted by Alex De La Torre during 2017 and 2018. They were edited by The Big Small Stories editing team during 2018 and by each interviewee. The stories are told in first person so as to keep the 'voice' of the interviewee.

We hope that you enjoy them.

Cecil Linehan and her
grand-daughter, Niamh.

Foreword

We will meet together, the tellers of the fine stories in this book and I. We will walk from
one integrated school to the next and in our mind's eye we will be joined by each and
every boy and girl who attended an integrated school since 1981. All along the length
and breadth of Northern Ireland we will be joined by all the committed and courageous
teachers who gave up so much time and often made financial sacrifices to teach in our
schools. Then come hundreds and hundreds of parents who attended hundreds and
hundreds of meetings to ensure the integrated school in their town and city was ready
to educate their children. Children from all different faith traditions and none in a school
which gave them the opportunity to learn about the richness of the varied cultures our
province enjoys. And what about the members of Boards of Governors and Boards of
Directors, sometimes unknown outside their own school but without whose tireless energy
the movement would not thrive? Every member of staff who has ever worked for the
Northern Ireland Council for Integrated Education and the Integrated Education Fund
now too join in the walk in their droves and are cheered and clapped along the way as
are all our benefactors and supporters. We also see in the shadows pictures of many dear

colleagues who have passed away but without whose contribution the river of pupils in integrated schools would never have risen to its current level.

But even as this gargantuan tide from all sixty-five integrated schools winds for hours through the whole province, we hear other voices shouting: 'Why can't we come in?' These are the voices of the hundreds of boys and girls who for the last thirty-five years have been turned away from our schools because they were so oversubscribed. This great river can never, ever cease until all pupils seeking places in our schools are taken on-board. Are they in? They must be for……..

'Ar scáth a chéile a mhaireas na daoine' – It is in the shelter of the other the people live.

Our story has not yet reached a conclusion!

Cecil Linehan MBE
Co-founder, All Children Together
November 2018

Clare Bailey, MLA, one of the first 28 pupils to attend Lagan College.

Changing schools

A friend of my mum's, Mary Connolly, had been involved with the All Children Together (ACT) movement, and had told her that there was another option. It was a long way away from the house. We lived in Antrim Town, which is about twenty miles outside of Belfast. I knew that it was Catholics and Protestants, that had all been explained. But I wasn't thinking Catholic and Protestant. I was thinking, 'You're going to big school,' and that was really, really exciting. And it was quite exciting to be going to Belfast. You felt you were doing something very different from everybody else. I was quite anxious because I didn't know what my school was going to be like. We didn't even know where it was going to be, didn't have any colours, didn't have any tie, nobody knew this school. I was trying to work it all out.

Very first days

I remember that whole feeling on the first day. This was the first time I was meeting the people that we were going to school with. There was so much media at the school at the time and there were protests. But it was very well managed by Sheila Greenfield, the Principal. She didn't bring us in the front door because the world was watching. She wasn't going to let us come through that. She had arranged that we would

all meet around the Shaw's Bridge, the Giant's Ring end, rather than coming up the front into Ardnavalley, around the Belvoir Road. We were walked up through the back along the Lagan River. It was nearly like sneaking us in. We were the first 28. We were brought into the hall which was going to be the school. It was a gym hall in a Scout centre and it was being used in the evenings by other groups. We were just being loaned these premises until we got something else set up. We had to set the school classrooms up in the morning. There was a cupboard in the hall and we had to go into the cupboard to get our desks and chairs. The blackboard was on wheels and we had to wheel it out. And the teachers pushed it around all day. You could see the school secretary typing on the manual typewriter and the Principal taking everybody in and out and doing all the meetings. That was just happening all in the same space. Then there was Mr Lambkin and his bell. It was a big brass hand bell, if you know them. He would come and do the 'ding-a-ling' because we didn't have an electronic bell to tell us one class had finished and you were going on to the next subject.

Settling in

It didn't take us long settling in and getting to know each other. As the weeks rolled on, we got a mini bus. Colin, the mini bus driver, would pick everybody up. And we would drive

Lagan College, 2017.

around to Central Station and then there would be another collection point and he would drive us up to the school. We would come up the Rocky Road in the snow, just for the laugh, just for the excitement. And sometimes the buses just couldn't make it up the road! The bus broke down so many times and we would be this wee walking train of kids. If we weren't in by a certain time, the school knew we'd broken down and the teacher would have to come and get us.

Open-minded

Those setting the school up had to pay very particular attention to what prayers were going to be used in the school and what version of prayers were going to be used. We were using a particular version of the Lord's Prayer because apparently there was a Catholic 'Our Father' and there was a Protestant 'Our Father' but I didn't know this. Also what Bible was going to be used? I remember Brian Lambkin, the RE teacher. With hindsight you realise how special he was as a teacher, he was very, very open. He would bring things into the class and allow the pupils to discuss amongst them. I remember, we were being told that we were going to celebrate all the cultures, that we weren't going to focus on one and we were going to learn about world religions because it wasn't just Christianity in the world. I remember the Jewish festivals coming up and I remember the Indian festivals

coming up. I remember celebrating the Jewish Passover in class and we were all sent home with something different to make. And I was given a recipe for making unleavened bread. I didn't even know what unleavened bread was. I remember having to go home to my mummy and go, 'I have to make this, I don't know what it is.' And neither did my mum, you know. So that was brought into our home, a bit of learning, a bit of cultural experimentation going on there as well. And then on the Passover day sitting down as a class and eating all the Jewish food on the table.

The media

I remember there was so much media attention and so there was always journalists coming through the school. Every now and again you would pop up on your TV, do you know? 'Songs of Praise' came, they came a few times. Once they did the programme from St Anne's Cathedral. We were a focus for the programme because there was an interdenominational service happening at the Cathedral and we were the only integrated school. So the cameras did a close up on us. Sometimes we would have to do a wee snippet of an interview. You would be called out of class by a teacher and you would have to go and speak to a journalist. John Craven come to the school and I remember being filmed. You were always getting asked the same questions so it was nothing new, you know. They would

Lagan College main building.

ask, 'What's it like going to an integrated school?' focusing on the Catholics and Protestants. I'm sitting at the age of about 11 or 12 thinking, 'Well, I've got Catholic friends and I've got Protestant friends and that's okay.' At the age of 11 it was just all ok. We didn't understand the big fuss.

Making it up

We had no idea at the time what we were starting or what we were part of. We had no idea. It was just our school and we really didn't know that we were different and that our school was different. We didn't see it with outside eyes, ever. Well, I certainly didn't. And I just loved going to that school, I loved it. There were just so many different people. We were a brand new school and with only 28 pupils and we were smothered in terms of everybody knew everything about you. The teachers knew everything about you and we knew everything about them. It was that sense of family and it was all experimental. Connor McClelland actually turned around to me one day, he was another one of the 28, he said, 'That wasn't an education, we didn't go to school. We went to an experimental lab, you know.' We were an experiment, we were brought in from all these different places and it is true, there was that sense of making it up as you go along.

Growing

I remember as the school grew, we didn't stay just 28, we got more and more people. I remember we couldn't extend the building but we got an extra green hut every year to accommodate the new intake. So we would come back every September and run down to see how many new ones we'd got and there was maybe another two or three. They were just sort of being built around a playground. Then the National Trust gave approval that Lagan could have their premises and we were saying, 'This is amazing, we've got a site.' We all had to write a thank you letter to the National Trust. I think it was after Christmas that we moved schools from Ardnavalley Scout Centre. We were leaving Loughview. The new intake would go onto the Lisnabreeny site. It was a primary school but we were going in as secondary pupils. Imagine the toilets? The toilets were primary school toilets and we were all 15 or 16 years old using primary school toilets. A lot of people were taller than the actual doors on the toilets. A few years later after we had left we were invited up for the official opening of the new school on that site and I remember walking in and just seeing the school and the hallway was so grand. It was a huge big space and it had an amazing staircase, the double staircase. And I remember standing with Anna and Johnny MacBride and we said, 'Oh my, look at this, it's amazing!' We moved upstairs and saw they had a library. 'Wow, they've got a library!' They had a staircase, they had a school to themselves, they had upstairs, they had downstairs, there was a staff room, there was a Science block, there was the HE block, these were all things that we never had. So we were completely blown away by that expansion.

Social differences

What was most interesting about Lagan for me? It wasn't the Catholic Protestant thing. It wasn't the religious interdenominational element. It was definitely the integration of different social classes. We were not a wealthy family, we were very working class, living on a housing estate, coming through the 80s. It wasn't pretty. There was no funding for the school back then either. So my mum had made great sacrifices to send us, you know. She was paying the bus fares and there was no help for any of it. At one point she had to sell the car because she couldn't afford to get us on buses and keep up with everything, you know, because of the financial pressures that we were under. But I was going to school with others who lived very affluent lives on the Malone Road, for example. Or with others who were coming from Holywood, County Down or from Ballysillan. It was in their accents, it was in what they had in their packed lunch, it was in their school blazer, who had a wool blazer and who had a polyester blazer because the wool blazers were more expensive. And because there were so few of us, we were all friends together, we were a gang. We just moved about in this wee hub. I remember Susan lived just off the Antrim Road and I remember that Karen lived up in Ballysillan but then there was Joanne who lived in Lisburn and there was us who lived in Antrim and then you had Louise who lived up the Malone Road. But we all stayed together. We all slept in each other's houses. I was from a housing estate in Antrim, sleeping on the Malone Road and then heading up on the train to Finaghy and Lisburn. When I think about Lagan I think about those days. And that will always stay with me. I loved that I went to Lagan. Lagan still pulls strings in my heart. I wouldn't have missed a day. By the time my children were going to Lagan the school had expanded to the point

that I didn't even recognise it anymore. It had grown again. And when my two had just left it had blossomed into the new build that it is now. It's absolutely outstanding. I was invited up to have a tour of the school as it is now. I can't explain to you how overwhelming that was. It is probably one of the best facilitated, the best resourced schools that we have to offer at the minute. Lagan College is top of the pops in terms of school resources and is beautiful. To see that happen for my wee school is just phenomenal. And it was also eye opening. It was really a huge education for me.

Personal impact

I'm an MLA (Member of the Legislative Assembly of NI) at the minute and my politics have been really shaped from my experiences at Lagan. When Lagan first opened, the political context at the time was hard. The hunger strikes were happening while my family still lived in West Belfast. That was still my family roots and where family connections were in the midst of all this conflict. But then, I would be out to Lisburn in my friend's house, a completely different town, completely different perspectives or I would be up in East Belfast or Ballysillan. The colours on the streets would change. I had all that going on in my formative years. And that was because I went to Lagan College. If I had gone to my local school, none of that would have been brought into my life. This is the most important impact that Lagan had on me because I was integrated into or had an experience of so many different communities and cultures. It was just going to my friends and they would bring me right into the middle of everything. I don't know too many other girls my age that went to school and had the experiences that I had. Who got to know this city in the way that I did, you know? I walked these streets from East, South, North, West. I walked them all and had friends living in them all. Greater Belfast, inner city, it all. I think that took away a lot of fear because it was all so familiar. And I never had a sense of exclusion from any part of the city like others at that time and I think that's because of Lagan College. So from the age of 11 I was able to see Northern Ireland in a context that I don't

First day at Lagan College, 1981.

believe any other 11-year-old would have had the opportunity to do. And not just Catholics and Protestants but how diverse it was socially and economically. Lagan had showed me Belfast and parts of Northern Ireland in a way that wouldn't have been accessible to me from any other educational background.

Hope

My hope for Integrated Education would be that it is understood for what it is in the wider society and in a broader context. There's still this notion that it's just about bringing Catholics and Protestants to school together. I think we have to get the message out about the different ethos, that different sense of how things are done which is different enough to create a cultural change. I don't think that's understood outside of the sector. I also think that resistance to invest and encourage growth is still strong. But we are 65 schools which are phenomenal. And we are 35, 36 years into this. It should give everybody, it certainly gives me, a sense of pride. We're still doing it. We're not going away, you know!

Eric Bullick was the Principal of Omagh Integrated Primary School and founder and governor of Drumragh Integrated College in Omagh.

From Fintona to Omagh

I grew up in a small village in County Tyrone, the child of a Northern Irish father and an Austrian mother. They had met in a newly liberated Vienna in 1945 so I was nurtured in a house where the concepts of conflict, stability, international relations, politics and education were the normal topics of conversation. I started my own education at the little controlled Protestant primary school in the village and as a child I was totally oblivious to the nature of our fractured society. The concept of segregation was not one that troubled me. Later in a Protestant grammar school I was certainly conscious of segregation in education but not of the historical reasons behind it or the inevitable outcome.

I did my teacher training college in Lancaster University. I like to think that someone was astute enough to decide, 'Let's take this young man who appears to have grown up in traditional Protestant surroundings and let's throw him into a Catholic primary school for his first major teaching practice.' And that was a very good move, a real eye opener.

A few years later I attended a lecture given by Tony Spencer and that got me thinking seriously about the issue of how normal / abnormal segregation in education really is.

After working across the UK in 1978 I was appointed head teacher of that same little controlled Protestant primary school where I had been a pupil. It was a busy job: only

120 children, but it involved both full-time teaching and full-time admin. However I became increasingly dissatisfied with the fact that I was turning out well-educated children, stretching them as far as I could in maths, english, science and computing, but in the end they were leaving me at age 11, well prepared for their next school but not well prepared for life in Northern Ireland. They knew nothing at all about the other 11 year olds who were just leaving the little Catholic maintained school on the other side of town.

I made many attempts to make my little controlled school as mixed as possible by attracting a small number of Catholic children, a tiny number of Catholic staff and one Catholic governor. That led to many heated discussions with the Board of Governors who felt that I was taking the school in a direction that some of them did not agree with.

Around that time, the Western Education and Library Board advertised for a Development Officer for EMU – Education for Mutual Understanding. I saw that advert and I thought 'Now that is a very important job.' Six months later the job was re-advertised; they had not appointed anyone. So I thought, 'That is interesting; maybe I should apply for that job.' Six months later, it was advertised for a third time. And I said, 'Right, I'm going to go for that.' I informed my chair of Governors that I was applying for a job. I warned him that I would be looking for a secondment and I would be away for a year. He said that would be problematical but he would put it

Eric Bullick welcomes 300th pupil to
Omagh Intergrated Primary School.

to the other governors to get their views. They said, 'Yes, but a year to the day we want you back here again.' My work with the Western Board was extended to two years and the Board of Governors gave permission for that second year.

The work with WELB was both challenging and rewarding but during the second year I again became frustrated because EMU is so very limited. On paper it looked good, because I had linked up dozens of schools, all across the west of NI, some with excellent partnerships. But I was conscious that I was bringing children together for an hour, maybe two, once a month and then they were splitting up again, going back to their own schools and almost forgetting until it was time to come together for another hour the following month. I said, 'This is really no good. This is only marginally better than having no contact at all.' There were no firm lasting friendships being made. Some of the teachers were becoming friendly, I have to say, but the children weren't getting much benefit out of it.

The WELB initiative was paused after two years so I went back to my school. I built a huge extension on to the school and that kept my mind more than occupied and, of course, pleased the governors no end.

Omagh Integrated Primary School (OIPS)

In 1989 I became aware that some parents were trying to open an integrated primary school in Omagh, eight miles away. I gave them some moral support but I didn't get personally involved. My wife was involved and some of the committee meetings were actually held in our home, but as the head teacher of a neighbouring primary school, there was something of a conflict of interests. Omagh Integrated Primary School opened in 1990 and the first Principal was Maureen Butler. I followed the successes of the school and wrote several letters to congratulate them on how well things were going. After three years Maureen announced that she was going to move to Loughview IPS in Belfast, and I applied for the vacancy. It seemed the most natural move and that was really the start of my involvement in Integrated Education. The year was 1993 and I had been in the village school for 16 years.

I had been Principal of a controlled primary school in Fintona with 125 children and I moved to the integrated primary school in Omagh, with 110 children. Although it was a slightly smaller school my work load immediately quadrupled. My old school had been a well designed permanent building whereas this new school was housed in a motley collection of dispersed mobiles. It was a huge shock initially that I was responsible for everything. Suddenly the local Education Authority, (the WELB) was removed from the situation as they played no role in the admin. of a grant maintained integrated school. The school was administered by the Board of Governors and the head teacher so we did everything. We managed the maintenance, the finances, we drew up job descriptions, placed the adverts, conducted the interviews, we even organised our own public liability insurance. I was shocked that all the Principals of integrated schools were being asked to do this, without any prior warning. The huge list of responsibilities is never mentioned in the job description. If there was a legal problem, I would have to phone around to see if there was a local solicitor who would take on the case. So, I had moved to a smaller school but my workload was just astronomical. And I was teaching full-time, a class of Primary 6 and 7, preparing them for the dreaded selection test.

My primary objectives were to promote high standards and growth and soon the school was expanding. We were constantly appointing new staff and then asking the Department for new classrooms. Children were sitting everywhere; they were even being taught in my tiny office. The constant pressure of having to manage growth, manage the budget, manage staff and teach full-time with no back up service was certainly a challenge. The Western Board did provide five basic services: library books, an educational psychologist, transport, school meals and educational welfare. You could call upon the Board to help you in those five areas. But there were 25 other areas of complex admin. where the governors and I were on our own.

We had excellent governors who all had children or grandchildren at the school, or who had some experience of cross-community work. We had an architect, an accountant, an HR officer and another parent who was just incredibly practical; if the roof fell in, (and it frequently did) he knew how to get it fixed. A good spread of talent and energy and enough commitment to sit until 11 o'clock at night discussing issues until they were as resolved as you could get them.

We focused on appointing younger teachers who were just coming out of college. So naturally we were inundated with applications. I remember on one occasion we had 110 applications for two jobs. That meant we were able to pick and choose very highly motivated, highly qualified people.

Our relationships with the other Omagh schools was somewhat fraught. We were the new kid on the block. We were still by far the smallest school in Omagh and we were out on the edge of town, so there wasn't actually a community in the vicinity of the school. But we nurtured relationships with all the neighbours. We did everything to invite the community in, to make sure that they didn't feel us to be strange and that we didn't have horns. We worked on very close relations with the parents and the grandparents and the carers and anybody who was connected with the child. The child was our central concern but the child has a whole circle of people around it; so we concentrated more on the child's community rather than the Omagh community.

The school had already established a link with the local Presbyterian minister who organised a rota of clergy who would come in on a Friday to take assembly. To expand that to include the Catholic clergy was a struggle but one local parish priest Father Kevin Mullan was very supportive. Whenever our Catholic children had their First Communion in Primary 4, and their Confirmation in Primary 7, we opened the school to that child's extended family circle. So whether it was on a Saturday morning or a Sunday morning that their special masses had taken place, we had a big party in the school. So we had aunts, uncles and grandparents; we filled the hall and those were great occasions. We invited the priest back to speak and to bless the children all over again and that was a good bond.

Drumragh Integrated College

I arrived in OIPS in September 1993 and by February/March 1994 the parents were being invited in for their children's transfer interviews, when they have to complete a form to say which post-primary they want the child to attend. I was shocked by the end of those interviews to find that my class of Primary 7 children were going off in several different directions. The children had only been together for four years and now they were going off in seven different directions.

Having now attained its target enrolment of sixty pupils

DRUMRAGH COLLEGE

will be opening its doors on 1st September 1995
The Board of Directors wish to announce that they may be in a position to offer a limited number of additional places for September.
Any parent of a pupil currently in Primary 7 who wishes to avail of this opportunity should telephone the college secretary at
OMAGH 242008
no later than
Monday, 5th June

And I thought, 'That's simply undermining the integrated message that we have been trying to establish.' So over Easter '94, I started contacting people who I thought might have an interest in expanding the concept from a primary school to an integrated college. I started off with the founding parents of the primary school and was surprised to receive a very flat, blank, 'NO!' Some of them were exhausted and didn't want to start another major project, a much larger project. Some were happy that their children would have attended an integrated primary but they had their eyes on one of the local grammar schools. The grammar schools in Omagh all had a good reputation so, if they were heading in that direction, they didn't want to muddy the waters with an all-ability integrated college. And some of them objected to the fact that they had just appointed me to lead and develop their primary school and there I was going off at a tangent to establish a separate school. I remember making 50 phone calls that Easter and got varying degrees of responses from, 'No way,' to 'That's a brilliant idea,' to 'That's a brilliant idea and please count me in.'

I organised a meeting of all those people who had been positive. Many were parents of children who were already at the primary school. We went straight from that to a public meeting in the local hotel and that was better attended than I had expected. We had a top table with five guest speakers one of whom was Colm Cavanagh from NICIE. There were enough

people who had expressed an interest to hold another meeting in the primary school to establish a steering group.

Governors may have been sceptical but two members of staff were very supportive. My Vice-Principal, Ruth Robinson, was there, fully committed and another junior teacher, Bronagh McCusker, was very enthusiastic and they became committee members and worked hard.

The Department said, 'You're going to have to have 65 children before we will even look at this proposal.' We advertised continuously and the number did creep up, but it came nowhere near 65. Then we went searching for a site. We toured Omagh looking at every field, every run-down factory and building. We looked at the idea of having mobile classrooms, just like the primary school. We looked at using the primary school site because it was a big four and a half acre site. Could we actually put on more mobiles and have the college on the primary school site?

We then organised a visit to Oakgrove College. Principal Marie Cowan opened the college on a Sunday afternoon and we took three car loads of the steering group members up and spent the afternoon looking around at what she had established in an old psychiatric hospital. And we thought, 'We have an empty psychiatric hospital in Omagh,' and so we went to visit it. It looked totally unsuitable. It was a much older Victorian building than Oakgrove, which had been

Eric receives the
Charter Mark Award
from Mo Mowlam,
2000

built in the 1950s. We kept searching for other possibilities but kept returning to the old hospital building.

Derry/Londonderry is a small city whereas Omagh is a small town. So lots of people tried to put us off to whole idea. Even some members of the Board of Directors of NICIE said, 'You've bitten off too much here. It's a small town where there are already six established schools with a good reputation. You'll never get your 65 kids to open this.' So I don't really know what kept driving us on: naivety, determination or a mixture of the two.

We eventually settled on the old run-down Victorian building of the psychiatric hospital in Omagh. The Department put us under immense pressure. They said, 'You can't appoint a Principal until you've got 65 applicants. You can't even think about this new building until you've got the 65.' The numbers eventually came and then the Department said, 'You must have a specific balance of Protestant and Catholic children.' And we didn't have the balance. They wanted 30:70 and we had maybe 20:80. So we had to focus in on the local Protestant community. Eventually it reached the 30% mark. And then the Department turned their attention to the accommodation: 'We don't like this building, it's totally unsuitable.' So we had to find an architect who would make it suitable. The hospital authorities, however, were very anxious to have a tenant. These were empty premises, costing a fortune to look after. So they were saying, 'We can

accommodate you. In fact, we can make some adaptations.' Eventually the Department ran out of excuses and gave approval for the new college.

Around March/April 1995 we appointed the first Principal, Dr. Kathleen Hinds, who was the deputy head of one of the local grammar schools. Following her appointment numbers gradually crept up until we had surpassed the 65 mark.

We opened with 85 students on the 1st September 1995

These families were sending their children to a post-primary school with no history, no reputation, no exam results, staff unknown apart from the Principal, no reputation, and in a building that was totally unsuitable. It was risky. Five years earlier a number of parents had taken a big risk to send their children to the primary school. But a primary school is probably less of a risk. Parents could easily change their minds and conclude, 'It didn't work out. We'll move back to our local school.' But they tend to put a lot more thought into choosing a post-primary school.

I could see however that the first six/ten staff appointments were good appointments. It was obvious from this early stage that the college was going to do well. So, I responded to the demands of my Governors and returned to concentrate on the development of the integrated primary school.

Growth

In 2000 Secretary of State Mo Mowlam MP awarded OIPS a government Charter Mark – the first primary school in NI to receive such an award. As a result of this and other awards, enrolment was growing rapidly and we had already established two form entry. After countless 'Temporary Variations' and a 10 year battle with DENI, direct rule minister Maria Eagle MP, in one of her final decisions before devolution, granted the OIPS Development Proposal to grow to a full 14 classroom school. From the smallest school in Omagh, OIPS was by this stage the second largest primary in the town. I had been Principal of the school for 16 years and on retirement in 2009 I was delighted to be able to say that with 350 pupils in OIPS and 650 students in Drumragh College there were now 1000 within the integrated family in Omagh. In 1989 that figure had been zero and only 20 years later in 2009 it was 1000. That was quite an achievement for such a small town.

Integrated schools: Stresses and achievements

It was very difficult and very stressful to establish the two integrated schools but I can't think of any way that you could have made it easier. All pioneering work is difficult. Anybody who does anything that hasn't been done before, it is just hard work and there's no shortcut.

Those children who went through the two integrated schools have ended up as adults who have a very positive outlook, a positive attitude towards education. They are better prepared for life in Northern Ireland; they're better prepared no matter where they are going. They have seen more and they've had a broader outlook and they can listen to views and they can make up their own mind about politics and social issues. They are much better rounded adults. They have been exposed to so much more than education. They have had a well-rounded education.

The vast majority of children who went through the primary moved on to the college; between 75% and 80% of the children in the primary school went to the college. We promoted the college in all our literature; we promoted the fact that this is a natural move. Yes, there are other schools in Omagh with a good reputation but this is the school where you should be going. If you've enjoyed and benefitted from the ethos, for the last eight years with us, if you want to continue that ethos, the integrated college is the place to go. I'm currently a rather miserable optimist about the future. I think Northern Ireland is more divided than ever. So I'm not sure about the future. I'm really not going to make any prediction about the future at all.

I would just say is that in a divided and contested society such as Northern Ireland, segregated education is just the worst possible preparation for life. Northern Ireland is already divided and every new generation of segregated children is adding a further layer on top of our already fractious society. Integrated Education is the only way to prepare children; if you want Northern Ireland to be pluralist and modern and outgoing and progressive, then it has to be via Integrated Education. You can't expect children to come out of a segregated society and then suddenly go to work in a pluralist society. It's crazy to think that you keep the children apart but at age 16 or 18, they all have to work together harmoniously.

However, it is not possible to market an integrated school on the sole merit of it being integrated. The school has also be an excellent school. You've got to be able say, 'This is an integrated school and it's also the best school in the area.'

Aurora Cacharro, founding teacher at Strangford Integrated College

The old castle

When we started in Strangford we had absolutely nothing. I mean we had no buildings at all. There wasn't anything but it was a very exciting prospect. I knew that Integrated Education was about educating children of both communities together and this ethos was what I was looking for long term. I suppose I had this romantic idea of starting something new and being a pioneer. The school we started was on the grounds of Carrowdore Castle. Mr Jennings who was the owner at that time kindly let us put some mobiles on his land beside the old castle. There was a walled garden right beside the old castle and our mobiles went on that. The principal's office and the secretary's office were in the castle. I remember there was no heating so poor Anne sat in the office with her coat on all through winter. It was a beautiful room, white carpet, high windows but freezing cold. The mobiles were actually quite nice. They had electric heaters so normally they were pretty toasty. We had four mobile classrooms, the office in the castle and 64 children. A tiny school really.

Parent help

There was no money to pay anybody apart from the teachers so to start with once the mobile classrooms came and the workmen got them wired and plumbed, it was really all down to us teachers and the parents and the kids. The first week in September was basically spent putting together the desks and cleaning the classrooms because the mobiles were quite old. They had to be cleaned from top to bottom and everybody had to muck in. There was nobody idle. All of the furniture came flat packed so we all had to put them together. The parents did the vast majority of that. We had equipment donated to us from various places and that's really the way we started. We had a little bit of money for resources that came from the Integrated Education Fund (IEF) but funds were quite tight. Parents did everything they could. They had a rota and would've come in on a weekend and cleaned the toilets, cleaned the classrooms and did other jobs. Up until the time when we had a caretaker and cleaners, they did all of that. Our bursar for those first three years was also a parent, Frieda Kirkpatrick, who is sadly not with us anymore. She put in hours and hours to keep us solvent and to administer the funds as best as she could on top of a busy job that she had elsewhere. I remember there was a great sense of common purpose. Everybody knew that we were there for a reason and that was to educate students differently in a way that maybe wouldn't have been available to them in the local schools. The fact that these parents put their trust in us and believed in what the school was going to be and do and that they took their children from mainstream education and put all that work in is nothing short of amazing.

'All hands on deck!'
Preparations for opening at
Stangford College, August 1997.

A broad curriculum

At that early stage we were an independent school. We really could've taught anything we wanted but we all wanted to provide the students with as much of a broad curriculum as we could so that they would not miss out on anything. Among the six of us we covered basically all the subjects. I don't know how we did it but that first year we offered thirteen clubs: rugby, athletics, a choir, a craft club and a computer club. Our aim was to be a grant maintained school and to offer the curriculum in all its breadth so that's the way we were behaving from the beginning. That meant that we all had to teach more than one subject, for example, I taught French, Spanish, Music and PE. Normally for PE we took everyone to the leisure centre 'cos we didn't have any sport facilities. I remember on Friday afternoon the whole school went to Newtownards on a couple of buses.

Resistance and support

We knew the Department of Education were not in support of us. They were very much against us opening here because I suppose there were enough schools in the area already. They didn't want to fund another school. So the board officers were asked not to help us. But a lot of them did help us on the QT because they said those children needed to be educated and have a full experience so we did receive help from a lot of good professionals. I received a lot of help from a Music advisor. I wouldn't even have known how to teach Music or the actual curriculum and she set me right with a scheme of work and gave me advice on what to buy and the things that I needed to do. For that I will always be grateful.

Good relations

The religious balance was always very good and the kids were remarkably good at mixing with each other. I think it's because there were only 64 of them. Our Catholic kids, of whom the vast majority came from down the Peninsula, from Kircubbin and Portaferry, would've been together in primary schools and knew each other reasonably well but all the pupils socialised really well together. I think when you are 11, it's all about whether this person can play football rather than what religion they are. I remember one particular wee fella who lived on the Ballybeen Estate and he got into hurling because his friends at school all played hurling. He got a wee hurling stick. One day he was going home with his schoolbag and the hurling stick and we asked him if it was safe for him to go home carrying this. He said, 'Yes Miss, look.' He actually had the big bit of the stick inside the schoolbag and the other bit up his sleeve. He said, 'Nobody's going to see it, this is the way I take it home.'

Differences

Students falling out over religion or political views came maybe later when the students got a little bit older. Sometimes there may have been a small issue but, you know, that's to be expected. It was more important how we dealt with it when it happened. Young people will often fall out about something. The difference between other schools and an integrated school is how you deal with it. How you seek to promote understanding and get to a point when the children understand that they don't need to agree with somebody and they don't need to believe what they believe. It's all about respect. Also we tried to have a discipline system that was more about encouraging positive behaviour rather than being punitive. When something like that happened we sought to talk to the young people and kind of help them through the thinking process. Also we tried to challenge views a little bit and make sure that they were thinking for themselves rather than believing what they heard somewhere or saw in the media.

Our philosophy

I believe students from an integrated school are more tolerant of other people because we make a point of making sure that they understand that there are different points of view out there. I think it also makes them more confident. I think in a school like Strangford College students will be listened to. Sometimes they say, 'Miss, you know in another school my friends they get punished for this and that and they never get listened to whereas you do listen.' Even if in the end we might end up saying, 'Well, you're not right here,' we attempt to explain why. I think in a way that gives them confidence. Also it's always about reconciliation. It's about giving students the opportunity to make things good again when things go wrong. Our school is more about educating the whole person and not just filling them full of subjects and knowledge, you know? It's about making sure that they go out into the big wide world and are able to get on and work and socialise with all types of people. And that they'll be able to cope with any

situation that life throws at them. I think we do that well. Also we are making sure that the students that we send out into the world are good ambassadors for the school as well.

Proud of our pupils

We still keep in touch with a lot of the early students via Facebook and they all meet up. The memories that they have are good memories of school and they are aware now as grown up people in their thirties, that they were part of something really special and they are proud of it. When I bump into them they say, 'Oh Miss, remember when this happened?' They are proud of it too. One of those students of the first year group, he's an officer in the army now. He told me that whenever he went for his interview for officer he talked at length at having been a founder member of Strangford College and how that affected him and how he looked at people. He said that he knew that that was part of the reason why he got into the officers' academy. He could see that the panel interviewing him were really interested in this. He believes the qualities that he had acquired at school made him very eligible to be an officer.

Popularity

In the first couple of years we did have some students that gave up grammar school places but our ability range would've been more like that of a secondary school. In the last three years we have introduced the grammar stream. I believe it's important and it's good to be educated with different ability to you. Also I think it's good for students who maybe are of a higher ability to not be educated in a bubble. It's good for them to see that there are students of all abilities. Some students may be very good academically but they will be in school with others who maybe are not that academic but would run rings around them in sports or artistically. Or maybe they are in the class with somebody who has special needs of a physical nature but they are good at something else. I think it's good for everybody to be educated in an environment where you learn there are truly all sorts of people. Also it's good for us because Roman Catholics are in the minority in this area and even with that most of the time we've managed to get our 30% balance which is not bad. But since we've had the grammar stream, that seems to have improved slightly because the parents know the grammar stream is not static; the students move up and down the classes all the time.

Challenges

There have been challenges over the years. Establishing ourselves as one of the main players in education in the area was difficult because we were the new school and maybe people had the idea that nobody knew what they were doing. We really had to do a lot of hard work promoting the school. When we first arrived in the area nobody wanted us here. Carrowdore is a wee village but it really was very much of one persuasion. You know, 'Bringing Catholics into the area? Oh my goodness no!' There were problems at the beginning, like we would've had flags put on the fence and buses stoned on the way to the school and so on. Gradually, I think the local community realised that we were a good thing. At the beginning when there was nothing here in the village, apart from the petrol station and the pubs, we would've tried our best to go and, you know, get our petrol down there, use the shop, go for a drink on a Friday afternoon after school and show ourselves around the area. I think the local community gradually accepted us because they realised we were bringing a bit of life to the village. The village itself has really expanded in the last 20 years, there's much more housing about the place. I don't know but I think it may be in part because of the school being here. I think we have come to the point now where we are accepted in the area as one of the leading schools and we definitely generate a lot of interest. We are having our open evenings at the end of this month and often it's really manic particularly the first night. We normally have 1400 people through the door and maybe another 600 the night after. I think that gives you an indication of the interest.

Reflections

I'm pretty proud of what we did and what I did actually. I'm pretty proud that I took the risk. Thinking back, it was maybe a bit of madness, leaving a permanent job and not having a school, not knowing my colleagues and not knowing the children but I'm pretty proud of it. We did the best we could definitely with what we had. I sometimes am amazed at some of the things we managed to do, like school plays and school trips when we had nothing but I wouldn't change a thing. My experience of being a teacher at Strangford Integrated College has made me proud of the difference that I feel we have made in the area of North Down & Ards. I feel that in a way it's my life's work. I feel privileged that I have been given the opportunity to be here from the beginning and influence what Strangford was and what Strangford has become, and I feel that no matter what happens I am part of the history of Strangford College and that makes me very, very proud. I think that the way forward for Integrated Education is that every school will be an integrated school and have an ethos like the one we started.

Noreen Campbell was a founding teacher of Hazelwood Integrated College, established in 1985 and Principal there from 1996 to 2006. In 2009 she was appointed as Northern Ireland Council for Integrated Education (NICIE) CEO and retired from that position in 2015.

I knew that we needed educational reform

My introduction to Integrated Education was at a meeting held in 1980 or '81 in the Quaker House on the Lisburn Road for parents who might be interested in setting up an integrated college. At that time my eldest son was 10 and we knew we didn't like the education system we had, and we went to that first meeting. I was interested in and supportive of this initiative and I followed what was happening but I didn't become actively involved at that point.

At that time, I was a teacher in a boys' Catholic secondary school on the Antrim Road. I was parent of four boys and my experience had led me to oppose the education system that existed. Although we ourselves were from a Catholic background, our children were not brought up as Catholics. They did not go to Catholic schools which was considered quite radical at that time. They went to our local state primary school. Moving on to second level education, what option was there for them? There really wasn't one, and that is why we were interested in the idea of an integrated school. From my point of view as a parent of four boys, did I want them to go to an all boys' school? No, I didn't. It seemed ridiculous that you would keep boys and girls separated. Equally, I deplored the 11+ exam separating children on the basis of a discredited test at the age of 11. I was teaching in a boys' secondary school and I saw the huge waste of talent this created, really bright, clever

boys and nothing expected of them because they had failed an exam at 11. I was totally opposed to the idea of selection and separating children by social class. I was totally opposed to separating children on the basis of religion. We wanted a school that would model the type of society we wanted to live in, inclusive, based on equality and tolerance. The concept of Integrated Education answered all of our concerns.

My first son didn't go to Lagan; he was only 10 and it was too long a journey given frequent bomb scares and ongoing violence. Then in 1983 my second son did go to Lagan; a neighbour had a son going and they were travelling by car back and forth and so that made it easy. In 1985 there was a meeting for a school in North Belfast and at that point I became involved. I went to that meeting excited at the idea that we were going to have an integrated school in North Belfast and prepared to make it work.

Lagan was the pilot

A sub group from All Children Together (ACT) was set up called Belfast Trust for Integrated Education (BELTIE), led by Tony Spencer. He took the view that Lagan was the pilot school; it had succeeded and now it was time to move on and establish more integrated schools. A well-attended meeting was held in the Lansdowne Court Hotel on the Antrim Road. There were a couple of hundred people at it, enough interest to say this is an

NICIE at Stormont
Integrated Education
Week, 2014.

idea worth pursuing. The aim was to establish a primary school and a college. The meeting was held in March, the schools were to open in September; it was a very ambitious plan.

My friend and I said, 'Yes, we'll definitely be involved in this as parents, but we're not going to get involved in this as part of the organisation because it would be too much.' But then we both did and spent the rest of our lives as part of the organisation! And it was too much!

I applied for the job of Principal because I believed completely in the vision, not because I had the experience for the job – I didn't. I knew well the person who was appointed; we had been on a course together and got on well and shared a very similar educational philosophy. I was more than pleased when he got the post. I was appointed teacher in '85, and then I was appointed Vice Principal in '86 and I was Vice Principal until '96, when I was appointed Principal.

Hazelwood approached integration from a different angle than Lagan. Lagan was set up as a school to bring together children from two denominations. Hazelwood was concerned more about the societal/tribal division. It was established to promote reconciliation and mutual respect in a divided society and to create a space for young people from both main traditions to learn about and with each other. We did subscribe to a Christian ethos but, essentially, the religious beliefs of the students were their parents' responsibility. To underline our mission of reconciliation, we held an annual peace assembly. This celebrated the work of Hazelwood, which was about accepting difference and challenging division, and accepting and giving a voice to all. We invited everyone from the community in, including civic leaders, politicians and clergy. However, the only Catholic priest who came to that assembly in Hazelwood in my time was Father Troy from Ardoyne. The Catholic church would have nothing to do with the school.

No children, no building, no money

It was an amazing privilege to have the opportunity to shape and create a school. We weren't fitting into what had always been and which had gone unchallenged. We were saying, 'Here we are with a blank slate, how do we do this?'

There was no building, there were no resources. There was nothing, I mean, there were no children! There was an educational concept, and there was a Principal and two teachers. There were various committees looking at various issues. But there were no children and there was no building and there was no money! All of those holes had to be plugged by people like me, who had just spent their time in the classroom, hadn't been out recruiting children!

My husband had been teaching in the same school as me and he left his job at the same time, to start up his own business. We took a big plunge. The first year of the school was very difficult, for a number of reasons. First of all, we were surviving financially from month to month and, secondly, we were in what had been a warehouse. The location was brilliant because we were in the city centre. I took the children out all the time to be educated in the City Library. The old peoples' home was beside us and we did a wonderful history project. But the actual building was totally unsuited for educating children. There was no natural light and no playground. I hadn't realised that I needed natural light to operate, I found that really difficult. Also, there was the difficulty of trying to create momentum with 17 children, of creating a school on a shoe string! My memories of the first year are really of everything being a challenge.

The Anglo-Irish Agreement had just been signed in 1985 and there were many protests and much tension; it was a very fraught time. There were a lot of those types of pressures and we were trying to build up children who had been plucked away from their friends to go into this new untested school; personally, I think the first year was the most difficult. We had good times, wonderful people who came in to volunteer to help and bring in all these activities for the children, the parents were really involved and came in to offer support to the students, offer their skills. There was all that type of moral support and much broader support than you would get in an ordinary school, so it was a deeper and more enriching experience.

Curriculum

In the early days, we took the view that the hidden curriculum had to be made explicit. Our classes were all ability. We had a non-punitive approach to discipline. We believed in the voice of the young person, in being open, democratic, accepting, promoting mutual respect and understanding. We knew, as a staff, we had to model mutual respect and understanding. All of that sub-structure, the hidden curriculum, was consciously created. We very consciously looked at the curriculum and what subjects needed preference in that curriculum to ensure that young people had an opportunity to learn more fully about each other. For example, Drama was part of the curriculum up until the age of 14, both because it developed empathy and allowed for the exploration of other points of view and backgrounds. History and English Literature were important as well. We had an entitlement curriculum in Hazelwood way back in those days; every young person was entitled to learn another language, every young person was entitled to a broad curriculum, regardless of what their perceived ability was. Now, the curriculum has been restricted and the entitlement has been whittled away in order to focus on exam results. So we were creating a value based curriculum at a time when society was changing to purely monetised values.

If you're starting a new school you have a clean slate, an opportunity to create a model of education in which integration naturally thrives. To me, integrating Protestants and Catholics was only one part of that educational model. I believed, if you got the learning environment right, then the individual as part of the community would feel accepted and nurtured and everything else: the acceptance of others, a respect for diversity, pride in one's own background and tradition, would fall into place. If you were able to get the elements of an educational community right, you would create the environment which nurtured the individual and promoted mutual respect, which enabled challenge and accepted difference.

When Hazelwood was established, five secondary schools in the area had just closed because there had been such a dip in the number of young people. And here was a new school starting, never mind a new integrated school; we were not popular and we didn't have relationships with other schools. There was a lot of hostility towards us. We had to concentrate on developing our school in the face of that hostility. But we had to connect in the community and ensure that all of our parents and children felt comfortable in the school, which in its second year had moved to a site off the Whitewell Road, itself a contested area. When tricolours went up at the school gates, it was imperative to ensure that they were removed.

Support for staff

As Principal, certainly in terms of appointing staff, it was a priority to ensure the staff understood that integration was

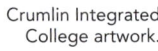

Crumlin Integrated College artwork.

lived out in the school on a daily basis. In that sense, the use of first name terms which we had adopted was a very valuable tool because it very explicitly said, 'This is not just another school.' There was a question we asked at interview; which went something like, 'In Hazelwood, we use first name terms – what do you think might be the advantages of this?' That enabled us to get an insight into the open mindedness of the applicant. I think that was a better test than, you know, 'Do you support integration?' Of course, everybody supports integration!

We believed that the staff are role models for the students, our aim was to create the environment that enables staff to be such role models. There were many challenging times and some extraordinary learning experiences. One example that stands out was the issue of the poppy. In determining our policy on this, staff engaged openly, and robustly, and with respect. You could hear people understanding others' well thought out views about the poppy, for and against, which had never been considered before. However, we didn't provide nearly enough opportunities for staff to explore their own biases because in the meantime we were delivering a curriculum and getting children ready for exams.

In 2002 two young men from the area were killed in violent incidents, a past student was killed in a sectarian attack. In our particular area it was a very difficult time. It brought to the surface all the depths of feeling in the local area. We had to deal with this tension openly and with sensitivity in school.

This challenged the school internally and the school community responded brilliantly because we were able to create a space which enabled difficult conversations. The trust needed to achieve this had been deeply embedded.

When I look back on my career in school and think of all the things I could have done differently, mostly I think in terms of work with staff. There were so many expectations piled on staff in their teaching and their leadership and not enough support. Staff need time and space to explore and recognise the depth of division that exists here and to be aware of their unconscious biases. I think that is critical to successful integration. Certainly, I don't think we did enough in Hazelwood. I think definitely as a school Principal, and as someone involved in the foundation of the school, I took far too much for granted in terms of what I expected of teachers and underestimated the challenge and support they needed. I think that is critical for integrated schools generally. Most people here still don't mix with other religions until they're 18 or 21 or, if they become teachers, maybe never!

I think this is a particular challenge for transforming schools. I think for schools transforming that, unless this reflective and self-exploratory work is done, you do not have the change from the roots which make the difference in the ethos of the school. That understanding informed a lot of my work in NICIE in terms of promoting relationships between integrated schools, and developing and sharing good practice and emphasising the importance of meaningful conversations with all people involved in a transforming school.

Moving out of the bubble

Retirement didn't suit me at all so when the post in NICIE came up I saw it as an opportunity to continue my involvement in Integrated Education, and I was lucky and privileged to be appointed to the post. It was a different type of work which was fascinating. I had to learn a lot because it is not the self-enclosed world of school with which I was familiar. It was a totally different type of role, but the principles and the mission hadn't changed.

Hazelwood had been extremely successful and what we had set out to do, we had achieved. But there I was working with people who were all within the same bubble and shared a mindset and were all speaking the same language and on the same path. To then come into a role where you're interacting with the outside world was both a shock and a challenge. The wider educational world in Northern Ireland does not accept the principle of integration; division is in its DNA: the aberration which is integration is to be controlled and contained, not promoted and encouraged. That total intransigence and resistance was a shock to me. I'd been living in a lovely little bubble for a couple of decades!

The future for integration

Integrated schools are now accepted; they are well established and respected; they are part of the educational landscape. I think integrated schools changed for the better other schools. I think because parents are such an important part of our schools that other schools, and Catholic schools in particular, learned from us. Catholic schools became au fait with the language of integration and they became more parent-friendly and started to use the language of inclusion. I think integrated schools present a model of how to create a positive inclusive and diverse school community. Integrated Education was a catalyst for change, although that would never be admitted by the educational establishment.

We continue to waste money in duplication and triplication of school sectors and at a time when there is real pressure on school budgets and the quality of education is under pressure. Leave aside the political arguments in favour of Integrated Education, leave aside the societal arguments in favour and just look at the economics. Value for taxpayers' money demands a more rational educational system; building and maintaining peace demands the same; recognising and responding to the wishes and preferences of parents demands an integrated system of education. The case for change is obvious. However, the depth of opposition to integration is so entrenched that it will require an independent commission on the lines of the Patten Commission to achieve change.

A simple solution

When I was CEO in NICIE I went to the Department of Education, to the Minister for Education and to the Education Authority (EA) with a simple and non-controversial solution to expanding Integrated Education. I proposed that parents are requested to nominate the type of school they want for their child when registering the child's birth. This would enable efficient and effective planning of schools. This proposal is very simple, and perfectly workable. The information gathered gives the EA five years' planning based on parental preference. The process of nominating a preference for school type embeds the importance of education and involves parents in education from the start. It may be that many parents will say, 'Well, actually we're going to stick with our own,' and that will be their choice. But for those who prefer an integrated school, and all of polling suggests that would be for the majority, the EA then knows that five years hence they need x number of integrated places in any area. The function of EA then is to provide those places and that can happen through the process of transformation.

The parents who established the grant maintained integrated schools were exceptional, they were prepared to devote time, energy and commitment to developing their school. Most parents do not want to have to create schools for their children, they don't want to have to be involved in developing a school. They're busy working, they're bringing up their children and they want a good school for their child. It's the role of the state, not parents, to ensure that schools meet the needs of society and parents. Rather than reflect our divisions, the government has an obligation to shape our future society. Our present system reflects and perpetuates a divided society. Since the two main parties are dependent on tribal identity in order to get their votes, it is in their vested interest to maintain that tribal identity. If, in addition, you have a lobbying body like the Catholic church, then the vested interests protecting the status quo are huge.

I think our grant maintained integrated schools are successful and well established because the culture of integration was embedded in the foundation of the schools. I think for transformed schools the journey towards integration is a more difficult one, because they have a culture to challenge, question and change. That requires patience and support and clarity about expectations and how they might be achieved. I think when there is an agreed process for transformation clearly communicated to all, transformations will be easier and deeper for those involved. If there were proper economic incentives for transformation, especially in this time of budget cuts, then I think there are any number of schools with a healthy mix of populations who ought to be formally integrated. We need more schools to transform and once you get a tipping point, then I think change will hasten, but we're not at the tipping point.

And finally…

I consider myself privileged to have been involved in a movement which has made a difference to the lives of the individuals and to society more generally. I have gained enormously from my experience of working with the full range of our society, of mixing with everybody and of being challenged personally to examine and be aware of my own biases. The experience changed and developed me. I think other people ought to have that same privilege.

I have witnessed how children and young people appreciate the opportunity to learn with and about and alongside each other. I think all children are entitled to that experience.

I have had the opportunity to develop and test an educational philosophy, I have had the privilege of working with inspirational leaders of integrated schools.

My early career was conducted against the backdrop of the Troubles. Those who were involved in Integrated Education wanted to make a statement, to say the violence was not in our name, to show that it was possible for people from across the divide to live in harmony and respect. Our schools proved that was possible. Integrated Education in Northern Ireland has been adopted and adapted in other divided societies. It has been my privilege to have been part of this movement for change through education.

Colm Murray Cavanagh, Anne Murray Cavanagh, Bernie Webster and Tim Webster are founder parents of Oakgrove Integrated Primary School and Oakgrove Integrated College.

Introductions

My name is Colm Murray Cavanagh. I visited South Africa at the time of apartheid and when I came back to Northern Ireland in 1972, the Troubles were at their height and there was a huge movement of people in this city. Derry was a city of about 100,000 people and 15 or 16,000 people moved house. It was obvious that the segregation in the schools was a contributory factor in my mind to the divisions in the community. In about 1975 I wrote an article to the Catholic Education Authority who were looking at reorganising education and I said that they should look at having integrated schools as well, not just look at the 11+ which was what they were mainly focused on. I was in contact with All Children Together after they started in 1977. Myself and another community worker, Eamon Deane, spoke to Londonderry City Council, as it then was, and a significant majority of the councillors agreed with Integrated Education. It seemed at the time in Derry that the schools were becoming integrated, but in fact it was only a snapshot of the movement that was taking place, as the Protestant people moved away and the former Protestant schools became more mixed. So, when the idea came up among some parents in 1990 that we should tackle the segregation in the schools, I became involved in the work that eventually became Oakgrove Integrated Primary School in 1991.

My name is Bernie Webster. I was born in 1955 and I grew up in Donegal. I was a Catholic and had Protestant friends in the street but we went to separate schools. I never thought there was anything peculiar about it. That was how it was and I never questioned it really. When Tim and I got married, we were living in Derry and we had our first child in 1982. September 1981 was the first time that I ever heard of integrated education. We were just discovering around those days that I was pregnant, having my first child. The news headlines one evening at teatime had the opening of Lagan College. I thought that was absolutely amazing, really, really wonderful, just such a marvellous idea. I actually remember the faces of everybody who was interviewed and what they said. It stuck with me and I thought that if I had children, that's what I would like for them.

My name is Anne Murray Cavanagh. I was a teacher and came back to Derry during the height of the Troubles in 1972. My original intention was probably to teach English and Geography, probably in a Catholic girls' grammar school. Jobs were plentiful at the time and there was a local school, Greenhaw Primary School, a controlled Protestant school. I asked somebody about that school and somebody said, 'It's a wee mixed school, they have Protestants and Catholics.' I thought this was quite interesting, so I wandered in and had a word with the Principal, Geoff Starret, who was a really visionary guy. He was from across the border, from around Lifford, had

First assembly at Oakgove Integrated Primary School.

been in the RAF and had gone into teaching. The Protestants had started to move across the river because of the Troubles. They were being shot and bombed out of the West Bank so they moved across to the East Bank because it was safer. So the school was decreasing in size and local children who were Catholic then started coming into the school. Geoff was encouraging that and he encouraged me as well, because I was from the Catholic community. There was a job advertised, I applied and got this job in a wee mixed primary school.

During the years I was there, I learnt a lot from Geoff. He had a great disregard for conventional attitudes. During the course of the time I was there, the school went from 3% Catholic to 3% Protestant within 15 years. The Protestants kept moving across the river. I worked there because I thought if I was in South Africa I would want to teach in a school with black and white children and I thought it made sense if I was in Northern Ireland I would teach in a school with Protestants and Catholics. I just always thought that some kind of integrated, mixed education was a good idea. That was basically where I came from and so when this conversation arose about how we divide children every way we can, by gender, by ability, by religion, by anything we can think of, I was definitely for joining the group that was going to try and set up a school. We didn't know whether it was going to be a nursery or primary or post primary or whatever, but I was very happy to join that movement. The other thing was that in the

late 1970s I joined All Children Together (ACT) and used to go to Belfast to their meetings as well.

My name is Tim Webster. Because my dad was in the army I was born in Egypt and grew up in London. One thing that resonated with me was that in my early teens, a politician, I think it might have been Michael Foot, gave a speech and talked about London being a melting pot of cultures and nationalities and then described how this interaction of cultures and nationalities stimulated creativity and innovation. I used to go up to Soho and walk around the streets and walk round the world: I'd go through the Greek quarter, the Italian quarter, the Spanish quarter, the French quarter and effectively go round the world in less than a square mile. I thought that was brilliant because I didn't have to get a passport or travel. When I left London I went to Cheltenham and studied landscape architecture. When I completed my course I needed to find a job, and was looking through the magazines at standard adverts of idyllic landscapes with, 'Would you like to be a landscape architect in Milton Keynes?' Four years in Cheltenham was like being wrapped in cotton wool. There was one advert which was a picture of Waterloo Place in Derry, just after a bomb had gone off. All the trees were scattered all over the place, the plant pots were cracked, the gas main was on fire and every window was broken. This was so different from all the other adverts that I thought whoever put an advert like that in must have a sense of humour.

I rang up and a gentleman called Brian Woods answered the phone. He was the manager of the landscape architecture department in Derry and he asked if I would like to do the interview on the phone. I said, 'Right, save a bit of time,' and he asked, 'Are you sure you want to come here?' That was the only question he asked. I said, 'Yes,' and that was it: I packed my bags and came to Derry. It was intended to be a six week job but a couple of days after I arrived, they blew up the railway station in Belfast and I thought it was a sign from God that I was not going back to England. So I stayed for six weeks and I have to say I was having a great time. I was in all parts of the city, building playgrounds, designing planting schemes for housing estates and working with a great bunch of people. Then we moved on to designing murals to cover bomb sites and working with community groups all around the city. I was thoroughly enjoying myself, so when they offered me a permanent job, I took it. As time went on it became quite exasperating because I was meeting people and making friends on both sides of the community and having great craic with them all, but they often weren't comfortable 'crossing the line'. There were just a couple of pubs in Derry where everyone could meet and there was a place called the Pound Club in Belfast where people from all parts of the community would meet up and listen to Blues and Jazz. We were all huddled together in this little oasis of sanity surrounded by the insanity of the Troubles.

That echoed with me until I met Bernie and we had children, and then there was the fateful barbecue where we all started discussing Integrated Education. I think, like a lot of people, I was very frustrated, that I wanted things to change, but I didn't see violence as being the answer. I was involved with Community Mirror for a while doing illustrations. Founding an integrated school just seemed like such a good project to bring children together to sit in the same classroom, talk about their differences, rather than just talk over a fence about each other. Once people are generalised as 'the other' they become the enemy very easily; far better to have them in the same classroom, at the same desk fighting over the pencil and getting to really know each other.

Getting the Integrated Project Underway

Bernie: It was the day in 1990 that everybody got the letter about what schools their children had been allocated for secondary level and we were having a barbecue and there were three couples sitting and everybody was giving out because there was a problem some way with the placements. Anne Murray said, 'What this town needs is an integrated primary school and secondary school,' And we all said, 'That's marvelous,' and we all began to talk about it. It started at a barbecue in our park, so for many years afterwards we had a celebration barbecue in the park because that was where the idea came. Anne can't even remember that conversation, but I remember it.

After the barbecue, towards the end of August, I remember Colm saying, 'If we're going to follow up on this, we're going to have to get people together.' The four of us talked about it and discussed it over meals. It was in September that we started getting people together. We got friends together first, because who else do you know but your friends? You ring your friends and tell them, and, yeah, they tend to be thinking along the same line as you. It got bigger that way and expanded into relevant people. Tim and Colm had the chair at the first meeting because they were a Protestant and a Catholic.

Colm: We held the first public meeting in Lisnagelvin Leisure Centre, which no longer exists. It was neutral and that was important. We needed a place that was accessible to everybody. We rented a room in the Everglades Hotel at least twice. Both were on the Waterside, which was mixed and over a hundred people came.

Tim: It was very funny actually because we had set out the chairs and were expecting 50 people. We thought if we got 50 we'd be flying. I thought it was nearer 200 that turned up.

Bernie: A lot of them were really interesting people. There was one couple who came whose family had been damaged badly by the Troubles. She continued to work with the schools, she's retired now, and it became her life. There was a group of teachers who actually came, I think out of curiosity, from

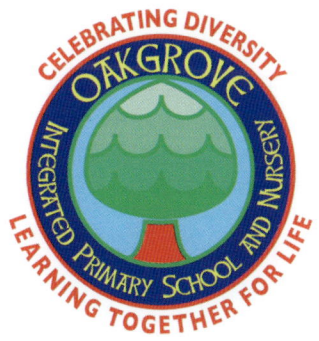

one of the local schools. One of them stood up and said, 'Mr Canavan, or Cavanagh, or whatever you call yourself, I want you to know that not everybody here agrees with Integrated Education.' Colm said, 'Thank you very much,' and she sat down. There was a policeman there who wanted no religion in the schools. He wanted religion completely removed and fought for that for a while.

Anne: The people involved were enthusiastic. So many of the people were there with you, trying to find out what it meant for their families because they would have had young children a bit like us.

Colm: Fiona Stevens, who was the Chief Executive of the Northern Ireland Council for Integrated Education (NICIE) and Fiona Stelfox who was the chair, were at the meeting. Some people at that meeting wanted an integrated primary school, some people wanted an integrated college and some people wanted an integrated nursery. So we got three groups together to look at those three different things. There were only two integrated colleges in Northern Ireland at the time and I went to talk to Lagan College and Hazelwood College, and some other people looked at nurseries and some people looked at primary schools, and it was very clear that the easiest thing to do was go for a primary school first. Nurseries were very difficult to get funding for and a college is just a bigger thing to set up, so we went for an integrated primary school. In 1989, the Education

Reform Order had been passed and that meant that parents who met the criteria of the Department of Education had a right to an integrated school.

However, the Department wasn't going to open the schools, it was still left to the parents. I remember speaking to a guy in the Department when we had started the process of applying for an integrated primary school and I said that some people were interested in a college as well. He said, 'Don't even mention a college until the primary school is up and running.' Then, about January 1992, we went back to the Department and said, 'Now we want a college. The primary school has been open since last year.'

Tim: I got three pieces of wisdom from those early days. The first one was from Colm when we were discussing a time scale and we were talking about two years. Colm said, 'If we give ourselves a two-year time scale, we'll faff around for 18 months and then do all the work in the last six months. So we'll cut out the faffing around and just do it in six months.' That has stuck with me for various other projects as well. The second piece of wisdom was from Anne Murray's mentor from Greenhaw, Geoff Starret, a wise old man. When we were getting a bit of flack from a few people, just verbal, nothing serious, he said, Just don't bother responding, just get on with doing the job of setting up the integrated school.' I thought that was great wisdom as well. And the third bit was Colm again, when we were having another bit of bother, Colm said, 'Success is the best revenge.'

Colm: I don't believe in revenge!

Tim: Maybe I was just wanting a positive outcome.

The working groups

Anne: We decided to have a working group. Anybody who wanted to could be in it. We got people to sign up and give us contact details.

Colm: There were about a dozen in the working group, parents who were looking for a place for their children.

Tim: We started an enrolment book for pupils, which we still have. We have the minutes of the working group meetings as well, once or twice a week.

Bernie: We had a lot of social events, dinners to celebrate everything: the roof going on the school, etc. We realised that the children were coming to the meetings with us and playing while we were having the meetings and we realised that, because they had no one to look after them, the children were sitting with clipboards, playing meetings, taking minutes, it's what you do. At the barbeque discussion when we had the idea of the integrated schools, I was just about to give birth and I took a lot of the phone calls over the next few months. It was the most active maternity leave I've ever had and most enjoyable, I have to confess. I was very busy with getting people on board. I was very busy with the baby. The baby fed away and the phone was in the other hand.

Anne: We brought the children together in the leisure centre for an afternoon and they would go swimming and afterwards we would have a tea party for the children and the parents. We got together to build up a sense of community and interest.

Tim: We had an Easter egg hunt in the square. I hurt my back trying to get one of the eggs.

Anne: That's right, that was an activity for the children and the parents got together, so those kind of activities became half social, half group work in a very informal way. Except you'll see from the minutes of the meetings that this was people saying,

right, what do we need to do, with NICIE backing us. That's when Kevin Lambe appeared as our Development Officer. Kevin was very supportive and he was very excited about the group as well. He was up and down the road once a week and then as time went on and it was getting close, when you know the advertising for staff and so on had happened, then he was in the middle of all that. He was very, very supportive of us, and he joined in with our enthusiasm. I think he enjoyed that the group was a particularly enthusiastic group who didn't see objects in their way.

Colm: We had to meet after work because we had jobs during the day, and so we would meet on Wednesday nights, every Wednesday night for a couple of years. But that meant that Kevin wasn't getting back home until after midnight in Belfast. I mean he was 75 miles away! We had to find pupils, we had to find staff and we had to find a place for the school: that was the work we had to do. We looked at a whole lot of places. We felt it had to be on the Waterside which was mixed and it had to be on an interface between two parts of the community so that both Nationalists and Unionists of all stripes felt comfortable walking into the school. Geoff Starret and I went to the City Council to ask them if they would rent to us. I had spoken to a couple of councillors before, both of whom were SDLP and one of them put his hands to his head and said, 'Oh Jesus, if you want support, don't ask us to support Integrated Education. Ask us for money, but don't ask us to support Integrated Education!' And the other one said, 'I don't think that Integrated Education is going to cure the problems of Northern Ireland, but it won't make it worse.'

So the feeling was that the SDLP, which was the majority party in the Council, was supportive. They eventually gave us the site for a pound a year, if demanded. The strange coincidence was that the Guildhall, the City Council's hall, had been bombed by the IRA early in the Troubles and the Council had moved to temporary premises on the Waterside, and that's why they had built these premises and mobiles. That was where the City Council used to meet and that was where the discussion had taken place in favour of Integrated Education in the 1970s. Then the Guildhall reopened and so they didn't need all these Portakabins. The Inland Revenue had wanted it, but the Council turned them down and agreed to let it to us. Then the parents came and did the work: they were derelict premises so we had to clean them.

Mushrooms in the corridors

Anne: There were mushrooms growing along the corridors and it was in state of disrepair. We had to have builders in to make it safe and then we had to paint it, clean it, do electrical work, cut the hedges and do all of that. We had parents in helping us do all of that and we had builders in. We were there painting or doing whatever was needed, up until midnight, we had whole families in. Each year after that we had to grow because we started with 68 children in September 1991 and ended the first year with 144. I think the Department of Education was a bit surprised at the speed with which it was growing, parents just kept sending their children during the year.

We came in on the back of the legislation and we met the Department's criteria for funding in a few weeks. It was really up to the wire, very last minute. They gave us a normal budget to run a school and we worked all over the summer to get it up and running for September. Every year after that we needed an extra something. There was another building and we had to get it done up and I remember being there past midnight with the architect, fighting with somebody who was doing the work on the school saying that the electricity wouldn't be ready by the morning. It had to be because there were new children coming in the morning. These were the conversations. We had families out there at midnight, cleaning toilets, getting everything ready for the next year because each year we were getting bigger and bigger. So parental involvement was enormous, there was huge enthusiasm.

Managing Growth

Anne: In the middle of this, I became Principal of the school. I remember during that first year, towards the end of the first month, I rang the Department at break time because I was teaching as well, and every day more people were coming in. I remember saying I needed another teacher next month. He asked how many children I had got and I told him. He asked, 'Where are you getting all these children from?' I looked out the window and there was a nice tree opposite, I said I was growing them in trees. I could hear a sharp intake of breath. This man thought there was a lunatic running Oakgrove Primary, which was probably right! We got our new teacher and then another because we were growing, that was the kind of speed of the thing. I always felt that Integrated Education in Derry was a door that was kind of partly open and just needed somebody to push it open.

While that was all happening in the primary school, there was a separate working group working towards a college for the following year. The primary school was doing whatever they had to do to grow and the other group had very serious work to do because the college was a whole different ball game and came up against a lot of objection.

Work begins on the college

Colm: For the college, the Principals of six secondary schools in Derry went to the Department of Education and said that there was no need for another school in Derry, that there were vacant places. The Department simply said to them that under the law, if the parents met the criteria, had the number of pupils and a site that the parents had the right to an Integrated Education and that was the end of the discussion.

Bernie: Once the schools were established, we became governors. We had the rule that only one person from each family would be a governor in the school.

I became more involved with the college and Tim stuck with the primary school. I was also secretary for the Foyle Trust for Integrated Education so I was organising meetings. I was saying to Colm, over the first week or two of the primary school opening, that we had to have the college meeting off the ground in order to get the college open for the following September. I actually did the radio interview to announce it, which I'm always very proud of. Colm made me do it!

Colm: Bert Montgomery, a brilliant man who just recently died, was an estate agent. I grew up very close to him and then he went to a Protestant school and I went to a Catholic school and his family moved away from the West Bank of the Foyle. He found something like 28 different sites that were possible, some of which weren't even on the market. It was really difficult to get a place to start the college because it needed to be bigger. We actually applied for planning permission for an empty factory in Newbuildings, and a group of parents came along and said that would not be an acceptable place, they didn't think their children would be safe there, that Newbuildings site was not a good place for an integrated school.

Anne: It was a flashpoint and it was seen as a Protestant village and sometimes when buses would come back from football matches they'd be stoned.

Colm: It was one of the places that they were building houses at the time of the movement of Protestant people, so a whole lot of Protestant families from the West Bank went into the new houses there and it became very much a Protestant neighbourhood.

Let's do it

Colm: At this time we had the first ever meeting with notice of a formal motion. The motion was that even if the Department of Education did not fund the college, we would open it anyway. We had to advertise for staff, we were going to recruit eight teachers and other ancillary staff and we couldn't recruit teachers and then say to them, 'Sorry, the college is not opening, we're not going to pay your salary.' This was about January 1991. If the Department refused to fund the school for whatever reason, we were going to have to raise a quarter of a million pounds to fund the college for that year. And if they still refused to fund it the second year, we would have to raise an additional half million pounds for that year. So that's what the discussion was about and it went back and forward. We had serious discussion and then we eventually went round everybody in the group and they all said, 'Yes, let's go for it. Let's do it.'

Bernie: A group of us had to sign to take responsibility for £10,000, to pay £10,000 if the school went under. I remember the two of us sitting looking out the window trying to estimate the value of our cars, thinking about £10,000, how would we pay? We all signed it, but we had no idea where we would find £10,000. At that stage of your life you have young children and you don't have £10,000, but we signed it anyway. It would have been another mortgage for us.

Colm: When we went to the Department of Education at the beginning of 1992, the Minister for Education was Lord Donaldson who chaired the meeting. They said, 'Well, of course you'll open as an independent school for a few years and if it proves viable, then the Department will pay.' We said, 'No': the big charities, the Nuffield Foundation, the Rowntree Trust, etc. that had helped to fund Lagan College and Hazelwood, had said that now that the 1989 Order was on the statute book, that there was no longer a role for charities and the government would have to pay. We wanted to open the school in 1992, and it's worth noting that after that the Department brought in a regulation that no college could open in less than two years. We were the last college that opened in one year!

Kevin Lambe was still the Development Officer and NICIE held a big meeting in Derry, its Annual General Meeting, and Derry people went to it obviously. It was in the Everglades Hotel and NICIE was saying we needed more than a year to do this. The Department of Education said three years. Our response was that we really appreciated all the help and support we had got from NICIE, but that this was not NICIE's decision, it was our decision and we wanted to open the school in 1992. NICIE then said we were absolutely right, if we wanted to open in 1992 it was our decision and they would give us any help they could. It might not be possible, but go ahead, and that's how it opened.

Anne: The Department only came through with the permission to go ahead with the college in August and we were opening in September. I remember clearly because we were on holiday and we got a phone call in France to say you can go ahead. We had about 70 or 80 children lined up for the school. A lot of people who weren't happy with their kids at other schools and wanted to have Integrated Education kept their children at their original school, but we had a few that came and repeated their first year in order to get to the integrated school.

Planning to grow the college

Colm: In the college we could only take first years, and then when they became second years, we took a new intake and then they moved up and we took another new intake.

Anne: That's how we did it. We had 11 Primary 7s that needed to leave the primary school and we didn't want them to have nowhere to go. That was a big part of it.

Bernie: Every year for the first five years we had days of interviewing from about 4.00pm to about 10.00 at night, to get the next new teachers for the following year because the staff number was going up that amount every year.

Colm: We ended up with the school in Northern Ireland with the most Portakabins! Somebody had suggested Gransha Hospital, the old mental hospital, as a site for the college. We got half the building and the hospital used the other part for storage. Then every year after that we had to put a row of mobile classrooms in the grounds beside it. So that was year three, four, five, six and seven. There were about 45 mobile classrooms.

Impact of Integrated Education

Tim: In terms of the impact on our children, we had a very concrete vision. Evidence of that was when my oldest daughter became a teacher in Aberystwyth. She was in the staffroom and realised that the North Welsh staff were talking in a very derogatory way about the English staff who weren't in the room. She raised the point with them. She said, 'Do you realise what you are doing?' I don't think that would have occurred to her if she hadn't gone to integrated schools and discussed difference with people of a different stripe. She challenges segregation and prejudice. I think my kids all have a strong sense of social justice.

Anne: I remember a story from one of my daughters. She talked about having gone into medicine and that the people she did medicine with were from grammar schools, separate schools, independent schools. She thought that she felt more at ease dealing with a variety of patients. On a particular placement in a mental health facility, she went with a colleague who was to interview one of the patients but this patient was silent, wouldn't speak to anybody. Her colleague had to go, and while my daughter was sitting there, she started to talk to this person and they had a grand conversation. That was great and when her colleague came back she realised that Nora (my daughter) was talking to this guy who wouldn't normally talk to anybody. This was a kind of breakthrough and her colleague was delighted and the hospital was delighted. Nora said she didn't do anything different, it was the way you just speak to everybody because that's what you do. I think that was part of integration because they were used to doing that and Nora didn't have any kind of fear.

One of my daughters, when I asked her what difference Integrated Education made, said she was talking to a friend of hers who went to the school. My daughter asked her what she thought, if she had to say what Integrated Education gave her. She said, 'A sense of fearlessness.'

If only everybody in Northern Ireland could be proud of everybody in Northern Ireland

Colm: There was a little girl who was eight at the time, and who had been to another school. Her parents were part of the group who opened Oakgrove Primary School, one was Catholic and one was Protestant. A few days after the school opened, the little girl came home and as she was taking off her school bag and raincoat, her mother said, 'How did you get on today?' and she said, 'Fine.' Her mother said, 'How do you like your new school?' and she said, 'Fine.' Her mother said, quite casually, 'What's the difference between the new school, Oakgrove Integrated Primary School, and your old school?' The mother was quite taken aback when the little girl said to her, 'Mammy, actually I never told you before, but at my old school I never talked about you. I talked about Daddy, but I didn't talk about you. At Oakgrove, I can be proud of both of you.' That what it's all about! Even at the age of eight a child knows there are things you don't talk about. If only everybody in Northern Ireland could be proud of everybody in Northern Ireland.

Introducing the ethos to staff

Anne: Right from the start, we met and had a training day for teachers where we looked at contentious issues. We needed to be able to talk in front of one another, to test things out because lots of us hadn't had to do that before. We had to do that among ourselves, and it had to be about contentious issues, it couldn't just be polite things. So that was done every year and it continues to be done and that's the basis of being able to do any of the work within the school with the children and with the parents. As we went along, we did have contentious issues we had to deal with. We needed the staff to have the skills to respond to things that happened in order that we could deal with it rather than sweep everything under the carpet, we bring it up and put it on the table.

Anytime I was involved with interviews for new staff I always felt that we needed somebody who liked children. Some people thought it was bizarre to put that in an advert, but for me it wasn't, because the key thing was that the children were the centre of all of this. The other thing was to get some kind of indication that the interviewee understood what integration meant, that it was more than politeness. Many, though not all, teachers in Northern Ireland were trained on a separate basis, but people bring integration from other directions in their lives, for example, mixed marriages. I saw an interview recently where somebody was talking about her sister who was married to somebody from another country, and how that had affected the family. Integration isn't just about education you know. It can come at you from different directions.

Colm: My original thinking was that the impact was on the children, but in fact it's on the parents and the grandparents and the teachers and the families of the teachers. There would

be examples of disagreements within families, that parents want their children to go to an integrated school and the grandparents don't. Sometimes the grandparents win and sometimes the parents win, but the impact is not just on the child in the classroom, it goes out. You can have absolutely no doubt that when the integrated primary school opened in 1991 and the integrated college opened in 1992 that there was discussion in every teacher staffroom and every college in the town about the integrated school. There was a kind of insult involved in that the other schools are not 'good enough' in some way, that they're deficient. They obviously won't be happy with being criticised like that. I think that every school in Derry now says they open to people of all traditions. They didn't say that in 1990.

Anne: I would question whether all schools ever sit down with their staff and do a session on contentious issues, the session a whole lot of staff don't want to be at. They always have too much to do and they're very busy and could I just miss that session. No, you can't. It's the most important thing that you do because you need to have the skills to deal with it. And you may need to hear things that you don't want to hear.

Bernie: That wasn't just the teachers. That was the Foyle Trust for Integrated Education as well. We all became extremely comfortable talking about issues like that, to the extent if you were going to something and you were a Catholic female and you said you needed a male Protestant to come with you, somebody would volunteer. We were very comfortable with who we were in that group.

Tim: When I look at the schools of Derry now, they all say, 'We welcome diversity, we are a diversity friendly school,' and that's a good thing. The language of integration has been adopted by all the schools, but, from what I've seen and heard, the practice hasn't always followed. The Anti Bias Curriculum could be a feature in all schools. The Shared Education Project troubles me because it's giving a big block of money to parts of this community so that their children can meet for a few hours a week, share a few non-contentious activities and then go back to their schools. To me, that's reinforcing segregation, it's not putting them in the same classroom on a day-to-day basis, which is where the real integration takes place.

Colm: On the other hand, it's better than not having anything.

Bernie: There was something we all did early in the process. We did the Investing in Excellence programme. It was learning about a positive approach to things and how to change things in your life. A lot of us did this and we were extremely positive as a result of it. I was speaking to the Chair of our Board of Governors at an event at the primary school one day, and he slapped me on the back and said, 'That's really great, that's marvellous Bernie.' This other woman, Principal of another school, came over and pointed her finger at the two of us and said, 'That's what you Derry people do differently, you're always telling each other how good you are.'

What would we have done differently?

Bernie: I would have kept better records from the very first meeting. Once I became Secretary of Foyle Trust I have the books. I have about five or six books, but it's from about a year and a half into it.

Tim: If I had stayed sober at the barbecue, I might not have got involved at all! I was saying, 'Brilliant idea!' It was like getting on a train to wave someone goodbye and when I sobered up, the train had left the station with me on it. Yes, it's been a fun project with a positive outcome, I've enjoyed it.

Colm: There were areas where people tried to start integrated schools that failed. My daughter showed me the change, the bell curve in the graph and you have the early adopters of new ideas and then you have the next group that does it and it seems that when you hit about 17, 18, 19% of the population, that's the tipping point and it becomes the norm after that. So now we are at 7%, so we have to do another 7, 8, 9, 10% of pupils into integrated schools before it becomes the norm. And it's not moving as fast as it was before, but it's still moving, so we just keep it moving, just keep it moving.

Anne: I think we were lucky to have such a great group of enthusiastic people who kind of thought the same way as us and who were prepared to do the work and who were prepared to take risks and who were brave enough to do all of that in the face of the community we lived in. It always made sense to me and I wouldn't change any of it, including the mistakes, warts and all, the bad times as well. There were times when we dealt with contentious issues that brought us to a different place. If we hadn't had the hardship, then I think we probably wouldn't have been doing a really good job. If this was easy, why isn't everybody doing it?

Personal reflections

Tim: The key thing for me is that the whole integrated school project has been a celebration of 'individuality, tolerance and joy'. The real pleasure for me is that art and drama and music, which are very undervalued in the curriculum, are prized in an integrated school. When we have a nativity scene the entire year group will be on stage, there'll be 63 shepherds instead of three, 14 wise men and 28 wise women as well. It's just the inclusiveness and the sense that it's a community; it's more than just a school, it's a community of the children, of the parents and the teachers, and it's a little oasis of sanity. For me it replaced Soho when I was 16 and the Pound Club in Belfast when I was 21. Now I've got Oakgrove.

Colm: I'm glad that I've been involved in it and glad I'm still involved. I went from being one of the parents and being co-chair of the Foyle Trust for Integrated Education on to the board of NICIE, then chair of NICIE. Then I ended up as President of NICIE and then I was asked by the Department of Education to co-author the Independent Review of Integrated Education. In the process of doing all that, I decided to join a political party, just before the referendum on the Good Friday Agreement. I looked through all the political parties that were at the talks at the time and I joined the Alliance Party because they were the one party who really seemed to be serious about reconciliation and were committed to Integrated Education. I'll be talking to politicians to try and move forward some of the

Oakgrove Integrated College, 2017.

suggestions and proposals in that Review. There is just so much to be done. We come from a divided society and we don't have to be divided. And so I'll just continue to do the work.

Bernie: I think looking back it was a marvellous project to be in. It was terribly exciting, it affected our whole family. One of the things that sticks with me is that everybody has the same fears and not to be afraid to do something. That's something that I see coming through in our children. When the government said that you can't open the school for three years, we went ahead and did it. Then at work, if something like that happened me, if somebody said, 'No, you can't do that,' I would say, 'What?' It probably made me more successful in life, workwise as well. I think the children have definitely gained from it. I see, especially our youngest, her thinking process is very like the thinking process that we had in the early days, where she just does it.

It changed our lives totally because, up to that point, I came home from work exhausted, managed to struggle to get dinner on the table, get the kids sorted, get them to bed. I'd be so tired I'd do the dishes the next morning and sit for the evening, watch television and go up to bed. Then suddenly I was doing the minutes, I was getting minutes out, getting ready for the meeting on Wednesday, cooking on Tuesday for Wednesday. Suddenly I wasn't tired anymore, so it changed my life.

Anne: My involvement in Integrated Education has just made enormous sense for me in terms of a just society here in Northern Ireland. In 1979 I co-ordinated a group of 53 people in Derry to go to India and we all went to different places. When we came back we reviewed the trip and really the outcome was that we had learnt a lot about how people live there and so on, but also that only people in India could solve their problems in India. For me, Integrated Education is a practical way of dealing with and addressing reconciliation in Northern Ireland.

Passing on the baton

Colm: There was a group of people talking about opening a college in Ballymena, and I said to them to call up and see our college, Oakgrove College. It hadn't been going very long at the time. They came up. I always remember the day. We showed them around the old red brick empty hospital building, and, as they were going away, I remember hearing one person saying to another, 'We could do that.'

Norah Connolly is a parent from Bridge Integrated Primary and New-Bridge Integrated College.

I got involved in Integrated Education in 1985, when we moved from West Belfast to Banbridge. I had wanted to move back to Belfast because I was so lonely. We were only here in Banbridge a year or two, when Bridge started. So that's where I got all my friends. There was a committee set up for a proposal for an integrated school and I got involved and decided to take my children out of their school and send them to Bridge Integrated Primary School. I became very involved in the Parent Council and fundraising and after a few years, I was invited onto the Board of Governors as a parent governor. My parents were very supportive and when I explained to them about Integrated Education my dad used to say, 'One of those schools that her kids go to.'

The founding of Bridge Integrated Primary School

In the founding group there was Wes and Cathy Beck and Frank and Sheila McQuade, who were Alliance Party councillors. The first Chair was Brian Henning and his wife Shirley was involved and there were lots of families involved. He, along with a lady called Agnes McConville, who has now passed away, would have been the two main people. He found the house for the primary school. Parents like myself, who had children going to the school, went in after work and knocked down walls, took kitchens out and decorated it. Another friend, Helen Mallon, who is a teacher and her husband, a

local GP, worked as a voluntary teacher and it was just one big happy family. These were parents who didn't know each other, but are now still friends. We were from different backgrounds. My friend Helen, the teacher, was from the Protestant community. We were really close friends. If I was minding her children, they came to Mass on a Sunday with me, and if my children were at her house, they went to the Presbyterian Church. It was just a community, and we made very good long term friends.

At the beginning with the primary school, we had to have public meetings. It was covered in the local paper that a committee had been set up as a steering group, inviting people to a public meeting to see if there was a need for an integrated school and there clearly was. Then enrolment forms went out, and you had to put your child's name down. You could have put the name down nearly from the child's birth.

Once we got enough pupils and secured a site, the steering group applied for funding. It was the Nuffield Foundation that actually lent us the money, and then it was paid back by the Department to purchase the school. In the early days the parents were supported in the process of establishing the school by Bernard Boyle and Michael Wardlow from the Northern Ireland Council for Integrated Education (NICIE).

There were a lot of challenging things going on at the time. It was said Integrated Education was only for the middle class, and it wasn't true. The parents bit the bullet and said

Carson Awards at
New-Bridge College, 2017.

Olympic Torch at New-Bridge
Intergrated College, 2012.

they wanted to create the school. A lot of people thought it would fail, but it didn't. I think it was perceived as a threat to education in the town. There was the rumour that integrated schools got more money than other schools, but we didn't.

Relationships with the churches were fine, though the Catholic Church wouldn't have been as supportive. There were seven children making their First Communion in the first year and my daughter was one of them. They were told by the parish priest that they would be making their Communion with the local Catholic primary school. We said, 'No, it's our day.' It took a while, but the seven children made their Communion and we went back to the school for refreshments. We had a barbecue in the local rugby club and the whole school attended, along with the families of the children. It was a celebration and then every year, when you went back to the school after First Communion for tea and sandwiches, it was the Protestant children's parents who organised that. They maybe didn't go to the Mass but they organised the sandwiches and the cakes and buns.

The primary school was open within two years and my five children all went there. I remember the first day of Bridge. The parents were all there with their children in their wee uniforms going into this house. P1 and 2 were together because there were only 58 children starting. Mr Graham was a teaching Principal and then there were four teachers and others who came in on a voluntary basis to help out. Parents used to go in to do reading. If you could, you did anything to help, in the office or walking the children to the swimming pool and walk them back. We had no money for buses.

Then came the College

When my youngest, Hannah, started P1, my two eldest children went to the local high school. I thought, 'Why are children going to an integrated primary school and there's no follow up?' A steering committee of parents from Newry and Banbridge got together and decided we wanted an integrated secondary school. So I was there at the beginning of both schools.

There were some parents from Newry, Newcastle and Banbridge. My husband went to the first meeting in Newcastle. He came back and said it was interesting but it was obvious you couldn't have one school in Newcastle to serve Banbridge, Newry and Newcastle, because there are great big mountains in between. How would you get kids to Newcastle in bad weather? Shimna opened in Newcastle. Then there was a meeting in Banbridge Leisure Centre for Newry and Banbridge parents. My husband was to go to the meeting, but he had a business meeting and said I should go. I said I wasn't interested in being involved because I was on the Parent Council of Bridge, on the Board of Governors and treasurer of the school. But eventually I did go to the meeting. There were quite a few people there, a couple or three men from Newry and myself from Banbridge and another guy, Tom Griffin. There were six main people who were going to drive this college forward. Everybody got their job. Mine was to find a site, but I knew nothing about sites. I went to the ordinance survey office in Belfast and looked at maps with farmers' fields and stuff. My very good friend, Frank McQuade, was a councillor, a member of the Bridge Board of Governors, and a farmer, so I went to him and said, 'Right, tell me some farmers' names who might possibly sell land.'

I want to buy your land

I looked at 28 sites. I just went up and knocked the door and said, 'I want to buy your land.' There was a site down off the dual carriageway. I knocked the door and said, 'We're interested in purchasing the land,' and he said, 'What's it for?' and I said, 'It's for an integrated school.' He said, 'An integrated school? What's that?' and I said it was for Protestant and Catholic children to be educated together. He then told me to get off his land, there would be no Catholic children sitting down in a school on his land. For the site here, I approached Mr Cousins myself. He lived just down the road and I just went to the door and this is how we got the land.

Because my two oldest children were at St Patrick's they couldn't move because they were in fourth and fifth year and you have to start the new school with a Year 8 class. My third child was to go into Year 8, but that year the new school was deferred. I approached Anne Hovey, who was NICIE Acting Development Officer. I said it wasn't fair that I had put in all this work and my child would miss out. We approached the Department of Education and we are the only school in Northern Ireland that started with a second year. We had a Year 8 of 78 and a Year 9 of 18, the only school ever to do it.

To recruit our numbers we went out to leisure centres, town halls and sent out fliers. We went to all the schools and stood outside giving out fliers. We were chased away but we did it anyway. We always put things in the paper and then we arranged the first meeting in Dromore. We had posters made and everything and we had two of my children in makeshift

uniforms to give everybody the impression this was going to happen, and nobody turned up. I don't know why. Maybe Dromore just didn't want it. It was an awful night anyway and it was soul destroying. It really was. We cried, and then I said, 'No, guys, keep going.'

Once we had bought the land, we got second hand buildings from the Department and they were terrible. There were drips everywhere; the day we opened there were buckets everywhere, but it didn't matter. We had parents coming in cleaning windows the day the school opened. In the August of that year, 1995, the diggers were in to flatten the land. This was August and we were opening in September and that's all there was. I was down in my caravan and was coming up to Banbridge and I thought I would nip in. The digger was there and the digger driver said he had been told he needed to go another five foot, and I said, 'Go for it.' He said, 'I'm supposed to be meeting some wee woman,' and I said, "That's me.' He said, 'Right.' I said if we needed another five foot, go ahead, so we did. On 13th August, the mobiles were put on site, two weeks before the school opened.

Then there was a commotion outside my house one day and my husband asked me what it was. There were desks, there were books all delivered to my house and left in the garden. I had opened an office in my house where I could work from and have a postal address. The driver said we were told to deliver it here, and showed me the invoice. We had to transport it all down to the school.

Such a proud day

We opened on the day, on time. We needed 60 pupils, but the 18 second years didn't count, we needed bums on seats on 1st September. We were all waiting outside and only 59 children got off the bus. And then another came driving in saying, 'We slept in, we slept in!' so there were 60. It was such a proud day, it really was.

Our first prize day was outside, because we didn't have the room. It was in the car park, which was a football pitch and a netball court. Then the next one was rained off and we had to come in. Parents were involved, though not in teaching like the primary school. We had parents on the Board of Governors. I'm still here.

'The Magnificent Seven'

I had no experience of project management or finances before I was involved. I had to learn everything on the way. We were looking for people with commitment to Integrated Education, a Principal and seven teachers. We needed a bit of everything. The ad went into the paper, and we got 15 applications for Principal, which was unbelievable. We had to learn how to shortlist, then went to training for interviewing. We interviewed for the Principal first. I was so nervous because I had never done it before, and all these parents were depending on me to get the best possible person. And we did, Peter Agnew, wonderful man. He got the job and then we interviewed for seven teachers. We had 78 applications. We interviewed in Bridge Primary School, on a Saturday and a Sunday, because we had no premises. And we got, I call them, the magnificent seven. They gave up their jobs, they handed in their notice and we still hadn't got a school. They knew that, and that there was always a chance it could fail. I think two of them are still here, Anna Loughran and Catherine Gorman. Elaine Lennon actually came to my house before the school opened and we worked in the office there. That's how we started.

A special school where Catholic and Protestant children were all friends

I have two grandchildren at New-Bridge at the minute and I have five at Bridge Primary School. They just go automatically. The grandchildren just take it for granted obviously because they didn't know anything different, but it had a big impact on my children. When we went up to my mother's and my son Desmond, the third one, asked his cousin if he was Catholic or Protestant, my sister was horrified. She said, 'Why's he asking that?' and he said it was because he had friends who are Catholic and Protestant and they talked about it in school. He

thought that was normal. He was only in P5 and he explained that he was at a school, a special school where Catholic and Protestant children were all friends.

Family and motivations

I was brought up in West Belfast, the youngest of 13, I didn't know what a Protestant looked like, if they looked any different from us, until I went to work. I worked for a Unionist MP, a solicitor. People used to ask me if I wasn't frightened, because the Troubles were quite bad. I remember I said, 'No,' that they were as frightened as we would be. Everybody's the same. He was a solicitor for a lot of Unionists who were up for murder during the Troubles. That's why I didn't tell anybody. But I did go to court with him and we'd have gone to prisons and taken statements. They used to say, 'Here's the wee West Belfast girl.'

Looking back, I wouldn't have done anything differently. I helped other steering groups, and you know my advice was to keep going. No matter what, keep going, dust yourself down and keep going.

I think the fact that not many schools are starting or transforming recently may be because there are a lot of integrated schools, but still not enough. Maybe Protestant and Catholic schools are amalgamating, sharing the building. I think it should be if they are going to share a building, a Catholic school and a Protestant school in the building, they should be integrated and bring the children all together and the staff. You can't have separate entrances. People say Shared Education is the same as Integrated Education, it isn't. You see it in Bridge particularly at Christmas or big events, all the children together. Every Christmas I sit and cry. Every year. When they start singing hymns, you know, I am so proud that there's kids from all different communities.

Grace Doone was a founding teacher in Mill Strand Integrated Primary School in 1987 and has taught there ever since.

A new job

I started work in Mill Strand Integrated Primary School, Portrush in September 1987. The interview was at a local hotel outside Coleraine because we had no premises. I was delighted to get an interview but I was very apprehensive because the integrated sector was completely new to me and to most people. The idea that Protestant and Catholic children and children of no faith would be educated together is such a natural thing, instead of children being divided. There was no school, as such, and I remember late, late that night a phone call came, and they offered me the post.

I had been subbing around the area because we had three young children and I had just come back to teaching, but always in the Catholic sector. The word was that if you left the Catholic sector, you actually don't even think about trying to get back in. So, it was a big step into the unknown to go to the integrated sector, and there was a lot of disagreement about Integrated Education and it was a risk, but a risk worth taking in my opinion. My family were remarkably supportive, because I am from the Roman Catholic background and all our history is within Catholic education. They were very, very pleased and would have told people and probably would have tried to support me in things people would have said to them, 'Why is she doing that? Why is she going away from, almost leaving your faith?' That is how people would have looked at it.

There was a lack of understanding because they didn't realise that there was a Christian ethos, and there would be sacramental preparation, and I had the privilege and still do, all these years, of preparing children for sacraments.

Where could this school be?

I remember very shortly after being offered the job, we drove around Portrush. There was a building somewhere, but we didn't know where. We had heard it was an old house, so turned up to the right and it wasn't the right place at all. Then we reversed out and drove to another place and, yes, it was Dhu Varren House, a big old, grey stand-alone house. There was nothing else there. That was exciting, that the school was going to be there!

So, there had been a Principal appointed, myself as an assistant teacher, the nursery teacher and an assistant, Mrs Nora Nevin. I drove to Dungiven, to meet the Principal, Dessie Irwin, and we met just in the car and chatted. I remember asking him, 'Do we have policies in place? What is our handwriting policy?' And he sort of looks at you, because there wasn't anything. We started in September.

Grace Doone gathering rushes.

Mill Strand 30th anniversary on Mill Strand Beach.

Early days of the school

There were two camps. There was huge opposition, we learned that as the months and years went on. But there was good interest as well, and a lot of people signed their children up for Year One and there was a good crowd for the nursery class. There was such an interest, desire and need for the school.

I had 12 children in my class. When I was appointed, I should have been taking P1, 2, 3, 4 and, I think, possibly 5.

Jane Stewart was in that first class. Nursery and Primary 1 were downstairs, and we were upstairs. Jane has a growth disorder, Spondyloepiphyseal Dysplasia (S.E.D.), a condition that meant she wouldn't be able to climb stairs or anything else. But she was accepted like everybody else. Do you know how Jane managed? I carried her. Nowadays you wouldn't do that. It would not be acceptable, but there was no other way and I carried Jane Stewart. I am sure she remembers it well because she was in my class two or three years, on my hip, up those stairs and down those stairs. Every day. Up and down. Down to go to the toilet, back up, etc. Jane is a terrific character (and an amazing young woman now with her own children at the school) but it was difficult in those early years because those stairs are pretty steep as well!

Anything that we had was basically what people were donating or throwing out

There were obviously chairs. There was no blackboard. On the table, there were jotters. I remember the jotters, they were that old newsprint. If you wrote with ink pen, or with felt marker, everything came through. It wasn't good paper. There was fluorescent paint. I don't know where they got this from, but there were tubes and tubes of green and yellow and orange fluorescent paint and that is basically it. There might have been a packet of pencils, nothing else.

My parents were market traders and I would have been used to going to Ballymena Market in particular, so anything that I saw for sale that might do my classroom, I was buying. I remember buying a big, big container of buttons and the children counted with those. Also, going off to Donegal and picking up shells, so they could count with those and lovely wee pebbles. We had those for a couple of years. Nowadays, it would be called outdoor classroom, but we were doing it way before that. I would have brought in burdens of stuff from the country where we have a wee place in Glenavy and just brought in lots of stuff from nature. It was such an exciting time, just so special in my life. I certainly don't regret it.

There was no school uniform nor school crest in those early years. I remember one afternoon during a staff meeting we started to talk about what might be good for a school crest.

Suggestions and ideas of using the school location as a crest-like the beach or waves or birds flying high. I remember that I scribbled a sketch of the school front door (the doors belong to the original Dhu Varren House and are pretty impressive double doors with a fan glass window above and steps leading upwards). I suggested, 'Why don't we use the front doors of the school with a child standing on either side of the steps?' and added, 'Let's have one of the doors open to show that our school is open and welcoming to everyone.' Mrs Cassells, one of the early team of teachers, was really good at art and I recall her drawing the 'idea' and saying, 'Something like that then!' It looked great and that became our school crest: simple and child-centred. It's been tweaked a bit over the years, with computer technology and all that, but that's how we got our school crest. That's something I remember very well.

A huge, huge battle

Within the whole Northern Ireland Council for Integrated Education (NICIE) Principles, there has to be a mix. Mr Irwin was Catholic. When they appointed the nursery teacher, she was from the Protestant background, as was Mrs Nevin, and Sally Osbourne, the nursery teacher. When they appointed the P1 teacher, Mrs Moulden came, and would have been from a Protestant background. And then myself, Catholic background.

Very quickly then we had to think about doing sacraments, because that was part of the whole contract. Children from a Roman Catholic background, if their parents chose, would still be provided with sacramental preparation, and although I had the experience of doing it in the Catholic sector, it certainly was very different when we started to do it in the integrated. We used the same resources, but we had a lot of challenges. A lot of bridges to cross.

Really, we weren't welcomed by the local Catholic churches. Our children weren't going to be able to make their First Communion. I couldn't really tell you the year, it could be '88, it could be '89, we started having meetings and meetings. These were innocent children. These were six and seven year old children whose parents wanted them to follow the Catholic faith, and make their sacraments, and we were making provisions for them to be taught by qualified teachers. But you can't really blame the local parishes and the local priests, because it is obviously coming from headquarters. But we certainly weren't welcomed in terms of sacraments. It was very difficult, and really it was a battle and meetings, after meetings, after meetings, to St Malachy's to meet a priest, over to Portstewart, down to Portrush. Eventually we would get an agreement that the children would receive their First Confession and First Holy Communion.

At that time, it was made very clear that the parish school had ownership of the First Communions. It is now regarded as a parish First Communion. We were made to feel like second class citizens. It was very, very sad. When you speak to some of the parents that were involved in it, there was a lot of heartache there. A lot of heartache.

Much more of a battle was to try to get our children their sacrament of Confirmation. That was horrendous. We didn't have Confirmation in the early days because we didn't have a P7 class. But it filtered up eventually, and that was a huge, huge battle. Newspapers and local TV stations wanted to get involved and the parents did their best to keep that out because they were looking to protect their children, whereas newspapers and media are looking for a story.

We went to Ballymena, a convoy of us and met the bishop's envoy or whatever; I have to say, that didn't go very well. He wasn't very supportive of women and most of the group, as you can perhaps imagine, were women because, 'If you want something done, ask a woman!' We came away feeling he didn't even want to hear what we had to say.

People that send their children to the integrated sector, not all are committed to integration but a lot of them, certainly in the early days, were very strong in their faith. Even if they were an inter-church marriage, they still wanted to keep the promises they made at their child's baptism and get their child raised as Catholic and make their sacraments. It was very, very difficult. Thank God it is a lot easier now.

Within the last 20 years, we're more accepted because in the early days, all the local schools were basically against us.

Apart from anything, we were taking their children, weren't we? When you think about it. It is bottoms on seats at the end of the day as well. So, if you look back through newspapers and stuff, there was a lot of remarks made about that school on the hill. No religion, and poaching our children!

Doing it our way: contributors and risk takers

The school was referred to many's a time as a test tube for the university, because there were a lot of far thinking university people involved in the establishment of the school. Alan Smith, Stuart Marriott, the late Bill O'Neill. Wonderful, wonderful people and very committed to integration. Alan Smith and his wife Elaine, and Dot and Derek Wilson, of course, were instrumental in founding the school. They were the seed that grew the school. But Bill O'Neill and Stuart Marriott, now I am getting a bit emotional, they gave so much time to us. We gave time to them, there was no such thing as measuring time in those days. I think when you start to measure things, it is not a very good idea. They were in the school, week in and week out, sharing their skills and knowledge and bringing us resources from the university.

I remember one of them bringing reading books, again, we only had old fashioned, out of date stuff that nobody wanted, really. When you buy books now, you buy a set of 10 or 12, or 15. But it was one of each and it was sufficient for 12 children in my class, and we were able to use that. And they shared their expertise and all the new developments in literacy. They were terrific, they really were. In those early days, any parent that decided to send their children to our school were taking risks. Even taking risks in their learning. We weren't established. All the local schools had many years behind them and we were something very, very new. We were very free. You obviously do your staple subjects, your core subjects. You know as a trained teacher what has to be covered, but there wasn't a core curriculum. There really wasn't anything that you could look up and say, 'I have to cover this, this and this.' You just covered what you thought should be done. That was the beauty of it because

you had that freedom to bring in so much more and step way out of your comfort zone.

In Portrush, I am sure it is still in existence, there was a residential home for people with special needs. We made links and three or four of them came up every week and were part of our school. Barney helped Tom with the caretaking, cleaning the floors etc. Wasn't that wonderful for children to experience that? There was a girl called Anna in my classroom. There was no such thing as a classroom assistant in the primary school, so Anna was supposed to come to help me, but, in fact, Anna just loved taking part in whatever the children were doing. And I have photographs of them in the wee gardens that we built. I would have brought loads of flowers to the school because mummy and daddy had a nursery down at home, they were market gardeners, and I would have just brought burdens, and burdens of plants and we would have planted loads of stuff.

At our first Christmas, I suppose we were still this odd school up on the hill, Mr Irwin, the Principal, with his great singing skills, took the children out into the community to sing around the war memorial in Portstewart. Wasn't that lovely? The war memorial has connotations of belonging more to the Protestant side, and we were standing there altogether singing around it on the first Christmas.

No doubt, and from the word go, it has always been inclusive in terms of the celebration, in terms of the choir. You would have children from both denominations and children of no faith, wanting to sing, wanting to attend the sacraments; which is lovely and that still goes on very, very much indeed. Likewise, their parents want to be involved. But the early days were tremendous, because we were like pioneers. We didn't really know where we were going. We only had a slight idea of what we were doing and with the good guidance of those men that I mentioned.

But it was a great place to be, it was an exciting place to be. We didn't measure time and we didn't really have a closing time. We just stayed. There was an awful lot of meetings, and the governors, with the early people that were involved in establishing the school, they were mostly the governors as well. They met and met, almost on a weekly basis, I would say. We would have known them face to face and first name to first name. All of those people.

The bond and the balance

I suppose we just had that bond, really, and they were in and out of the school and if things needed done, and if we were having any sort of fetes or celebrations or very wee basic things; nowadays it is much more elaborate perhaps, but it was very simple in those days. But those people were involved in everything – baking and selling wee bits and pieces and helping with art. It was such a good time.

Each teacher would bring part of themselves to their class, that is the beauty of Integrated Education: somebody from the Protestant background, they share something with somebody from the Catholic background. There is no mystery about the mass, there is no mystery about the sacraments – things are open and honest and shared. Early on, we said we need to have a church service to balance it. So, we had established a harvest service in Ballywillan Presbyterian Church in Portrush and that is still going and that has been a great success. We decided that we would, in a big way, recognise Remembrance Day. It is certainly more inclusive now, Remembrance Day in November, but in those early days and just coming out of conflict, – I often wonder, 'Are we really out of it yet?' I don't know! But we were very close to the conflict in '87 and to wear a poppy really labelled you as Protestant. There is no doubt about it. We said we were going to recognise Remembrance Day in our school and do something about it, and we still do it every year. Children make little poppies, and each class makes a poppy wreath and we remember those that have lost their lives in all the conflicts, to try and take it away from belonging to one side. We also hold our annual School Carol Service in Holy Trinity Church of Ireland here in Portrush. The service is open to the whole of the local community and last year we almost filled the whole of the church - isn't that great altogether? So, that was three ways that we deliberately, and still do, make sure that we're trying to balance things.

We have done quite a bit of work with the help of NICIE also on flags and emblems. I have to say, there is not nearly as much done now but certainly then, there would have been. Maybe we had more courage or energy perhaps back then! If you had gone to a workshop run by NICIE, that would have enthused you to come back and do things with your class. So, talking about football teams and emblems and flags. Again, it is because I am from the country and I was reared in country crafts. I would make the St Brigid's Cross with the children. I would, and still do, bring rushes in every beginning of February and help the children. I have to say, they hardly ever pick up how to do it, but we work through making St Brigid's Cross and they know that Brigid didn't belong to one side or the other. She was a Christian saint and that sort of thing. So, symbols and emblems of Ireland and of Britain.

Changes over time

I can remember our 10th anniversary. There were great celebrations and we had a service in the Methodist Church in Coleraine. A terrific crowd of people turned up. I can remember myself doing a lovely reading. The idea of our school and the steps that we have taken and how a chrysalis turns into a butterfly, and it was a beautiful reading and it was quite emotional, and I can remember doing that.

Shortly after our 10th anniversary, Mr Irwin retired and we then had a period of instability. It wasn't a good time for our school. And then we started to rise up again like the phoenix. I could have moved away to another school during those dark days and dark years but I felt, 'Why should I?' I was there from the beginning, from the very first day that the school doors opened. I didn't think I would be there 31 years later! I thought to myself, I was the first teacher appointed and I was very determined.

We had a lovely man for a year, a temporary principal called Mr McKim. He was a retired principal from the secondary sector. A wonderful, compassionate, energetic man that just brought joy to the school. That helped a lot and that gave the governors time to pull the school back together and think about an appointment for a new principal.

Then they appointed Mr Reid who has been in our school, maybe 14 years? Certainly, the school is in a very good place in terms of numbers. We started off with 50+. I talked about my first class of 12, by the summer time, there was 19. They are talking about double intakes for the school, they are having to bring in more accommodation. There is a very serious possibility of a new building. That new building kind of breaks my heart a bit, because they are talking about relocating and Mill Strand has a beautiful site, and we look over that Mill Strand beach, which we have adopted as a school, environmentally wise. We look after it. It is a very special location, but there is a very big possibility of relocating to a new site.

The school is oversubscribed, so you can't be sentimental about it if you haven't got the space and facilities. When we started, the parents and governors did a wonderful job at preparing the old house, cleaning all the other chairs, sandpapering and painting. They did all of that. There have been four new classrooms built on in those early days, but we have outgrown our space.

There is a good atmosphere in the school now and there are a lot of very good people, particularly young staff as well. A lot of new young staff. I do think that they need to be maybe more aware. We can't always dip back into history, but we can't forget about what happened, and why we are here, and I think they need to be maybe more aware of that. The young people have no real understanding or recollection of what the Troubles were, and that conflict, and you don't want them to put a lot of energy and thought into it, but there is division in our community. And it has not gone away. So, I do think there needs to be more work in the schools about the division. Not to divide our children, but to be aware of the division, because how can you have mutual understanding and respect for people if you don't really understand where they are coming from?

Children that go through our school generally, by hook or by crook, they have something special. Now, not necessarily the real understanding about division or conflict, although they are aware of that, but there is definitely something that has crept into their being that makes them more tolerant, better at relationships, more understanding of other children and other adults and you can't put your finger on it, but sometimes you can say that child must have been at Mill Strand, because there is something special. So, we must be doing something right. Something is piercing them, going into their hearts. And maybe it will make a difference in our wee part of the world in future years, because they have something specially planted in their hearts.

A privilege

I love teaching. I think I might have been born to teach. I could never see myself doing something else. To get the chance to share your inner being as well and the freedom to do that, that you can be brave enough, courageous enough to share part of yourself; I think that is perhaps it. I think it is a privilege to help children with their religious instruction. I have a great liking for the Irish language too and I would use a little bit of Irish in my classes all over the years, quite a lot in these recent years because the children just love it.

So, wee bits of me goes into the children, is planted into the children and that is so rewarding. I don't know if that is any different from any other teacher that loves their job, but we have the freedom in the integrated sector, when we sit around the table, at lunch time and break time, as a group of people, different age groups, as teachers and assistants; as staff, and we have the freedom to talk and joke about what is going on in the world or what is going on in Northern Ireland or what we believe or what we experience, and we have the confidence to talk together in an open and honest way.

That might be the beauty of Integrated Education. It is important for the children, but I look at the staff as my second family. We have the freedom and confidence to talk to each other and joke to each other about virtually anything, and you don't get that in many places, because I am sure people have to hold back and say to themselves, 'I will not say that because I might offend somebody.' It's a safe environment. That is probably the big thing about Integrated Education.

It appears to me that the drive seems to be now to transform schools. I suppose it is all to do with finance, but the establishment from the word go of an integrated school is very exciting because you have that core of people that want to be part of it. I suppose you would have to work very hard on keeping the balance between Catholic and Protestant backgrounds, for staff and pupils. But we in our own school have to also, because I would be aware that our balance is not as good as it perhaps could be. In terms of how many children from one faith and another, or the balance of staff, because I think as a school gets older, they forget the old qualities that we have to maintain, and I think maybe we need to be reeled in a wee bit and look at our intake here. You don't want to turn children away. Everybody that wants Integrated Education should have that choice but we need to maintain balances as well. We want to have our children balanced and we want to have our staff balanced, otherwise then, we can't bring to our table, to our staff room that sense of being safe because we're not sharing our experiences. It is never going to be ideal. There are areas in Northern Ireland that are very predominately Protestant and predominantly Catholic, of course there are, but nevertheless, we do need to remember and regard the balance as important.

I think areas are getting very greyed, and schools are claiming they are integrated. They are doing a little bit of this, and a little bit of that, but they are not really integrated.

So, I think that certainly is a challenge for the integrated sector. There will always be people that are against it. The Catholic Church will, I imagine, continue to support their own church schools, of course. We need to remember our history: that Ireland had to fight very hard for Catholic people to get education at all and generations of Catholic people in the 18th and 19th century suffered powerfully under penal laws and weren't even allowed to attend school. So, I know where that is coming from. I think integration is just another choice. I don't think it should ever be imposed on anybody. We certainly have our Catholic sector. They do a terrific job. We have our state sector. They do a great job. We have an integrated sector and they do a great job too. I feel that integrated is the right choice, of course, but people have to have their choice.

In the early days there was a huge amount of investment from America. I imagine that is not available so much anymore; I wouldn't have thought so.

I started in '87 and this is 2018, so this must be my 32nd year. I don't think there are too many other people who have spent that long in Integrated Education.

My journey into Integrated Education has been a privilege, exciting, often very challenging, sometimes heart-breaking, but, apart from my family, my husband Hugh and my four sons, it has been the best experience of my life and I am still here.

Olwen Griffith was the Principal of Blackwater Integrated College. She also taught in Lagan College and was a Deputy Principal at Ulidia Integrated College.

Of course you can talk to each other!

I grew up in a mixed area but teaching in a school in inner city Belfast, I very quickly learned that being separated was important to some people and I thought that was very sad. My journey in Integrated Education started when I taught in that school. I had taken children away on cross-community trips to London and we were going to go to another school for a joint assembly. When we were at the other school, some of the girls said to me, 'Miss, we were able to talk to them!' And I thought, 'Of course you were! 15-year-old girls and boys: music, clothes, make up. Of course you would be able to talk to each other!' And at that point in time I decided I needed to be involved in something that deliberately brings these young people together.

A short time later Lagan College opened and I said to a friend of mine, 'I'm going to teach there one day.' In 1985 I joined the staff in Lagan College, the first planned integrated school in Northern Ireland, which was a great experience. One of the earliest memories of Lagan College I have is when we came up for an open day one Saturday morning and all the windows had been broken in all of the mobiles. We got our dustpans and brushes out and we cleaned up the glass. Fortunately, it was a nice morning so we had our open day in mobiles without windows! And that was just part of, I suppose, almost pioneer spirit, you know, 'We're not going to let this

beat us!' So I had 15 fabulous years in Lagan College and I really enjoyed that.

Special days at Ulidia College

I loved my job as head of Maths in Lagan College, I had a fabulous department that was working really well. It was one of the best departments in the school due to the people with whom I was working. However, I needed a challenge, so that's when I moved to Ulidia Integrated College as Deputy Principal. Eugene Martin (Ulidia IC Principal at that time) was head of Maths before me in Lagan College, so there was a friendship that continued when I got to Ulidia and what was great about that was we didn't have 'getting-to-know-you-time', we were able to get stuck into work immediately and that was very exciting.

Ulidia had just received its funding when I went as Deputy Principal. We were in the mobiles and all the fun that happens with that and then getting into the new school was just absolutely incredible. Those early days in Ulidia were very special days. The children were very prepared to talk about how they felt about things. I was discussing with children one day the various terms we use: Unionist, Nationalist, Republican, Loyalist, what all these terms mean and a child suggested that a Unionist was someone who wanted a united Ireland. Which sounds logical but is not correct! I had another

Ulidia Integrated College
sports day, May 2014.

wonderful experience where we were discussing about lilies being on display at Stormont at Easter time. The discussions started with, 'Well, sure, it's going to be closed so it doesn't really matter.' That led to, 'Does it matter, does that still make it okay?' We talked for quite a long time about how the lily is a symbol of hope. One of the girls in the class, who came actually from a very Loyalist background, said, 'I would like the lilies to be there as a symbol of hope that the Good Friday Agreement would work.' I just thought that was incredible. It is those kind of wonderful stories that makes it all worthwhile, because they are altogether in the classroom and talking in a sensitive way about their experiences, it allows them to learn about and from each other and that's really important.

Ulidia, after a number of submissions, eventually had government funding by the time I joined so for the parents it was less of a risk than other schools were, to some extent. In the early days of the school, the parents who took that risk with their child in sending them to an integrated school were committed to Integrated Education. As time goes on, parents will choose a school primarily because it's a good school, very often. Some still choose it because it's integrated and it's close by and all of those things but the fact it's a good school is very important. I love those parents who weren't initially committed to Integrated Education and I love those teachers who went just because it was a job, and then they became fully committed to Integrated Education. I don't want to always

preach to the converted, I want to have people coming along to the schools, both children and parents, who initially don't see the full value of Integrated Education, and then learn in the process. I think that's very important.

The journey of Blackwater Integrated College

I was seconded to Armagh Integrated College as acting Principal for a short while and shortly after returning to Ulidia, I was thrilled to be appointed as a Principal of a new school, Rowallane Integrated College which opened in 2006. That experience was absolutely amazing. I had heard about a new College possibly opening in the Saintfield area and I went along to the public meetings about it and I was very impressed with the steering group, a fabulous group of people: John Hagan, Anne Carson, Denise McBay, June Wilkinson, Bailie Thompson, and Frank Murphy were the main steering group members at that point in time. When the job was advertised I applied for it and I was delighted to be appointed. I went along to the first meeting and I just came out so excited because I just knew it was going to work.

We didn't even have a piece of chalk!

We didn't have a school building, we didn't even have a piece of chalk! But I just knew it was going to work. September approached, when we were opening and in August we still hadn't found premises. We had considered a hotel, we had considered church halls, but that was going to one side rather than the other so that wasn't really an option. In August, about two weeks before we opened, we were able to tell our parents that we had found a site.

How did we get the site? I'm not quite sure who found it! The steering group were always out looking and Belvoir Park Hospital had just closed at the time. I think maybe it was June Wilkinson because she was in the health sector in the civil service at the time, I think maybe she had found it. It was a perfect place and each day at lunchtime we used to go through an open tunnel in Belvoir Park Hospital, which ended up as an area where pupils could play at lunchtime. We started off with a small number of teachers and a couple of classroom assistants and a secretary. And I often say it was bound to succeed, because every single member of staff gave up a full-time permanent post to take the chance in coming to Rowallane. We got our 50 pupils and I will always remember our official opening. The television cameras were there on our very first morning, watching those children walk in. I could cry even now!

Watching them walk in that first morning was an amazing experience. We had a fabulous time that first day. There was great excitement but the kids just took it in their stride. I did so many interviews! May Blood was there and the American Consulate General and it was just an incredible morning.

The parents took a big risk

The parents were taking a chance on their child's education because they were sending their children to a school that they didn't know was going to be there the next month, or the next year. They were such a fabulous group of parents. Those parents came from around the Saintfield and Carryduff area. Some of them had had children at Millennium Integrated Primary School, some had had children at Cedar Integrated Primary School but some hadn't and had just heard about Rowallane and thought it would be a good way forward.

Some of the parents had children who had additional needs and the very small school attracted parents in that situation. Although their children might have had difficulties in other schools, they were able to cope in the smaller environment. We had one boy in particular who had Down's syndrome and he was amazing. He had been through mainstream primary and he stayed with us right the way through Rowallane and Blackwater; his mum actually became his classroom assistant. She was great and encouraged him to be very independent. It was great to have him but the effect that he had on the other pupils was incredible! I mean, no one would have dared to bully him, because the kids were just so supportive of him. It was just wonderful, the way they treated him, and treated each other. He brought a lovely dimension to the whole situation.

When we were recruiting staff for the various posts in Rowallane Integrated College, we were looking for people that had an enthusiasm for their subject but more than that, enthusiasm for teaching young people, for teaching children. Sometimes people will say to me, 'What did you teach?' and I say, 'Children!' Although my subject was Mathematics, children were the centre and the focus of what I was doing. We were looking for that when we were employing the teachers. We had to look for people who could offer a range of subjects and what would be the best fit to be able to offer the full curriculum. We also asked them, 'What do you understand by Integrated Education? How would this impact on your daily interaction with the young people?' We were looking for them talking about it being worthwhile and being very child centred but their enthusiasm was important. If they didn't excite me as they were sitting in the interview chair, they weren't going to excite the children.

That first year was very special and we got 60 children to come into our Year 8 the next year. We had to move up the site a bit and the Integrated Education Fund (IEF) provided us with mobile accommodation so we looked a bit more like a school at that point in time!. Those two years were, without a doubt, the most exciting in my entire teaching career. People said to me, 'What would've happened if you didn't get funding?' And I would've said, 'I could go and stack shelves in

Baronness May Blood celebrates a 'green light' for Blackwater College, 2008.

Tesco.' It wouldn't matter, it still would have been worth it for the experience that I had those two years.

The challenges of bringing together two schools with quite different ethoses

The school didn't have any government funding. We were funded at that point in time by IEF and we will always be grateful to them for putting us on the map. Rowallane, unfortunately, didn't get funding from the government and we joined with Down Academy to form Blackwater Integrated College.

We had to meet with the governors of that school and talk about how we could move this situation forward. Were they prepared to join with us in this? Were they prepared to go through the interview process again for a Principal? Would I be prepared to go through all of this process? Down Academy was a transformed controlled integrated school that was on the journey of transformation. I think that when a school transforms it is not immediately an integrated school. It is a journey and I would say possibly 10 years is a reasonable amount of time that is going to take.

It was not easy bringing together two schools which had quite different ethoses. The two sets of staff hadn't known each other, and the children by this stage were Year 10. Year 10 children can be challenging at times so bringing them together and expecting them to immediately become friends

had its challenges, but we got there. My secretary kept saying to me, 'This time next year, Olwen, this time next year!' Every time I would've been stressed about something, she said, 'This time next year!' and that's how it was.

Sometimes I think when we got approval for the development proposal to open Blackwater and close Rowallane that there was a sense from the Department of Education that they could get rid of two thorns in their side at one time because at that time Down Academy did not have a good reputation. Whether that was justified or not, it did not have a good reputation and it didn't have good numbers. I think to some extent there was a plan to make Rowallane go away and to make Down Academy go away, but we weren't prepared for that to happen so we decided we would fight. Blackwater is an excellent school. It has great results and when you look at the young people who come in, maybe feeling that they are a failure, and then they have a great experience and come out with eight GCSEs. I think there's a lot to be said for the work that goes on in that school. I often used to say to people that as a Principal I didn't have any passengers in my staff, they were all committed and all extremely good teachers. And there aren't many schools that could say that.

What we are doing is different

As a Principal, you need to make sure that integration underpins everything. Simple things like making sure that if you're writing questions that you include names from both sides of the community and other communities. The displays you have up in the classrooms, how you talk to and with the children. I'm not saying integrated schools are the only schools that have a child-centred education, they certainly aren't. What I kept saying to the staff is that what we are doing is different, and you need ways to keep that to the forefront. The opportunities that you have will be different in different schools. I mean going back to the Lagan experience, one time we had mock European elections in the school at the same time as they were going on in the rest of Europe, we had all of the political parties represented. Every single one of them from Northern Ireland was represented and it was interesting to watch the young people. We were a little concerned because they got into their tribal camps to some extent and we were worried that when they went back to class that there would be divisions. But we smiled broadly as the children got up from their camps and went over to each other and just went over to their friends and talked about what they had heard and it didn't divide them at all.

In Integrated Education we actually address the issues

Having taught in Lagan in the early days of the Troubles, I remember once I came in on a Monday morning and it had been a horrendous weekend. I came in to teach my Maths class and the tension that there was in that room, I thought, 'I can't teach Maths.' It was actually my form class so I had to say to them, 'Okay guys, put your pens down and talk to me.' We talked it through in a very open way. People were able to talk about how they felt but by the end of the class we were in a situation where we weren't personally attacking each other any longer and we all agreed that what had happened wasn't okay. But it wasn't 'your-side-did-it-to-my-side' any longer, we

were able to make it not so personal to us. And that's what I would say is one of the big differences about integrated schools. You talk about issues, you talk about things. I mean, people will say their school is integrated because it's mixed. In fact, it's usually more assimilation than integration because the young people don't feel confident to be who they are, whatever their background might be. They just are assimilated into the ethos of the school. Whereas in Integrated Education we actually address the issues and talk about them.

Integrated schools were set up initially to bring together children from Catholic and Protestant backgrounds. We've got to be honest and realise that the divisions in our society have really not gone away, you wouldn't have to scratch too far under the surface to find some really quite unpleasant thinking within our society. I have to be honest, sometimes things happen and I would have that gut reaction and then I'm surprised; I almost look at myself and say, 'Did you really think that? After all that you've been through and whatever!' It's just something that can be deeply ingrained into you.

I think it's very important that we continue to address the Catholic and Protestant coming together but I think that the diversity that's coming in our society with other religions, other cultures and no religion coming in as well, that can be a significant part of children learning about themselves and learning about other people. I think you have to look at the 40:40:20 balance. To me that is the ideal, but it depends where the school is situated. When I was in Armagh Integrated College for a short while, I found it had quite a big migrant population and a lot of that population are Lithuanian or Polish. I think you have to look at the individual school, I don't think that there is a template that suits all schools.

Engaging the whole community in the process

Getting the children out into the local community helps you to manage relationships with the local community. If you have the children out doing a litter pick, if you have the children out doing a beach clean, a bag pack, even doing a sponsored walk, you're not asking the local community to sponsor them but they see these pleasant young people walking around the place. Inviting the community in is very important too, so in Blackwater we used to have a Christmas fair each year and we would have gone to the houses that were just immediately around the school and given them VIP invitations to come to our Christmas fair. They would get free tea and coffee if they came along and presented their ticket. Trying to have a connection with the local community is very important. In Downpatrick on Remembrance Sunday all of the local churches will be there at a service at the cenotaph. So we would've had our head boy and head girl go along and lay a wreath at the cenotaph. And we have been quite fortunate in that each year our head boy and head girl were from different denominations, so one has been Catholic, one has been Protestant each year and we haven't planned it that way! It just has happened. And that has been good to have them come along in that way and involve themselves in what's happening in the local community.

I think one of the good ways to engage with the churches is to have your school carol service in the local churches. In Blackwater our first year we had our carol service in Down Cathedral which is where it had been held for Down Academy. My secretary was a choir mistress in the local Catholic church and I got her to arrange a meeting for me with the Canon who's a lovely gentleman. I asked him could we have our Carol Service the following year in his church and he said, 'I don't see any reason why not!' So that was great, it's a beautiful building. I was thinking, 'How am I going to do my Integrated Education bit here?' but I didn't have to: he stood up and said that the Christmas story was in fact an integrated story. That people had come from different backgrounds, different countries and different cultures.

The hopes for Integrated Education to become the norm

I would hope that Integrated Education would become the norm, and that all children would eventually be educated together because I think it is the way forward for any society. Segregating children just re-enforces generations of bias. The future of Integrated Education? I don't think it will be that utopia that I'm hoping for, not for a very long time anyway. I hope that there will be more schools that transform when they see that it is a good thing. We don't have a Catholic school that has transformed – yet!

In our political situation, I think that people think, 'I can't agree to that because I'm losing something' or, 'Look what they have gained, or what they have got.' I think that is one of the difficulties, because there's that sense of being under threat. In the more extreme parts of our community, people still feel that they are under threat of losing something. So I'm hoping that more schools will transform. I hope that, as more children come through integrated schools, that they will be the catalyst and more schools will transform and cause a growth in Integrated Education.

For me, choosing to teach in an integrated school was one of the best decisions that I have ever made. I have absolutely no regrets about my time in integrated schools, and I would encourage anyone to consider Integrated Education for their children and, indeed, for themselves if they are looking for a career in teaching or in the school environment.

Kevin Lambe trained and worked as a teacher before working for the Northern Ireland Council for Integrated Education (NICIE) as a Development Officer during a period in the early 1990s of exciting growth for Integrated Education. He then went on to become Principal of Shimna Integrated College in Newcastle, County Down, a role he has now held for 25 years.

Career decisions

I studied Spanish at university, and during my PGCE in 1976 I went into two schools, the first ever comprehensive school in Northern Ireland, St Louise's, which is 2,500 working class girls on the Falls Road. The second school I went to was Rathmore which was a Catholic grammar school in the suburbs. Basically, two Catholic schools, one selective, one non-selective.

Philosophically or ideologically I was always in favour of all ability education so there was no choice for me, I wasn't going to teach in a grammar school, I wanted to teach in a comprehensive/all ability setting. St Louise's was a great school and the first school to make a bold statement about all ability education. After 11 years there, Lagan was an obvious extension of my commitment to all ability education. This was boys, girls, Protestant, Catholics and others which I absolutely believed in. There's also a political thing for me. I would be quite political but I felt totally disenfranchised in Northern Ireland because everything, including education, ended up coming down to the constitutional question, which related directly to the religion question. Our troubles here were never specifically related to religion. Like everything else it is related to power and land and all the rest of it. But let's not go there!

When I decided in 1986 that I was going to shift to the integrated sector, some of my colleagues, some of my friends, even some of my family in those days would say, 'What are you doing that for?' It was like, you're taking a risk, moving over. Very much in professional terms there was the reality that if you moved from the Catholic education sector to the integrated sector, you were walking over a bridge and you were cutting that bridge behind you, there was no going back. I remember when I was moving from the Catholic teaching sector to going to Lagan and I liked all that I read about it and I was thinking to myself, 'Well, you know, what does it mean for me? Or, what do I want from this personally and professionally?'

And I thought about it like this: I will bring my duffle bag full of my memories, my culture, my things and I will go to Lagan and what I want is that I'll be able to set my duffle bag on the table. This is me, who grew up where I grew up, who believes what I believe. This here's my politics, here's my football team, here's whatever and that's my duffle bag. Would you like to have a wee look? And then I asked, 'Can I have a look at your duffle bag?' So I look at their duffle bag and in doing so we simply grow as individuals and as a community. Maybe that's what I think integration brings.

Lagan was really a natural extension of where I wanted to be. I spent just under three years in Lagan and then I looked around for the next big thing in integration because I was totally committed to it. NICIE was reorganising at that time and I applied for the Development Officer's job. It was just at the time when the 1989 Education Order was coming out so it was a very exciting time. That was the legislation which enabled

Image of Kevin Lambe courtesy of Down Recorder

Cranmore Integrated Primary School, 2015.

people to set up Grant Maintained Integrated (GMI) Schools. I was fortunate enough to get the job and I helped 13 groups of parents set up 13 GMI schools. 11 primary and two post-primary.

Friday nights and every other night

I was working day and night for four very intense years from January 1990 to June '94. There were really big characters in Derry/Londonderry with Oakgrove Integrated College and they decided that they would change their meetings to a Friday night and as I said to Colm Cavanagh at the time, 'As it is, I work every night of the week and you're going to have your meetings on a Friday?!' I said, 'Look, Maire's seven months pregnant, so we're going to be heading up in the middle of winter, up the Glenshane Pass to your Friday night meetings?' And he said, 'Sure, it's good fun, bring Maire!' So Maire and I set off with her heavily pregnant, sometimes through the snow in the Glenshane Pass. She was always glad to get to see Altnagelvin Hospital just as security, you know? But she did really enjoy the meetings and they were good fun and they were great people.

The Cranmore parents came to me in January 1992, saying that they wanted to open a school that September. My first child, Ciaran, was born in April '92 so I suppose I was a founding parent as well. I acted as the Development Officer and part of that job was putting a bid in on the house

which was interesting. One thing I love about the integrated movement is that they haven't just accepted the status quo, they haven't said, 'Oh, that's all there is, that will have to do.' They've actually taken the bull by the horns, taken control.

I used to say that for every parent who wanted to set up, or who set about setting up an integrated school, there was a different reason for doing so. For some of them it was an idealistic thing, for some educationalists they looked to Finland, and the fact that their schools were usually up in the top five in the world and people just basically went to their local all ability school. Some of them had an abhorrence of the segregated system or of the selective system. Some of them had experiences in traditional Protestant, Catholic grammar, secondary schools which had influenced them to decide there must be something better. So, I always like to say that for every person there was a different incentive.

The kernel of my educational belief

Other schools had succeeded, parents had seen this, had seen what appeared to them, for whatever motivation, to be a better alternative. It's all very nice and jolly and isn't it nice to have children together when they're primary school and isn't that lovely? But then in Northern Ireland we come to this huge obstacle, the abomination which is the 11+, the qualifying test, the selection process, call it what you will. And you know, it's alright having the wee children together, but then they really have to separate because you have the smart ones and then you have the other ones. There are far more middle class people achieving higher results in the test because they get tutors. The very nature of the test is flawed. Flawed as an exam in itself, it's flawed as a predictor of academic achievement. I mean, one of our students did the test, didn't get it, came through to Shimna, to our school, went to study medicine at Queen's, finished top of her year. So what sort of a predictor was that exam?

So, if parents do have a choice to set up a school, of course they're going to set up an all ability school which all of their children can attend. And not some of them can attend if they 'pass' an exam or only those who don't 'pass' that exam. You know what I mean, so of course you're going to set up an all ability school. I think for the original people, first would have come bringing Catholic and Protestant children together and educating them together and letting them live and grow and love together. All ability naturally flows out of that.

On a personal level, all ability was the kernel of my educational beliefs, if you want. But also there was this disenfranchisement from politics. I wanted to do political things that didn't depend on us being separate or acting as if we were totally different tribes or that there was nothing we could do. So, on a personal level, it was political as well as educational and that was important to me because politics for so many years had been in stasis in this place.

If you think a thing is right, you've got to do it

Today I was down talking about our Gay Straight Alliance in the school and people were saying, 'Oh, you're very brave.' I thought there would be much more opposition to, the Gay Straight Alliance, for example, but if you think a thing is right, you've got to do it. You know on one level you could say that people, myself included, were brave but it just gets to the point where you want to do something, it's not about being brave. I mean, I would never want to teach in anything but an integrated school and so it was a deliberate, it was a Rubicon to be crossed and to heck with what's back there, I'm moving on here.

I think when people started off integration and integrated schools many just thought, 'Look, are you mad starting a school in a scout hut? Are you mad taking a reduction in salary to go and teach somewhere where you don't know whether it's going to be successful or not?' No, you're not mad, probably passionate, you're probably committed, you're…you know, I often only slightly jokingly call myself an integrated zealot!

I always joke that the parents who set up the schools were all ability too. The only one thing they had in common is that they wanted something different for their children. That is a huge motivation and I think when they came together, I mean, for example, let's take Cranmore where my own children went to primary school. There you had people who were academics, like Bill and his wife and Anna and a member of that group who was a great Gaeilgeoir, a great Irish speaker. I remember another lady, Margaret, who was a very down-to-earth working class parent and she just wanted something different for her child. And she was determined to do that. I remember one of the first parents in Cranmore was an absolutely working class, young single parent and she was as determined as anybody, so, there was a real social mix as well. I think that's important too.

Cranmore was an interesting one. When I look at some of the other ones, maybe the profile was more middle class but as soon as they started bringing parents in, the class profile changed totally. So, at some of those 13 schools, you might have had a middle class demographic to start off with but that rapidly changed and was embraced because that's what you want. It's not just about religion, it is about class as well.

Becoming a school Principal

It was never an aspiration to be a Principal and not that I didn't want it, it just wasn't on my radar to want to. It was an unusual career path. I ended up leaving Lagan to come to NICIE and taking on the Development Officer's job. I knew quite a bit about teaching, I knew quite a bit about all ability education,

I knew a lot about teaching Spanish and French and some English and, you know, all those things. But right from the very start people would say, 'Kevin, how do we do this?' Or, 'What should we do here?' Sometimes I was able to tell them exactly what they should do but often I had to say, 'Look, I don't know, but I'll find out.' So it was a real learning experience for me too, you know, dealing with the Department, dealing with planning and how we do the interviews. So, I ended up helping these parents to appoint Principals, to appoint Vice-Principals, to do training then with the newly appointed Principals and other staff. They would then come to me and say, 'Well, Kevin, what do we do about A, B, C, or D, in school?' So in a very short space of time I gained that experience and knowledge, gained I suppose all those contacts too, in the Department and so on. Tony Spencer and I worked together on drafting the memorandum and articles. So we knew all the behind the scenes stuff. I worked with the ethos development with the Principals and I saw people applying to become Principals and, you know, I was telling people what to do and I suppose there comes a point where you say, 'Look, you know, you're still telling people what to do, how about you tried to do it?'

And so it became like a personal and professional challenge. And I suppose that was it. It became the ultimate challenge which I had never contemplated. And then, when the group came along in Newcastle, Newcastle is such a beautiful place apart from anything. There was no post-primary school in Newcastle and I just thought I'm going to go for this, see if I can do it. 24 years later I'm still seeing if I can do it. And I still don't know!

When people come to our school, Shimna Integrated College, they often say there's a lovely atmosphere here. Now, loads of schools have lovely atmospheres. I sometimes say, 'Well, you know, what is it?' And they say, 'Oh, people just seem happy to work there, to learn there, to be there, they seem friendly, they smile.' I do think that whoever is the leader in the school, it's really important. If, and how that person gets across their ideas and vision. I think mostly it's by example and I decided early on, that I would teach and every year I've

taught, except one year and that was a mistake. Every year I teach and I try to teach the wee ones, the Year 8s, so that I get to know them, they get to know me and they get to know my expectations and I get to know their expectations. In doing that, it also says to teachers, I'm not somebody sitting in an office, I'm doing the same job as you. So, no-one could ever say, 'Kevin doesn't know, he doesn't teach them.' Of course I teach them, I teach every one. So, in a way you're modelling the way you want. The way you interact with people is very important. The uniform policy is based on choice and was non-gender specific at the very start in 1994. There were trousers for everybody or just, pick a bottom, pick a top and we offered choice. I, as Principal, set high expectations for everybody. The structures we use now aren't the same as other integrated schools, we have all ability teaching in all ability classes. We have tried and succeeded over the years but it's now becoming more and more difficult.

People in integrated schools don't agree, that's the point!

In assemblies I ask if there are any announcements this morning. If a teacher puts up their hand I won't say, 'Well, Ms Smith, what have you to say?' I'll say 'Well, Ellen, what have you to say? Well, Karen, what have you to say? Yes, Rory, what do you want?' It seems like a very small thing but I think it's really important. One person said to me, 'Oh, I'm not sure everybody likes not being called Mr or Mrs in assembly.' And I said, 'Well, I'm sorry, but I will be calling you by your first name in assembly and I want to be called by my first name.' That says something about the status of student and member of staff as well. Assemblies are hugely important in our school and have been over the years, from the very early days and remember we did open on the first day of the first IRA ceasefire. The assembly very quickly involved traditions; St Patrick's Day was a one huge, big whole school assembly as was Remembrance Day. We didn't try to equate the two things but, you know, for one reason or another, the one community became associated with one, the other community with the

Bill Rolston (founding parent),
Mo Mowlam and Helen Hamilton
(founding Principal) at Cranmore
IPS, 1998.

other. Staff came together to bring their different takes, for example, at this year's Remembrance assembly we focused on women's role in the war. In one Remembrance Day we brought in the Spanish Civil War.

If something happens out there, if it's the Omagh bomb which had happened, I will be talking about the Omagh bomb in assembly the next day. And I will be talking about it in the knowledge that there are people of all traditions in front of me. And that's really powerful and that's really important. Any big issue, be it a violent incident or be it a political incident, or a political setback, I was determined to talk about that the next day. Contrary to what people think, people in integrated schools don't agree, that's the point! We don't agree, we agree to come together in peace and openness and celebration, but we don't always agree. And we don't support the same teams and we don't have the same family histories and we don't treasure the same memories. Sometimes we do but it's coming together in the knowledge of who you are with and this stands for parents and staff and everybody else. You come together in the knowledge that you don't agree but you want to celebrate the fact that you don't agree. You want to have structures that allow you not to agree and celebrate your thing. And for your friends to be with you and not even necessarily agree with your celebration or what you're doing, but to say, 'Fine, you're my friend and I'm happy for you to do that with me in here.'

The future

I think one huge and important thing that has changed in 35 years is that we aren't seeing any new plans for integrated schools. And I think that's difficult because the only schools now that are changing to integrated schools are from one particular side of the community. The Protestant controlled sector. Some controlled schools now have a good mix and it is good that they're acknowledging that and moving towards that, but some Catholic schools have a mix too. And, you know, it could be seen that it's one side of the community which is making all the concessions or making all the changes and then the Catholic sector isn't doing that. Well, actually, if you read some of the promotional material, if you read about the ethos of some Catholic schools you would think they were integrated schools. You can't be a Catholic school and an integrated school. You can't be a grammar school and an integrated school. And I know people disagree with me, but there you are. As I said, we don't all agree. I don't think you can have an integrated grammar school and I don't care what the balance is. I don't care if it's perfect. The fact is that you're excluding 50% of the population before you open your doors. You cannot have an integrated Catholic school, you can have a Catholic school with a mix of students. I don't think there should be a single new school approved that isn't integrated.

Bangor Central IPS at
Euro Conference, 2008.

Every single school in Northern Ireland is underfunded at the moment. There is a surplus of seats in schools so clearly one of the things that has to happen is that unsustainable schools will have to be closed. But that could be seen as an opportunity. If, for example, in a small town there's a smallish controlled school and smallish Catholic school, well, let's bring the two of them together and we will have a shared school. I don't care whether they call it integrated or not. You can call it a shared school if they want, that seems to be the language. But you know perhaps there are such situations, maybe there are three or four tiny Catholic schools scattered about the place and there's maybe two small controlled schools or slightly bigger controlled schools, bring them all together. I think it's been proved over the years that the people want integration. The people of Northern Ireland want their children educated in integrated schools.

So, if you're amalgamating schools, why not take it a wee bit further and make it an integrated or shared amalgamation? Because we do need to cut down on the number of seats, we do need to have economies of scale. Well, let's do it, let's make it policy. I think it just needs somebody with a bit of courage and a bit of vision, a bit of leadership. I know that's like wishing pigs could fly in this country.

I suppose that the largest stumbling block would be the Council for Catholic Maintained Schools (CCMS), if we're honest about it. And I'm not saying that accusingly of them,

I can understand why they would want to hold on to 'their' schools, as they would see it. I have thought for many years that in a divided society it's understandable why people want their 'own' schools. But in a post-conflict society I don't think we have that luxury anymore and I think we have to find a way to integrate, to share and I don't mean share, going in the same gate in different uniforms and then parting, that is not what this is about. And it's not what it should be about.

If I could change something in the last 35 years of integration, it would be that somehow we could have better or more productively harnessed what was clearly the will of the people at a time, at a time of conflict, at a time of division. If we somehow could have harnessed that more but, I mean, look at the time, for example that I was with NICIE. 13 schools in under four years. A small group couldn't do much more than that. And had it been the Government doing it, it wouldn't have had the same success because half the population didn't trust the Government. Or didn't invest in the Government, so, it had to be someone like NICIE empowering parents to do it. And I thought that was a great strength. But those parents could only be empowered while there was the will and the instruction on the Department of Education to, you know, but we're now being led simply by money and there is no money. There was a ground swell of enthusiasm for integration as all those polls showed.

I think we have reached a plateau where people think we simply are not having any new integrated schools. If we look back maybe 10 years ago, suddenly the word 'shared' was the thing. Wasn't integrated any more, it was shared. That was an ideological thing and it wasn't the integrated movement who did it. The Integrated Education Fund (IEF) did good things and invested in schools really sharing. But this top down emphasis on Shared Education, it has stalled the progress of integration. On the whole, we're investing in Shared Education and that I'm afraid is not going to change society here. It really isn't. Whereas integration really has had a great effect. I think things like the Good Friday Agreement, things like Ian Paisley and Martin McGuiness, as First and Deputy First Ministers, I think those things, I think the integrated movement had a huge influence on those. The idea that we don't have to agree but the idea that we will set up structures like balance and integration, like all those things that we set up in integration, they were paralleled in the institutions that were set up.

I'd love to say the future would be many more all ability integrated schools. I'd love to say that but I don't see it at the moment. I see the funding situation for all education as being horrendous, inadequate. But I don't think people will continue to accept that we have to live in different silos and different areas and with different schools.

Shared Education as in going in the same gate and then to different schools is slightly better than segregated education but it isn't Integrated Education. I don't see in the near future any huge expansion of integration. But in saying that, I think we have to keep fighting to see that true integration, integrated schools, whether they come from transformation or whether there are four small schools, well, let's make one big integrated school. I think we have to keep fighting. Just because we're not physically fighting in the streets, doesn't mean we shouldn't be pursuing integration and a better society. I mean, we've seen in recent years how little it takes for the whole structure to fall down. And I do think structures are really important. Both in politics and in our schools. So, I'm going to say that I'm optimistic but we need fighters. I think we need zealots, we need the next generation to step up like our integrated alumni, you know, it's nice to see them coming forward.

Impacts of integration

Every year I emotionally wish my Shimna students well for their exams, for their final A2 examinations and give then their last talk before they head off to do those exams. I always say to them to go out and be successful in the world and to bring their sense of equality, their sense of justice, their sense of integration, their sense of celebration of diversity, their high

Gordon Wilson cuts the first sod at Shimna IC with founder students Darren Stockdale and Janine Johnston.

expectations of good treatment which will not depend on your sex, your gender, your race, your ability, your physical or academic ability, to bring those high expectations which they have lived with for 14 years, to bring those into their universities, into their work places. What I know it means is that they will go and do that, they will bring those higher expectations with them. With the expectation that while somebody may not agree, that they will respect that opinion and they will not put it down.

I heard today and you would think I was making this up, I'm not making it up, I heard it today and I hadn't known it, I was talking today about our anti-homophobic institutions and so on in school. And a person who had talked to one of our people had said that they'd heard the story and this is exactly what I'm talking about. One of our students who had come out quite early on, as being gay, had gone to university and he'd enjoyed the support of the Gay Straight Alliance in our school. He had gone to university and he had found that in his university that there wasn't a similar society or group. So he decided that he would set one up. But interestingly, he set one up with a Christian Union, alongside the Christian Union and Gay Straight Alliance and he worked with these people to set this up. So, to set up this new society which up to then hadn't existed. And to me that was him bringing his hugely high expectations of equality of treatment, of celebration of diversity. I think that's what integration offers people. And it

also offers people the wonderful opportunity to get to know people from all walks, classes, belief systems and so on.

Are you making this up?

When I grew up in Belfast, I didn't go to East Belfast. I was from West Belfast and people from East Belfast didn't come to West Belfast. Even before my children got to post-primary, I was bringing them to their friends in East Belfast, I was bringing them to places and that's just a very simple thing. If I can tell another wee story which is a story that I love. When my son got to age 10 and he was at Cranmore Integrated and he actually said he wanted to do this 11+. And of course, me being a liberal parent said, 'Alright, yeah.' I thought, 'Well, I have to show him all the schools that he might go to,' and I brought him to a local, well established controlled grammar school, which has a mix within it. And you know it was all singing, all dancing and so on. I told him about this grammar school I went to, that you did the test and, you know, depending on what you got on that test meant they offered you a place or they didn't offer you a place. And he took that in. And then maybe the next night it was up to another school, just up the road, a popular and well established Catholic grammar school. We went in there and we talked and when we came back from the Catholic grammar I just said, I said to him, I said, 'Look, you know the way that first school we went

Founding parents of Cranmore
Integrated Primary School.

to, you know it's grammar so it means you have to do this
test, and that depends on whether they offer you a place?' He
said, 'Yeah.' And I said, 'Well, that school we've just visited,
that works in the same way except that it's all Catholics.'
And he just looked up at me and he said, 'Are you serious?'
Because coming from where he'd come after seven years in an
integrated all ability primary school, he said, 'Are you serious?
Are you making this up?!' Maybe that's what integration does
for people. And then, of course, both my children chose
Lagan, which is wonderful and they have done really well. You
know, they're good rounded people with high expectations.

Errol Lemon helped establish Brownlow Integrated College in Craigavon and later went on to become Principal.

Craigavon: new town, new school

My personal involvement with the school goes back many years before integration was mooted as a possibility. I arrived at the school the year after it opened in 1973. It was part of the new city of Craigavon which was designed to connect the towns of Portadown and Lurgan and make a single, bigger metropolis. The fact that it was a new town gave the opportunity to think quite radically about educational provision. It was designed in a way that was quite ambitious at the time. There was an educational zone within Craigavon, which involved a cross-community approach. A large Catholic comprehensive school was constructed and in the same zone, Brownlow High School was constructed. Further along there was a Catholic primary school and there was a leisure centre. The idea was that all the schools would share leisure provisions, including sporting facilities.

In the event there was actually relatively little cooperation between the schools. They basically did their own thing and unfortunately the sporting provision that might have encouraged more cooperation wasn't completed because the city concept didn't quite develop the way it was hoped. We're talking the 1970s here and we were right in the middle of the Troubles. The area was not exempt from the problems associated with that. So for all sorts of reasons the schools developed quite independently. Brownlow was a controlled school, a state school.

We had some experience of a form of integration in the early days because the Vietnamese boat people were billeted in Craigavon for a time and somewhere between 30 and 50 Vietnamese children came to Brownlow. We had to modify our approach and our curriculum to suit them because very few of them could speak any English when they arrived. We set up a sort of an independent unit to assist the children of secondary age to learn English and then we gradually fed them into the mainstream school as their level of ability in English improved.

We also had for a time quite a large number of army children because one of the estates was an army barracks and they fed into the school. The children very often were not in the school for very long because their parents moved. The teachers developed a sense that they needed to be flexible in their approach and that they had to be very pupil-orientated. After two or three years the Vietnamese children left Craigavon; their families simply moved, mainly to England and, of course, the army children also moved. So, the numbers in the school fell quite considerably. We've now got into the mid-1980s and at that stage there were some concerns about the way the school was going in terms of numbers and economic viability.

The integration debate

A new headmaster arrived in 1986 and as far as the integration process is concerned, that gentleman played an absolutely vital part in it. His name was Frank Loan. Frank came to the school already very firmly of the opinion that integrated schools were the way forward. At that particular time there were no transformed integrated schools. Any schools that were already in existence were green-field site schools. By the mid-1980s, the amount of money that was required to set up a new school on a green-field site was no longer available. It appeared at the time that the future would be in transformation rather than green-field site schools.

Now, coincidentally, at that period, quite independent of the school, a group had been set up in Craigavon called NAGIE, the North Armagh Group for Integrated Education. It consisted mainly of middle class intellectuals whose original idea was to set up a green-field site integrated school in the Craigavon area. But realising that green-field site schools were not an option, they became interested in the concept of transformation. They called a public meeting; I think this was '87, maybe early '88. Frank Loan attended the meeting and raised the issue that Brownlow might well be interested in exploring the idea of transformation. A couple of their prominent members became converted to the idea that they would support the transformation of Brownlow. The leading member of that group was Chris Moffatt. Along with Frank, she played a very important role in the longer term because she had contacts with a different sort of constituency than Frank might have had. She provided the intellectual, philosophical underpinning of the idea of integration. That was her background. She was an editor of an intellectual magazine.

We're now up to 1989. At the first Board of Governors meeting of the new academic year Frank informed the meeting that there was this move towards at least investigating whether the school should transform. At that stage the school was not mixed as such because it was a state school but there was a minority of Catholics, somewhere between 5% and 10%, who did attend the school. There was a very large, very successful Catholic comprehensive school 200 yards from the school. So it obviously was a big magnet for the Catholic population. Due to the population movement because of the Troubles, the two main contributory primary schools to Brownlow, although they were both state primary schools, had become increasingly Catholic. One of them became 100% Catholic.

I was a teacher's representative on the Board of Governors and I already knew that Frank was going to raise this matter at the Board. I put my pennyworth in; I was very supportive. The counter argument was raised that it might actually lead to a lot of the existing children leaving because they had obviously not signed up to an integrated school.

They had signed up to a state school. Although that was a factor in people's minds the real debate centred around the whole philosophy of integration, whether the Board of Governors felt they could support the concept of integration. Basically, there was uncertainty as to what integration actually meant. What differences would it make within the school in terms of the make-up of the Board of Governors, of the management; what effect it would have on the teaching staff of the school and other ancillary staff? And, of course, the most important, the effect it would have on the curriculum of the school, what was taught and how it was taught and the ethos of the school. The received opinion in Northern Ireland was that Catholic schools were there to promote Catholicism and Protestant schools, maybe not so much to promote Protestantism as such, but certainly to support education with a British cultural dimension whereas the Catholic schools were considered to be presenting education with an Irish cultural dimension. So, if you accept that there was this fundamental difference between the two types of school, then the question arose, where does integration come into this? What cultural dimension and religious ethos does the integrated school nurture?

There were integrated schools in existence but they didn't have the experience of changing from one type of school to another. They had a blank sheet to start with, so they could do their own drawing. We already had a drawing. What we were going to have to do was change the template and modify it in line with recommendations that were already in the public domain as to what an integrated school was. The main assistance was the Northern Ireland Council for Integrated Education (NICIE) Statement of Principles; it was like a checklist of things that should be done, could be done or ought to be done. We had very close liaison with Kevin Lambe from NICIE. He and others came to the school to help organise staff training days. We also received financial assistance from the Integrated Education Fund (IEF).

Transformation

The legal process was that nothing could happen until the Board of Governors voted. The Southern Education and Library Board (SELB) as it was then, which was in charge of the school, would be informed that the Board of Governors wished to bring forward the idea that the school would become integrated. It was not actually the Board of Governors in total that had that vote. It was four members of a nine person Board. The four members were the transferors' reps, the representatives of the feeder primary schools. They had by right a seat on the Board of Governors; the primary schools nominated them. The complication was that the transferors' reps were clergymen; they were ministers of the churches that had run the school as a contributing primary school and because we were a state school they were Protestant clergymen. The process was that Protestant clergymen have got to vote for changing the status of the school from a Protestant school to some sort of in-between integrated school. If they had voted, 'No,' end of story. It wouldn't have happened. It is to their great credit that all four of them voted unanimously to allow the process to start. The four of them voted to forward the proposal to the Board. When they sent a proposal to the Board, the SELB did not know what to do because nobody had ever asked them to do this before. They then contacted the Department of Education. There was quite a considerable delay but eventually the Department agreed and had to go back to them and say, 'Right, you have to run a ballot of the parents now.'

By this stage the newspapers had caught on, and transformation had become a huge cause célèbre in the local area. The papers were publishing letters for and against integration. Craigavon Borough Council, who had no educational responsibility whatsoever, debated the issue. It was raised by the DUP councillors on the Council. A proposal was put forward that the Council would condemn the move by the school to become integrated and it was voted for nine to nil in favour because all the other parties had left the room before the vote took place.

Where the frist pupils of
Brownlow Integrated College
came from.

We had meetings with parents and informed the parents about what changes we imagined would take place. The same issues were raised: was it actually a good idea from a practical point of view? Would it help the school? Would the numbers increase? Would the existing pupils be happy to stay in the school if the school changed? What did it mean in terms of the make-up of the Board of Governors, the staff? And you've got to remember that this is in the context of a very virulent anti-integration campaign at this time, where the opposition were scaremongering. You know, this was a plot to destroy Protestantism in Northern Ireland, pupils in the school would be forced to learn Irish!

The Catholic school's position was, 'This is nothing to do with us. We will not get involved at a local level.' The position of the Catholic Church was very opposed to Integrated Education. That was well known, but as far as the local debate was concerned, the Catholic schools and churches simply kept out of it and didn't pass comment one way or the other.

There would be absolutely no point in going through with the process if the staff were opposed to it. So, we did have an informal staff vote. It was a small school; we're talking about 15, 16 staff. All but one of the staff were in favour of the process. The person who was opposed was opposed on philosophical/religious grounds. In the event, he stayed and continued to teach in the school for a number of years. The

staff, right from the beginning, were strongly in favour. The opposition that we experienced, the nature of the arguments that were put forward and the scaremongering roused the staff to be more actively involved than they might have been. If the opposition had been quiet, they might have not been so much involved. There was a number of staff who were strongly in support of change; there were some who were moderately in support; there were some who didn't care what school they taught in as long as they had a job and there was one who was against transformation.

We had the ballot and the SELB refused to release the result. The argument was that the procedure had flaws, that a number of the parents had not received ballot papers in time. There was a requirement for a 75% 'Yes' vote of the actual voters. A second ballot was then organised. On the second vote we got 66% but we didn't get 75%. We'd lost the ballot and people thought, 'Well, is that it?' In the meantime the legislation changed and now required 51%, a simple majority. The earlier requirement about the transferors' reps having the vote was wiped out as well. The process now was a simple majority of the Board of Governors and a simple majority of the voters.

We felt justified in going again. So, a third ballot was held. At this point we made a big mistake because we thought as we had 66%, that we were home and dry; we would easily get the 51% required. The vote went ahead; we got 40%.

This was a disaster. Third ballot; surely this is it? But no! There was provision in the new legislation that if 20% of the parents petitioned the Department, then the Department was required to run a ballot on the back of the petition. We got the 20% in three days. So the parents are going to be asked again. We were worried now. Will they even bother? We said we're not just going to sit back. We're going to write to the papers, put up posters, send out information to the parents. The week before the ballot, a member of staff and a member of the Board of Governors visited every parent's house. Myself and Meredith Scott who was a member of the Board of Governors visited 20 houses in Parkmore estate. We deliberately chose Parkmore because it was the most loyalist estate in Craigavon and that's where we would have expected the anti-integration argument would have been listened to most. At that stage there were about 180 or so pupils at the school altogether. We were well received, even in houses that would have been taken as being quite loyalist. Out of the 20 there were only two houses where we were told in no uncertain terms that they weren't going to vote, 'Yes'. The other houses did have genuine worries. There are going to be priests in the school taking religious education. Is that right? No. My son is going to be taught Irish history? No. British history isn't going to be taught in the school anymore? No. These are the sort of things that were being said. We said, 'It may be that a priest will be coming but they'll not be taking Protestants for denominational Catholicism. We will be offering Gaelic football but it'll be on an optional basis. We will have Irish but it'll be an option like French or Spanish.'

The day before the vote one of the parents came in in a panic. The 'Anti-Integration Concerned Parents of Craigavon', as they called themselves, had put out leaflets to all the parents, saying, 'Say No to Integration.' We got the leaflet and put, 'Say Yes' and stuck it over the 'No'. We crossed out their name at the bottom and put our name and re-copied it and sent it out to all the parents. The vote went ahead and this time we got 60% in favour. That was it; we'd finally got our majority. In March of '91 that was put forward to the Department along with the development proposal. In August, just before the start of term, the Department said, 'We agree that you can designate yourself as a controlled integrated school.'

An integrating school

Nobody was under any illusion that in September 1991 we were an integrated school because we weren't. We had changed the name. There had been a lot of discussion and debate and meetings and the staff were quite well prepared for what would be expected of them. But they were well aware that this was a process. You just didn't switch a light on and become integrated overnight. We started to use the term 'integrating school', not an integrated school. Of the three main constituents, the Board of Governors, the staff and the pupils, change on the Board of Governors was the easiest one but it wasn't as simple as it should have been. The Board went from nine to 14. The crucial difference was that there would be at least two representatives from the voluntary sector, who would be nominated by CCMS. The Catholic authorities refused to nominate anybody so there was a default mechanism that meant that the SELB could recommend in lieu of them. Quite unbelievably, they nominated a gentleman who had been very prominent in the anti-integration movement, a well-known DUP politician! The understanding was that they would nominate Catholics and they nominated this man! We appealed right up to the level of the Secretary of State for Northern Ireland, Jim Prior. He eventually informed the SELB that this was totally against the spirit of the legislation and that they would have to nominate somebody else.

Change to the Board of Governors was relatively easy and could be done fairly quickly because it was a procedural change. The staff was a much slower process. At the time of integration one member of staff was a Catholic. No staff would be made redundant in order to create space for a Catholic. We got assistance from the Joseph Rowntree Trust through the IEF. A Catholic, Terry McMackin, was seconded from Lagan College as a second VP in Brownlow. He was initially supposed to be seconded for two years; I think he was here for about six years. We couldn't have had a better man at that particular time in that particular position. He was a gentleman and a diplomat; he poured oil on troubled waters and was very good at bringing people along in a conciliatory and sensible way.

I became Principal in '94. The school grew quite rapidly which meant we were able to take on new staff. We now got applications from a lot of Catholic teachers that we wouldn't have done before. We now were seen to be an integrated school so we got applications from both sides of the community. Quite often the new teacher appointments were newly qualified; they were not people who had taught in one type of school or other. They came without much baggage. It was always made clear that the expectation would be that they would participate in the process of integration.

In Northern Ireland teachers don't move very much in comparison to England. You get people teaching in the same school for 30, 40 years. It can be positive, but in our context, it wasn't necessarily so. It would have been a major problem had we not grown. But the fact that we did grow quite substantially meant that we were able to recruit a lot more Catholics. From the management point of view relative numbers are quite important. If you're in a minority of two in a group of 20, the likelihood is that you're going to feel somewhat intimidated, even if not deliberately. When we got to the stage where a third of the staff were Catholic, the interpersonal dynamic changed. The debate became more robust and more genuine. I don't want to sound critical of the existing staff because they were very good but with the best will in the world, some of the things that they thought were good ideas in relation to integration, the Catholic staff, when in a minority, might have found somewhat patronising. They were doing things as Protestants that they thought Catholics would like. The Catholics didn't feel in the position to put forward their position strongly until they got to about a third of the group. Then we introduced policies that sub-committees, curriculum groups and so on had to be half and half Catholic-Protestant. Decisions were taken in sub-committees where the Catholic representation would have been similar and then brought to the bigger group to be ratified.

Mistakes and successes

There were a lot of things that could have been done differently. I think the biggest mistake that I made as a Principal was that there were occasions where I assumed that everybody was agreeing with what I was saying and I didn't clarify sufficiently. I could have explained where I was coming from better. I would present decisions which I had worked out in my head and I assumed that everybody else would agree with my position, but they had not necessarily travelled the same road. One of the issues in a transforming school is to bring the staff with you, from where they were to where you want them to go. Those people have been educated in a segregated system and whether or not they're completely aware of it, you do imbibe a certain amount of that sort of ethos. The pupils don't. Secondary might be slightly different, but they're coming into an integrated school. They don't know any different. They think that all schools are like this. The pupils are very often a few steps ahead of the staff in that respect.

I'll give you an example. We would have non-uniform days every now and again to raise money for charity. At the start the staff said there might be a problem. What happens if they come with what would be considered 'sectarian' t-shirts. So we said, 'Okay, we'll make it clear; we'll say, let's be blunt about it, you're not allowed to come in Rangers shirts or Celtic shirts.' Where we are is a very strong Gaelic football area and Armagh won the All Ireland Cup, the Sam Maguire, for the first time for several years. The whole county was in uproar. The big Catholic school near us, Lismore, closed the next day to celebrate the win. Now, the question was what did we do? Would we close or will we not close? If we closed everybody would say, 'There, I told you; Brownlow is a Catholic school.' If we didn't close then, 'There, I told you; they're a Protestant school after all. They're only saying that they're integrated; they're not integrated at all.' So what do you do? We decided that we wouldn't close but we would have a non-uniform day and they could wear their Armagh shirts. Now, funny enough, Armagh play in orange. I got the phone call that I knew I was going to get and it was from one of the Protestant parents.

Vietamese 'Boat Children' at Brownlow College, 1979.

'What's going on over there? All these children going to Brownlow in Armagh shirts.' And I explained. 'Well, alright. I can tell you now my wee fella's going to school and he's going to be wearing a Rangers top.' I said, 'Right, that's fine.' And about half a dozen arrived with Rangers tops on. So we had all these Gaelic tops and Rangers tops. There was absolutely no trouble whatsoever. I have photographs of Armagh supporters with Rangers scarves around their neck and Rangers supporters with Armagh tops on. The point is that the children were ahead of the staff. The next non-uniform day we said, 'Wear whatever you like,' so Celtic and Rangers tops and Armagh ones came in. They wear whatever they like and there's never been an issue with it.

You might imagine that the main problem would be the religious curriculum. In actual fact it was not because an agreement was reached between the two main churches in terms of the GCSE R.E syllabus. The pupils were all taught more or less the same thing. Prior to integration, we would in the morning have an assembly which was a sort of a semi-religious assembly. It wasn't really all that religious but once a week a Protestant clergyman would have come in and taken the assembly. But we realised when we went integrated there would be an issue if it was only Protestant clergy coming in and it was clear at that point that there was no way that there was going to be any Catholic clergy willing to do it. So we stopped clergy coming in. We still had our assembly but it

was not in any way religious as such. There was in the school a Scripture Union and it was very popular with the pupils. So we didn't want to stop that. David Crawford, who was in charge of it, sat down with Terry McMackin. They came up with the idea that they would change the name; it wouldn't be the Scripture Union; they would call it the Ichthus Society. And I said, 'Where did you get this Ichthus from?' Ichthus is apparently the word for fish; it's the idea of being a fisher of men. So the Ichthus Society was created instead of the Scripture Union and the activities were as non-denominational as he could make them. The Catholic children were invited and they did come in big numbers.

Every head of subject when they produced their action plans for the year had to incorporate within the plans how they proposed to introduce integration into the curriculum in their subject. At first they were saying, 'There's no Catholic Maths is there? No Protestant Maths; there's just Maths.' But they were very creative, so when they were doing statistics it was statistics about integrated schools. History was my subject for most of the time and we found that much easier. We could simply include Irish history but also did an awful lot of local history. We found that the local history got away from the obsession with this denominational thing.

When I retired in 2006 the school was just on the point of being oversubscribed. It had moved from about 130 to 150 pupils to 460. And a 60:40 balance had been achieved. Now, I know since then it has tipped the other way and there's now a big majority of Catholics. There's much more of a balance on the staff. The balance on the Board of Governors was achieved in the early days as I've said. Relations between staff and pupils were always very good. One of my biggest disappointments was that I had wanted to introduce A-levels and we were refused. Many of our pupils transferred to the local grammar schools to do their A-levels and they would come back to us and say they were shocked at the sectarianism that they had encountered in those schools. They would say, 'I never really understood what an integrated school was about until I went to that other school.'

I have to tell this story. There were two boys, non-academic boys and they wanted to leave school and join the army. One of them was a Catholic, one a Protestant, one came from Mourneview estate in Lurgan which is extremely loyalist, the other from the Garvaghy Road in Portadown which is extremely nationalist. They became very good friends in school. One of them joined the Irish Army and one of them joined the British Army when they left school. They came back then and two or three years later, they're 18, 19 and they were on leave at the same time and they'd kept contact with each other and they came out to visit the school together. One of them had been with the Irish Army in the peace line between Israel and the Lebanon and the other had been in Afghanistan. And then one of them said, 'Wouldn't it be a great idea if we came out to the school in our uniforms and you got a photograph?' I thought, 'That would be a great photograph but I'm not sure that it would really be a good idea from your point of view.' And then they realised what I was talking about, that it was a non-runner.

Looking forward, looking back

So I have no doubt that integration works; it definitely works and sometimes in the most unpromising circumstances. I had the best job in education in Northern Ireland for at least 10 years and I was very privileged to work with a lot of people who felt the same way as I do.

In terms of disappointment. I suppose, that there aren't more integrated schools in existence, given the fact that 35 years down the line and they are still 7% of the population. No Catholic school has transformed. So, you're taking 50% of the school stock out of the equation straight away. The strength of Catholic opposition has simply been overpowering and has succeeded in preventing any of their schools transforming. No grammar school has transformed to integrated; there's no integrated grammar school as such. Some of the grammar schools like to say that they are because there's Catholics go to them. I went to a leading state grammar school and they would say in the papers that they're integrated. They're not. How do you get transformation into the Catholic sector, into the grammar schools? It's difficult to see just how it could grow substantially until you have those sectors on board. So you take all the Catholics out, you take all the grammar schools out. The 7% that we're talking about is 7% of 50% because that's the sea that they're swimming in. That's the only place where they're having any chance of any success.

So, having said all that, what's the future for Integrated Education? I believe that unless there is a change in attitude at the political level that you will not affect the degree of change that is essential to make a change in society as a whole. It would be very naïve to think that was going to happen very soon. But it is so important to keep pressure and keep lobbying at the political level for structural changes. Otherwise you're going to be in this situation where you're chipping away over a long period of time.

I was fortunate to be in the right place at the right time. I ended up doing the job that, had I been told that I would be doing it when I was a young man, I would have been delighted that I would have had that opportunity. I ended up doing a job within an Integrated Education system that I very strongly believed in and believed was important for the future of the country. I hope that the relatively few people I influenced feel the same way.

Lorna McAlpine is a Senior Development Officer with the Northern Ireland Council for Integrated Education (NICIE) and has been an employee for 21 years.

My job has always been to look at the hurdles and get over them

My father was a policeman and he always used to say the problems in Northern Ireland will not be solved unless the children are educated together. He saw it as the way forward and part of the solution for Northern Ireland. I started off as a Development Officer in August 1997 and then in February 1998 I got a Senior Development Officer post. I actually applied as a job share with another colleague who happens to be Catholic and had kids who were at integrated schools and we would've been the dream team! Then she decided not to do the job share so I came in just on my own. I started when we had just newly opened four independent schools: Oakwood, which opened in '96, Ulidia, Strangford, and Malone. Strangford is all of about nine miles from my home so that's where I started. My job was to work with that group and access full funding for Integrated Education.

In those days there were about 31 integrated schools and about 10,800 pupils and now there are 65 schools and about 23,000 children. My job has always been to look at the hurdles and trying to get a group over them, around them, behind them, sideways. Whatever hurdles the government was putting in their path. At that point they had increased the number of children required to start a post-primary to 100 per year. Some people went off to Westminster and

protested and eventually got that down to 80. When Martin McGuinness became Minister of Education he dropped it to 50 children at post-primary and the numbers of children needed for a primary school from 25 down to 15 in the cities, which was Derry and Belfast, and 12 in the rural areas. This was helpful because it meant that we could get more schools. For example, Sperrin was going to be independently run and in the last day we got the 50th child. That was how it worked. We moved away then from being independently funded by the Integrated Education Fund (IEF). Sinn Fein did support us in that sense but that applied to the Irish Medium schools as well, so it made it easier for them as well. That made a big change and we started to get more schools through, but there was always an issue about us being too successful. That is why all of the schools from '95 on were built as core plus mobiles so the only permanent building they got was their administration block and their assembly hall, all the rest of the school was mobiles.

I'm trying to advocate for bringing children together and I will be quite outspoken about it. I will have my facts and my figures together and I will produce an argument which is pretty well unassailable. At a meeting recently they said, 'Why are you advocating for more places in X school when there's all this Shared Education on down the road here?' and I'm going, 'Well, I think Justice Treacy said that Shared Education and Integrated Education were two distinct things.' I'm arguing for

Frances Donnelly, Lorna McAlpine and
Denise Morgan with Nuala McKeever and
Robyn Scott (past pupil of Hazelwood).

children to have access to capital monies to stop them having to run around in the rain and in the snow because there's no internal corridors, that's what I'm arguing for. I'm arguing for children to have a decent education in a mixed environment, and a decent building to be in. It's my privilege that I will advocate for that and put forward the argument as strongly as I possibly can based on evidence. Some of those schools that we got through have already bust the numbers again. I was with a school today and it has already exceeded what we got it.

The early growth

Around that time that I came in, Integrated Education grew exponentially. We had a system, an arrangement with the banks in Northern Ireland which were willing to lend money in a 'club'. If, for example, we got a new grant maintained integrated (GMI) school proposal approved, it only brought with it the revenue money, so that was to pay the teachers and it was based on the number of children within the school. It didn't bring any capital money so we had to borrow money from the group of banks to build the schools. We would've borrowed enough to put several Portakabins on the ground and that would've done. So, say we had had approval, for example, in February, between the January and the February we would've made sure we had the children all recruited properly. We would've recruited staff and a Principal, and

teachers and got the curriculum started up. We would've put policies in place, at the same time a colleague of mine, Lawrence, would've been looking for sites, looking for a building, trying to get a building organised and over the summer time there would've been a field where we had finally got a site. And he would've developed that field, say, in the May through to the August, into a school. So you were trying to sell nothing concrete, it was an idea you were selling.

Even when the GMIs were going quite well, you had to test for transformation so your first step was to make sure that if you got a group going, you would say, 'Right, your first step is to write to the schools in your area and ask if any of them are willing to transform.' The Department's view was to transform an existing school was cheaper than to build a new one.

Then in 2008-9 the financial crash occurred and we had three or four schools in process and we owed money on all of those. There was a hugely expensive site in Armagh for the new Integrated College, it was about £8million so we ended up owing, I forget exactly, but it was probably about £19 million on all of those projects. We got the money back on two of them. We were a very small organisation with a huge risk. Sadly, Armagh (Integrated College) just didn't catch and the site was sold much later on for an awful lot less, when the market had collapsed. The club bank facility died. There was even talk about NICIE folding, there were all those legal and accounting terms being bandied about. The IEF helped pay some of the debt off. So, they were sad times and it put paid to us being able to start a school from scratch. It meant that all we could do then was transform schools and then sadly even that stopped for a while. It broke my heart when schools closed. I was terribly cut up about Clogher IPS. Lir IPS wasn't directly my project but I was cut up about that too. Armagh IC nearly broke NICIE financially.

The right thing to do

A lot of parents, and people who were not parents, were sticking their head above the parapet in their own area. Some did it because they were in mixed marriages or were motivated by the fact that this was something that they could do for the future of Northern Ireland. They put a lot of hours into it. We would've met two or three times a month with some of the groups at the start and then there would be sub-groups looking at this or that. They would've gone out at the weekends and talked to parents and run events. The typical thing would've been teddy bears' picnic and events in leisure centres to bring parents and children in and try and get them to complete expression of interest forms. It was tough and often we weren't popular in what we were doing. For example, in one area there was a point where the parents were having a bit of difficulty and it turned out the difficulty was coming from the local paramilitaries. I brought the question back to my boss at that

time and I said, 'You know we are getting problems from local paramilitaries, they are not happy about this school opening.' He went to the political people and they got them to back off in order for us to be able to do the work. It was tricky and you can imagine explaining that to a group of parents!

They really had to be dedicated to keep on moving. In the end they won through because they had a belief that this was the right thing to do for their children. This was the only way their children were going to meet people from a different background. So many of us have gone through a Catholic or a predominantly Protestant system and maybe not met anybody (from a different background) until university days. Teacher training is separated as well so students maybe not met anybody at all from a different background. The parents and families have worked really hard to do this. For us it's been tough. I've been on the receiving end of some of the vilification at times as well. But we just kept going. We felt we had no choice but to keep going because it was the right thing to do.

There are still sectarian attacks, there are still sectarian things going on, people only live in certain areas, only feel comfortable in certain areas. I was doing the statistics not that long ago and there are about 1100 schools in Northern Ireland. Other than the integrated schools there's only 90 odd of them that has a mixing at least 10% Protestant in a Catholic school or at least 10% Catholic in a controlled school.

Mo Mowlan at
Ulidia College.

Including the integrated ones brings it up to 150, but you see how rare that actually is and it's only a tiny level of mixing.

There's a story that is told about the guy who wrote the original Statement of Principles. His son was a pupil at a big grammar school and he (the father) was on the local TV news programme and said, 'You know, I'm an English Catholic,' and the son came home from school and threw the schoolbag from the front door to the back door and said, 'Thanks very much, Dad, you broke my cover!' He had been passing as a Protestant in that school for a long time. A Catholic child going into a predominantly Protestant school or a Protestant child at a predominantly Catholic school will pass as the majority just to be safe unless there's a sufficient number there in order for them to be able to articulate their needs and desires. So that's the issue that we're dealing with.

Political will

The Alliance Party certainly have supported us. They raised the moral issue about it, saying this is why we have to work to try and educate our children together. If we had a period of direct rule, often it worked in our favour, because the direct rule ministers understood what we were trying to do. In England it is the norm that you're educated with people from a different background. Even in the church schools there's a mixture of religions. We have a very strange perception of normality here

in which we separate children by religion, we separate them out by gender, we separate them out by ability and everything else. My old boss used to say we find five or six ways to separate people out, which is not right. A lot of that is around socio-economic reasons and the grammar thing is still there.

Children will mix in integrated schools and they will form friendships and perhaps relationships. And the politicians are picking up on that and saying there's a risk if children are educated together that they may form mixed relationships in which land or property may go the 'other way'. It's incredible! It would have been commonly talked about in rural areas. But I remember people beside me in North Belfast where I grew up, selling their house in the 70s and being convinced that they had sold their house to a Protestant family. It turned out they were a Catholic family and the owner was annoyed about it. And so I knew that it wasn't just a country thing. I remember telling the story to somebody else and they said they were buying a car off somebody, in the country, and the person wanted to know what religion they were. They dug and dug to make sure and it was only a car! And it's not just Protestant to Protestant or Catholic to Catholic, it's both sides.

Integrated Education is not generally supported by the DUP. Certain people within the UUP have come over to our side on occasions, but a lot of people think that Shared Education is the answer. And I think Shared Education is good but will only really work as long as the money is available.

First day – new uniform at Kircubbin IPS,1998.

Once that money runs out, where's the incentive to continue to share? The thing that we should remember is that 43 of the 65 integrated schools are involved in Shared Education. The research shows that the integrated schools that are involved are helping to show that Shared Education's working because they are finding moderate attitudes amongst the children in integrated schools. I've seen cross-community projects and holidays with children being sent away, Education for Mutual Understanding and latterly, Shared Education. Whereas once an integrated school has started, it will continue to do the work that we've talked about. Shared Education is maybe once or twice a week at the very most, some of them met six times in the whole time of the project. What I'm trying to say is that the only way you're going to get that all day every day mixing is in an integrated school. It's very limited but the politicians see shared as being important and the numbers involved look good. Shared might roll into integrated. It hasn't happened that way yet but we've got the capital money that's going into both integrated and shared. I'm very optimistic about those things.

We're still having difficulty with being allowed to grow because of the impact it will have on their schools and that continues to be one of the factors. The Department are asking us to come forward with area solutions but some of those area solutions are very hard to define. You're kind of saying, 'Hang on a minute, it's about maintaining the institutions and therefore maintaining the political situation that goes behind those institutions?'

Nursery places

I've taken a huge interest in the nurseries over the years because I could see that the division started early. Professor Paul Connolly said that children from as young as three can make sectarian remarks so the integrated schools have understood that. The 1989 Education Reform Order didn't allow for nurseries to become integrated. I helped to get that piece of law overturned in 1998. I've also put arguments together that have eventually ended up in a judicial review which went the way of Integrated Education so I've helped to change policy as well. I'm very proud that we've managed to get nurseries funded, and children are being brought together earlier.

It was very unfair that we weren't allowed to have funded nurseries from 1989 up through to 1998. The law had been written because the feeling was that nursery schools are very mixed and, true enough, they are but as time has gone on, there's been less mixing in some of the newly established nurseries, nursery schools and nursery units. Last summer I put a paper to the Department of Education about the nurseries and what we've come out with is that the authorities have been told that they have to support Integrated Education and they have to recognise demonstrated parental demand.

That is very strong for us, we hope to get more nurseries out of that. I'm very proud of that. When we get development proposals through too, I'm just delighted.

Growth of Integrated Education

Up to 2006, there were smaller school transformations come through because people were aware that that might be a way of keeping themselves alive. Then the Bain review came in at about 2006 and eventually a sustainable schools policy in 2009. You were getting transformations that were for altruistic reasons but also you were getting smaller schools that were just trying to do it to survive. Once the sustainable schools policy came into play I would've said, 'Look, you're not sustainable as far as the policy,' and some schools weren't allowed to transform, for example, Donaghadee and Conlig.

What really heartened me was it was announced in 2016 that there was to be £50 million a year for 10 years for capital. They only spent about £8 million in the first two years of it. My job is to create development proposals which are strong and robust and trigger something. The last announcement under that Fresh Start Agreement was March 2016 and that's incredibly exciting to be able to say that we've 15 schools in that programme at the minute. In 1995 they stopped building brick buildings in schools for us. They only built core buildings for administration and assembly hall, and mobiles for everything else. That's going to change the game completely for those schools. What we need is more and more announcements but you know that also depends on the political situation as well and how that can be managed without a minister. I'm very excited about that and that's why we're constantly going out to people (in schools) and saying, 'Do you need a proposal, where are you with this? What about your growth?' I think the Department has changed significantly its view about integration and it is 'alive', as they would say, to Article 64 which it really wasn't to the same extent five or 10 years ago. They really want to do something. It's looking better than it's looked in the many years that I've been doing it.

As long as the numbers are good, the schools will still be doing the good work of bringing children from different backgrounds together and educating them in their differences and their similarities and letting them learn from and with each other. Over the last couple of years we've managed to create the capacity for another 1200 places within the schools. I think we are on the up.

I'm very excited about our future, really excited. I'm going to be brutal about this, the parents who set these schools up didn't really care about the type of building they were going to. They are going to get new buildings. How much more attractive is that going to be for parents? You're still going to get the hard-core parent who'll say, 'Integrated is the right thing for me,' and then you're going to get the parent who's saying, 'Aye, integrated and look at the lovely building they've got as well.' Look at Lagan, in a horrible building for years, it's beautiful now. You could build another Lagan beside it and still fill it. They turn away as much that would fill another school, so I see the future as being very rosy if we can get the money spent. To line up the projects that the Department, the Northern Ireland Office and the Treasury are going, 'Right, here, come on! Take this, get this spent.' My job is to get the money spent.

Ulidia and the kitchen table

I was only in NICIE about two years when my marriage broke up. I had a development proposal had to be in at the end of the month so I went into the office and took the papers and brought them home and worked on them. I was supposed to be moving house as well at one point, and it was all done in my kitchen table in the middle of my divorce, putting the paperwork together. We went to the opening of that school, Ulidia, in September 1999. Mo Mowlam, the Secretary of State for Northern Ireland, came to open it. She had just come from discussion with the prisoners and she talked about the release of the political prisoners. That was totally unpalatable to many people: that the price of peace was going to mean there was going to be early release of prisoners. I was sitting there going, 'Oh my goodness,' but at the same time knowing we're going to get funding for this school. The tears just came down my face when the penny dropped with me, that she was going to force their hands and make the Department give it funding. A story that Eugene Martin (Principal of Ulidia) told that day also made me cry. As a young Maths teacher he had gone to work in Dundonald Boys' High School and they said to him, 'What's your first name?' He said, 'Eugene,' and they said, 'Well, you can't be Eugene here, you'll have to be Gerry.' He was a Catholic teaching in a Protestant school and he couldn't hold his own name. I was thrilled to hear his story, thrilled to see her and even though I was going through a personal hell at the time, it was amazing, it was just utterly amazing. To some extent I was putting the needs of those children in Ulidia ahead of everything else as I was sitting writing it at home in the midst of trying to sort out a separation and divorce.

The future

I think the future is very strong for us. We're at 7%, okay? That's all we have. How much more so will we be able to make a big difference when we get all those development proposals through and we get all the new buildings, how much more difference will we be able to make? I've been doing this for 21 years, I know this is a slow system, but I am delighted about where we are now. Because the money is there, they are talking about shared sites and this and that. I put the ideas out there and wait for them to come back. There are lots of possibilities, there is definitely more to be done so I'm very excited by it, I have rarely been as excited about it.

It's important to recognise the trans-generational aspect of the Troubles. Northern Ireland has the highest level of post-traumatic stress disorder (PTSD) in the Organisation for Economic Co-operation and Development (OECD) countries and the highest level of suicide in the UK. Professor Siobhan O 'Neill says that parents who've been through the Troubles or have PTSD cannot parent properly because they don't produce a proper attachment with their children, the children don't have a proper attachment to them and that then means when they start to go to school or in social circumstances, they act that out. Her feeling was that Integrated Education can break the cycle because children have the chance to develop empathy. I think this is one role that Integrated Education needs to explore. I think it's really important. Integrated Education has the capacity and the potential to be able to do something about that trans-generational aspect of the Troubles.

I think NICIE has made a difference. I think the IEF and integrated schools have made a difference to this country and will continue to make a difference. We need to learn about each other because we have to co-exist. And we have to co-exist in friendship, not in fear. So, I couldn't be more excited about it. I couldn't be more thrilled about what I've done, the last 21 years!

It's been an honour and a privilege to be part of the creation of a different future for Northern Ireland because that's what I believe we're creating here. There's been times when it has been very difficult, and there's been times when it has been an absolute joy. I couldn't be more thrilled to have been able to support parents, children and schools. We're the small group that have made the change. We're still growing in the most difficult of circumstances. This would not have happened without the commitment of other people. To create something which would never have been created without the commitment of all those people, it's been a privilege to be part of that.

Denise McBay has been a governor of Millennium Integrated Primary School in Saintfield for almost two decades and a founding parent and governor of Blackwater Integrated College in Downpatrick.

Early Days in Millennium

I got involved in a very roundabout way. It was my partner who was the avid Integrated Education person. We had just returned from living in Holland for five, six years. We were used to a different education system over there. My first child was already in a Catholic maintained primary school and the second child was due to start school. We had moved to Carryduff and a leaflet came through the door. There was a proposed meeting about setting up a new integrated school in the Lough Moss Centre. I was the working person in the family. Sean was the mum, basically, and so he had more time on his hands than I had, so he took this on board and started going to the meetings. Out of the first meeting he became one of the original steering committee members. He and Margaret Marshall, Christine Truman and Adrian McNicholl and a couple of others formed the steering committee for what ultimately became Millennium Integrated Primary School. That steering committee started in February, March 1999, so by the following year, they were looking for premises. Unfortunately, Sean was killed in a car crash just before they were about to open the school.

So, even though I wasn't actively involved and I wasn't one of the ones who thought about it, I thought this was something he was so passionate about that I needed to take the next step in memory for him. I had one child at the time who was about to start primary school, Cailin, so I put his name down for Millennium and he became one of the first 10 children to start at the school. And I became one of the first governors of the school. That is 18 years ago and I'm still there.

I wasn't particularly au fait with Integrated Education because I had just returned to Northern Ireland and it sort of happened in my absence. But the more I got into it, the more I understood it and the more I wanted it. The bottom line was I liked the mindset of the people there; I liked what they were trying to achieve.

At the beginning it went through the normal process with the Northern Ireland Council for Integrated Education (NICIE) and the Belfast Trust for Integrated Education (BELTIE) and the Integrated Education Fund (IEF), the traditional supporters of Integrated Education. We also had support from various political parties. Dawn Purvis from the PUP was on our first Board of Governors.

By sheer luck it was the first time we had the Northern Ireland Executive. Martin McGuinness was the Education Minister and his very first role was to grant the development proposal for Millennium and for one Irish Medium school. We seemed to arrive at the right place at the right time. From 10 children to coming up on 400 children. It's been a remarkably successful school.

We didn't have a building when we were selling the idea and this was weeks before the first children were meant

Millennium IPS at NICIE
Stormont Walk, 2017.

to start. We're trying to get these parents to commit their child to literally nothing because we didn't have a building. I think that we were all equally mad at the time, but we were so passionate about it. We didn't get the building until about three or four weeks before the start of September.

It used to be a hostel up Breda Park in South Belfast, those old Victorian, three, four-storey houses. The front living room of the house became the classroom, the kitchen became the canteen and the room at the back became the office of the first Principal, Mary Roulston. There was a lot of work to be done just to make that habitable in the space of three or four weeks. It was difficult for me because I had a baby the week before, the 25th of August, and I had a child starting school the following week. The potential parents and Mary, obviously, were getting stuck in to get the building habitable. They were taking down curtains, sticking them in the washing machine, painting the walls, doing all sorts of things. I just stood there in the background. They managed to get it done on time for the first children arriving.

I'm surprised 10 parents actually took the risk to send their children. You can understand the worries parents would have arriving at what is effectively a house that we turned into a school and thinking, 'We just passed three good schools with proper buildings and facilities on the way down to come down to this.' You have to take your hat off to those parents who drove past all that and came to us.

Building a reputation, building a school community

I had this overriding sense from day one that this was going to be a success. I can put my hand on my heart and say I did not doubt it, not for one second. I know it sounds a bit stupid, when Sean died it was almost like we had a guardian angel and I just knew that school was going to be a success. I think a lot of the parents had the feeling that this was going to be a success, even though it was hard work. And the proof's in the pudding, as they say.

We were very lucky because there was such a short time between the initial steering committee and us actually getting the school up and running and getting Departmental approval. Literally that all happened within a year, whereas other schools in the same situation had steering committees and groups for years before they got to that point. We got to it very quickly. So that group became a Board of Governors very quickly. It was quite a diverse group, especially the first set of governors. We hadn't a notion what we were doing. We had to learn, learn hard and fast. And there was a whole mixture of personalities. Some people liked what we'd done, some people didn't; some people found it difficult, the decisions we made. The governors' meetings were very intense but we managed to keep a fairly even keel over the years. I don't remember anybody storming out!

The first couple of years I did the wages for the staff and then the accounts and I'm not an accountant. You were doing that when you were coming home from work. It was all very busy. You had to learn a lot about HR, what you could and couldn't do. And you had to learn about governance.

It helped me as well. It was a bit of therapy at the start. It kept me busy and kept me thinking on the positive all the time because Integrated Education is such a positive thing. That kept me very motivated and kept me focused. I could have lay down after Sean died and just give up the will but it was part of the therapy. We had great fun in those days; they were really good times with people and it was a beautiful experience trying to convince people to give me your child!

Mary became known very quickly as excellent. Mary has a gift with parents and children. In a small community like Carryduff there was a big curiosity factor. People became curious; more and more were coming out of curiosity and then getting sucked in because they could feel the vibe and the ethos of the school. Carryduff is a mixed area; there's a lot of mixed marriages. So people came for different reasons. A lot of people came because the controlled school or the CCMS (Council for Catholic Maintained Schools) school didn't quite suit them and this was a viable alternative.

It was hard work in the third year particularly because at that stage we were still in the house in Breda Park. We'd been telling parents, two and a half years, we'll get the school, and nothing was coming of it at all. Our numbers dropped and we knew that the parents were getting a bit anxious. So it was just a matter of keeping your foot to the pedal and pushing, because we knew that people couldn't live on a promise forever.

NICIE had a building officer, Lawrence, and he would have been responsible for purchasing the site. They had a special set up with the bank that allowed the purchase of sites and then the construction of the buildings. Then the Department would pay when the school was vested. We knew the site had been identified quite a long time before but it was getting to that point where we needed the plan, we needed people to see something was happening on that site, should that be just demolishing the existing house that was there. So it was a great relief to us first day when they came up and demolished that house. We could say, 'Look, it's starting.' We moved from Breda Park to a temporary school while we built the permanent school. We had mobiles, but at least we were on site.

The construction programme was about 14 months. It's about to be demolished and we're about to get a brand new one in the next year and a half or two.

Battling for Blackwater

It came out of a group of parents who had children at Millennium and Cedar whose children were getting to the age like mine. Those kids had not much hope of getting into Lagan. Lagan was over-subscribed and at that stage didn't have in their criteria the fact that you went to an integrated primary school. The same as Shimna; it was very over-subscribed. The parents still wanted to maintain the child through an integrated secondary school. So a group of about eight of us got together, a mix of parents, Cedar and Millennium, and formed a steering group to push ahead with a new second-level school in the mid-Down area. There were three schools there – Cedar, Millennium, Drumlin – feeder schools that we could have secure numbers.

Millennium arrived at the perfect time. Blackwater arrived at the most difficult time. It was coming out of the Bain Review, the review of sustainable education and there was a lot of nervousness about. Blackwater didn't get its development proposal in the first instance. Lagan and Shimna objected to the development proposal, which was shame I thought. They had their own agenda; Lagan were in the middle of a PFI, and I think they thought that another school might mean the possibility of them losing their new-build. But both schools were hugely over-subscribed so it wasn't really a numbers game.

Blackwater had probably the most difficult path of all, because we had huge numbers of people wanting to come. We had 40 children come into the first year. For the first three years I think we got at least 40 a year. The IEF very generously got us a site in the old Belvoir Hospital and provided us with what was then state of the art mobile accommodation. We were in the old part of the building; it was a bit like Harry Potter. It was one of those old red brick buildings in the first year. Second year we needed bigger, so we had a couple of mobiles and the building. It was very successful. We submitted the second development proposal the following year and were unsuccessful. We had about 120 kids. The governors at Blackwater had such a stressful time. It made some of them ill it was so stressful, because we all felt this massive responsibility. It still makes me nearly cry; it was an horrendous time for us all.

We put in the third development proposal. Down Academy numbers were falling; they weren't sustainable at all. They were a controlled integrated school. The possibility was that we would shut down the Academy and shut Rowallane and we would open a new school on the site of Down Academy. That was the last thing we all wanted but we went for it. We had a great Principal, Olwen Griffith, who managed to pull us through that. I can't think of anybody more perfect as a Principal than Olwen, a very strong woman who steered that really difficult ship through a very hard time and who suffered greatly for it herself. It was very difficult years: you had that problem of two different staffs, two very different ethoess, two groups of kids, two groups of governors merging.

Millenium IPS signing the peace wall, 2014.

Obviously, we lost a lot of children when the second development proposal was turned down. People left, people got anxious, nervous. Then when we heard we were joining with Down Academy, that was the nail in the coffin for quite a few. Down Academy had a very poor reputation. It was a poorly performing school and it was the complete opposite to what we were trying to achieve. Down Academy was a controlled secondary school with the pupils predominantly from the Protestant community. Then it transformed but was never good. In Downpatrick you had De Le Salle and St Mary's on the CCMS side so there was not a lot of Catholics attracted to Down Academy.

That was a time when I nearly lost heart. I had always seen the integrated sector, I suppose, as the independent corner shops whereas the other schools were the Tescos. What happened should not have happened. That was my single biggest disappointment in Integrated Education. How could one school go and do that to another when we were all in it to grow the sector and to provide for more children? It just didn't make sense. We were never going to be a threat to them. They were so big and so over-subscribed.

Millennium has got a fairly secure future. We're on P7 or P6 of our second intake. Blackwater is a different ballgame. Fundamentally, the reason it's not succeeding at the moment is its location and the building. You're going into an old building that's falling down round us, has very little facilities,

has no playground, has no pitches. Parents want more now than an ethos; they want to see the iPad, the interactive white boards, the best equipment. If it was vested and had a new building, it would become a success, I have no doubt. As it stands, we've only got capacity in the building for 300, 250 children. Under health and safety, we couldn't fit 500 in that building if we tried.

Blackwater has produced the most astounding results for children who were destined never to get anything. We have one of the highest rates of SEN in the whole of Northern Ireland, and those teachers are nothing but miraculous, what they produce out of those kids.

Commitment to integration

I can't believe I'm still on the Blackwater Board of Governors as well. But my baby is Blackwater. To me it's a child that started off disadvantaged. Millennium was born with a silver spoon. Blackwater was born with a few deficits; with the right nurturing and the right direction it will get there. I'm much more emotionally attached to Blackwater, even though I have the whole Sean thing with Millennium. It's like having two children, one child you know is going to be a success and they've got a good head on them and you have one child who'll always worry a bit more about.

Blackwater College with
the Olympic Flame, 2012.

I'm not that type of person who looks back and says, 'I could have done differently,' because there's no point. What's done is done, it is what it is. I think we did everything in our power in both schools. My dream would have been that Blackwater would have been more successful.

What are the challenges now for parents wishing to set up? Numbers, bums on seats. That's always been the fundamental challenge. It's much more difficult to get parents who have free time. It takes a lot of time and hard work and it's getting parents who are so dedicated and have that time on their hand. Not a lot of people have that nowadays. There's political factors as well, but the bottom line is, if there's a will, there's a way. But there hasn't been the will from a lot of parents and that would worry me more.

For me, Integrated Education has been a life style; it's been so integral in my life, not my younger life because I never knew it existed, but in the last 20 years. I have seen the real benefit of Integrated Education and it's almost tangible.

When you walk into an integrated school, it's that child-centeredness. As a parent, I knew that no matter how bad things were going to be that they were approachable. You could talk stuff through; there was nothing off limits. It was an extension of your family. I don't think other sectors offered that. And I loved the mixed ability, the children that come from every quarter. They all add, even children that you have great difficulty with. The kids learn from each other.

I really wish it would grow more in Northern Ireland because I think it's the only way forward. It's the lack of vision in some people that they don't see it. People don't like change in this country, and Integrated Education is change. It would be lovely if all schools in Northern Ireland were integrated, wouldn't it? I don't think it will happen in my lifetime, or my children's lifetime, unfortunately. I'm not even talking about integrated, but just, come together in whatever form that is, and that is not Shared Education, by the way; I'm not an advocate of that at all. I'm one of the thoroughbred integrated ones.

Terry McMackin has been involved in Integrated Education for more than 30 years. He started as a teacher in Lagan College, continued his career as a Senior Teacher in Brownlow Integrated College, and worked in the Northern Ireland Council for Integrated Education (NICIE) for about 10 years. He currently continues to support Integrated Education through his role as a NICIE Associate.

I come from the Falls Road, Belfast; a very Catholic area. I grew up in a very mono-cultural, mono-religious background. I first met Protestants at university. I became a teacher and initially taught in St Malachy's College, a Catholic grammar school. I was there for about two years and then I got married in 1968 and my wife and I decided to go to Uganda for two years to teach in a mission school. I was moving from a very insular society to a country with blue skies and sun shining, so it was like a window being thrown wide open and, of course, there was the whole cultural richness. I'm a committed and practising Catholic and the African church was so much more alive and vibrant; so those two years in Uganda were a very formative experience in my life. They were also the first two years of our marriage; our first child was born in a Ugandan mission hospital. It was a very significant period in my life.

We returned home to Northern Ireland in 1970. By then the Troubles had begun. I taught in St Malachy's from 1970 to 1977. But there was something about teaching in a grammar school setting, an all boys' grammar school setting, that struck me as very limiting. The highlight of each school year when the staff returned was whether the GCSE results were at 95% or 93% or whatever. If they weren't sufficiently good, we were urged to ensure they were better next year. So, there was something about this very limited focus on academic achievement that at some level troubled me.

In 1977 I applied for St Louise's Comprehensive College which was expanding at that time. Eventually it had over 2,000 pupils. It was non-selective and so for me a more open and inclusive situation where the school wasn't focusing just on academic achievement for the pupils. I stayed there from 1977 to 1985. The Troubles were raging during this period and I became conscious that I had an important role as a teacher but was not particularly politically involved. I was nevertheless aware that the Troubles were causing great division and pain in Northern Ireland society.

A long career in Integrated Education

Lagan College opened in 1981. In 1985 they were looking for a head of Religious Education; that was the post I held in St Louise's. I decided I would like to have a go at this. There was a further inclusiveness about Lagan which appealed to me. It was co-educational, it was non-selective, and it was open to children and staff from both traditions. I think in a real way that's what was driving me and was what led me to Lagan. I was in Lagan from 1985 to 1991, I was a joint head of RE with a Protestant colleague. That was a good experience in itself. Then in 1991 Brownlow College in Craigavon decided to transform. The College was looking for a senior Catholic teacher to join their management team to assist in the transition from controlled to controlled integrated and I was appointed to the post. I was in

Denis Taylor at
Glencraig IPS, 2008.

Brownlow from 1991 until 1996 when I retired from teaching for health reasons. I stayed out of teaching from 1996 until 2000 when I was appointed to a Development Officer post in NICIE. I worked in NICIE with schools which were considering transformation or were in the process. I retired from NICIE in 2010, but I still do some work for them as an Associate. The two main areas of my interest in the integrated sector continue to be Religious Education and transformation.

Teaching at Lagan College

I joined Lagan College when the college was still on the site of what is now Loughview Integrated Primary School. They had moved from the Scout hall at Ardnavalley, but the buildings were quite primitive. I mean St Louise's was a beautiful school in terms of buildings. Lagan was largely in mobiles and they were very cold in the winter! I suppose what really kept me going was the radical nature of the venture and it was something totally new for me. For the first time I was rubbing shoulders with teachers and other staff from different traditions to my own. RE is a subject where you must, of course, have sensitivity. I was faced in Lagan with classes with a range of pupils from different Christian traditions, other faith traditions or of no particular faith. Previously my assumption had always been that all these children in front of me were Catholic. So, there were normally no delicate issues, you didn't

need to be particularly sensitive when you taught. In this regard Lagan was a real learning experience for me. I believe of all the teaching periods in my life, Lagan was probably the one that was most stimulating. There was a presumption that everybody who was there was of a like mind in terms of really wanting to be respectful of and understand others' views. But just meeting with and working with people with different views, political views, religious views, from different cultural world views, all of that was immensely stimulating.

Developing an integrated ethos

Every year in January during Christian Unity Week, we held a religious service in Lagan. It happened in my second year that members of the Maranatha Community, a fellowship of Christians from different traditions, were visiting Northern Ireland. I met with them and told them about Lagan College. In those early days the Christian ethos of the college was seen to be of great importance but there was no obvious symbol of that in the college. One of the Maranatha Community was Lord Hilton. We were just talking about what might be a suitable symbol. He said that he knew a Greek carpenter who was Orthodox in religion. We came to the idea that this Greek carpenter would be commissioned to carve a cross. Just a plain wooden cross with a Celtic motif in it and the Maranatha Community would pay for that. That cross hangs in the foyer

Martin Lynch, NICIE patron at Saints and Scholars IPS, 2008.

of Lagan College now. For the Unity Service we laid the cross on the floor of the assembly hall, surrounded by lit candles, with music of the Taizé Community playing. It was a very simple service which drew together parents and teachers and governors from the main Christian and indeed other traditions.

In those early days one of the practical questions was how to celebrate differing religious traditions. For example, should the distribution of ashes on Ash Wednesday be confined to the Catholic pupils or be open to everyone? The way in which the Lord's Prayer is said, that was one of the ways in which Lagan tried to respect both Protestant and Catholic traditions. The Catholic version of the Lord's Prayer is different from the Protestant version. If you said it one way you were a Catholic, if you said it another way you were a Protestant. The way that Lagan managed that was to say the versions alternately at assemblies. So there were issues like that, that had to be worked out.

The first transforming integrated school

Brownlow College was the first school transforming from controlled to controlled integrated status. There was a lot of local opposition to it. I think it's probably fair to say that the original motivation of the school to become integrated was to increase pupil numbers although both Frank Loan, the Principal, and Errol Lemon, Senior Teacher and later Principal,

were personally in favour of integration. One of my tasks was to help to steer this process in terms of moving the school from a controlled ethos to a controlled integrated ethos. The approach that I took to that was very much 'one small step at a time'. I remember very clearly back in 1991, a gathering of the staff, and I was talking about integration and the difference that it can make teaching in an integrated school. I said, 'I might consciously take a risk and say to you that my favourite political person is John Hume, leader of the SDLP.' I looked at the body language and it was like, 'What is this man saying? John Hume? He supports John Hume?' What I took from that experience was that to most of the staff in this recently controlled integrated school, having someone who supported John Hume was something that they couldn't quite take in.

There were two members of the local Orange Lodge on the staff. Drumcree was going on at the time and one of the issues in moving to controlled integrated status was setting up a chaplaincy team that would be representative of all the traditions. Until transformation the pattern was that essentially the local Protestant ministers came in and spoke to the assembly and there would be a certain number of Catholic pupils present but they had to listen to him or her, whatever was being said. Sometimes thinly veiled anti-Catholic views were coming from one of these ministers. Because the school was becoming integrated, one of the ministers said to me, 'I'll not be coming again because there may be priests coming into this school.' One of the first Catholic chaplains was associated with the Drumcree situation. He was working with the residents' group in the Garvaghy Road and was known for that, but he said he would be very willing to come in for the Catholic pupils. A member of staff objected, and I think a number of parents said they would withdraw their children from the school. In the end maybe five left over this or other concerns about integration, certainly no more than that.

As time went on there was less anxiety about change. As one of the ways of marking change I decided that I would make the sign of the cross, which, of course, is a very Catholic action, at the start of the school assembly. I explained to the pupils what I would be doing and why I would be doing it. And that was fine. One of my Protestant colleagues was anxious that the whole thing would succeed and was very supportive of me. He said that several of his fifth years had come to him after the assembly, asking, 'What's that happening here, this Catholic sign of the cross being made?' He went out of his way to explain to those pupils, 'This is what integration means; it's respecting all these different practices.'

Over the five years that I was in Brownlow College, relationships were always good. I think that's maybe a key point I would make that, in transformation and all of these situations of change, getting the relationships right first is vital. When people realise that you're not a threat, either because of what you're actually doing or because of the kind of person you are, I think that they will more readily accept the little changes, knowing that they're coming from a reasonable place.

The challenges for transforming schools

When I first came to NICIE, there was a certain amount of funding available, I think through the Integrated Education Fund (IEF), encouraging schools to explore transformation. There was quite a significant amount of funding available in terms of providing for staff development, but very few of the schools considering transformation or that had recently transformed, had taken this up. One of the first briefs I had was to visit those schools and try to encourage them to take up this staff development. There was consequently a good take up of NICIE training because of those visits. I think the key challenge in that was overcoming the school's sense of being seen as second class. The initial view when someone from NICIE came in to a transforming school was, 'Oh, here's someone from the pure brand of integration coming in to tell us where we're doing it wrong.' I would start the conversation by looking at existing good practices that were taking place in the school, without it being integrated. In most cases, the management genuinely felt that when they were doing these things, they were implementing integrating principles. Once they realised that this wasn't an attack or that they weren't being regarded as second class and that this funding was available, then they came on board.

A school that is intending or hoping to transform, especially primary schools, needs to be aware of the requirements for sacramental preparation. That is probably one of the big changes that a controlled school will make, to have to provide sacrament preparation for Catholic pupils. I remember one school that was just exploring the idea of transformation. We met in the board room of NICIE and as soon as that requirement of sacrament preparation was put on the table, they almost immediately got up and left! So, for schools considering transformation there can be certain things that are just no-go areas for them.

The personal journey in the road of Integrated Education

For me the journey has been stimulating, challenging and humbling, particularly when I think of the efforts of parents. I've been involved recently with Mallusk Integrated Primary School's transformation and I really admire the commitment and tenacity of that group of parents.

I can remember years ago watching (on a black and white television) Cecil Linehan being interviewed, about a conflict with the local Catholic bishop over arrangements for reception of the sacrament of Confirmation, for Catholic children not attending Catholic schools. Of course, the good Catholic that I was, I thought to myself, 'That woman has a nerve! Who does she think she is challenging the bishop?' But now I know she was right! Cecil went on to be one of the founders of All Children Together (ACT) and then of Lagan College. I have enormous admiration for her and those early pioneers.

Through involvement with integration I've met good people. People that have stood up to be counted and even in the early days re-mortgaged their houses! I don't think I could have done that. But it was the realisation of that tremendous investment that kept me engaged. It's a source of inspiration for me even now.

Tony Macaulay was a founder parent of Spires Integrated Primary School and Sperrin Integrated College, both in Magherafelt.

Growing up: Protestants, Jews and Catholics

I went to a primary school at the top of the Shankill Road in West Belfast where everyone at my school was a Protestant. There were no Catholics at all at my school. Catholics lived at the other side of the peace wall. So I didn't meet Catholics. There were football tournaments between the primary schools in Belfast at that time and I just remember it was really important that we beat Holy Cross in Ardoyne which was the nearest Catholic primary school to us. But I didn't play football so I didn't even have that experience. My first experience of meeting Catholics was through the School of Music in Belfast. I learnt the violin and went for lessons there on a Saturday morning. I was from the top of the Shankill Road playing the violin beside people who grew up on the Falls Road. I thought it was fascinating; I thought, 'They're just the same as me, they just wear different school uniforms. Sadly, they're better at the violin than me!'

Unlike most people from the Shankill I got through the 11+ system and went to a grammar school, Belfast Royal Academy (BRA). BRA was interesting in that it was seen as this prestigious Protestant grammar school but at that time it was the nearest school for the Jewish community which lived in the Antrim Road. While I was there, there were more Jewish students than Catholics; it was mostly Protestants and Jews. So we had Jewish assembly in BRA. As the Troubles

developed there were some businessmen murdered from the Jewish community. A lot of the Jewish people left and went to Israel. So by the time I left BRA there weren't enough people to have a Jewish assembly anymore. The number of Catholics at BRA started to increase slowly at that stage.

I remember my first day at BRA and there must've been, like, a handful of Catholics in my class. I was really interested in making friends with them because I was fascinated about meeting people from a completely different background. My first mate on my first day was wee Thomas from Ardoyne who, a bit like me, against all the odds ended up at grammar school. We both felt a bit different because of where we came from – me because I wasn't from a middle class background and him obviously because he wasn't from a middle class background either and was from a Catholic background. I suppose I felt a bit of a connection with him.

BRA was on the Cliftonville Road. All hell was breaking loose in the streets around us. I remember having to go to school without a school uniform and finding it hard to get home. The school was this sort of oasis away from all of that. But it was also a place where you didn't talk about differences; you didn't go there in terms of their politics. We didn't really talk about the issues. I was involved in the Christian Union in BRA and I remember at one stage I was on the committee and some of us wanted to invite a Catholic priest to speak.

Sperrin IC Opening Day,
September 2002.

It was forbidden. We weren't allowed to invite a Catholic priest to the Christian Union just to ask him some questions! So that said to me: although it was saying it was open, it was ultimately a Protestant grammar school and obviously with the name and the heritage of the school, very much a British identity as well. I never had experience at school of actively learning sectarianism or to distrust or hate anyone from the other side. I heard positive messages at primary school and grammar school about respecting people and being tolerant, but at the same time, there was this divide.

I remember when I was quite young watching on television that there was going to be this integrated school, Lagan College. I remember watching news reports of protesters standing to try to stop this school happening and I remember at the time thinking, 'But sure, nearly all the schools in Northern Ireland are not integrated so why would you protest about just one?' I remember thinking this was bizarre; it just seemed to me to be the most obvious thing to do it, seemed to be the right thing to do. Why would you protest against something so obviously good?

I got involved in youth work and community development in my career in the 1980s and into the 1990s. I was very involved in cross-community youth work, bringing young people together for contact and learning experiences. Part of what I was doing was almost compensating for the education system, the fact that the children or the teenagers

didn't know each other because they were at separate schools and lived in separate areas. A lot of the work I was doing was making up for the fact that the system was creating this division and keeping the young people apart from the age of four. My wife, Lesley, and I were both involved in this sort of work for many years, and we felt that when we had children we would want our children to go to an integrated school. It seemed to be the obvious choice and we're both Protestants. I know a lot of people in those days who sent their children to integrated schools who were in inter-church marriages but we're both Presbyterians and we just felt that it was the best thing for our children to grow up being at school and having friends with people who were different from them. If they were to go to go school with other children who were Catholics or other faiths or no faith, they would have a broader understanding and respect for other people. Ultimately, we thought this country will really never become a truly integrated society until we have Integrated Education as the norm rather than the exception. So partly for what we wanted for our own children but partly for what we felt was the future, we wanted our children to be at an integrated school.

Spires Primary School

At the time, the 1990s, we were living in Magherafelt and there was no integrated primary school and no integrated

{102}

Sperrin IC new building, 2007.

college in our area. So, we got in touch with the Northern Ireland Council for Integrated Education (NICIE) and talked to other parents who were like-minded; some were like us, others were in mixed marriages. We realised that the only way our children were going to go to an integrated school was if we got together and started one. That shocked me at one level because I never thought I'd be involved in starting a school, never mind two schools! But I thought, 'If we wait for the government to start the school, it ain't gonna happen. The Department of Education aren't going to make it happen. The only way it's going to happen is if we go out and do it ourselves.' So we got together with other like-minded parents and that's exactly what we did.

A few of us talked to NICIE and they organised a public meeting in a leisure centre in Magherafelt. There must've been about 300 people came along, mostly parents like us who were interested. There were also people there who came to oppose it. There was a man who came who was obviously on the Board of Governors from the local Catholic school and he dominated the whole meeting; he shouted people down. And I was thinking, 'But you've got a school for your children to go to. You've got what you want. We don't have what we want! So why are you coming here trying to stop us have one little integrated school in this area?'

One of the other key founders who became the Chair of the Governors, Anna Clarke, was very much involved in

community development work. But in the primary school it was mostly women, mostly mothers. There was probably about eight of us in the core group. We met every week for a year. NICIE Development Officers would come up and support us, help us to understand the process. None of us were from an educational background or a teaching background, so they were helping us through the process. I remember doing a lot of door-to-door leaflet drops. We did stands in the local shopping centre, giving out leaflets and chatting to parents. And we did family events to bring people together, to let people know what we are doing. I remember one event where I was manning the bouncy castle, giving out leaflets, doing a speech about our vision for the school, selling burgers and sweeping the floor. We all pitched in. We had a competition for the name of the school and we had to design the logo and the uniform. We had to persuade 28 parents to register their children for the school. My daughter was number one, but we needed another 27. We got the final one the day before the Minister of Education was to give approval for the school. So we just made it.

We had to get a site and that was interesting because people are funny about land up the country; you don't sell land to the other side. So, even if the site was available, some people wouldn't sell their land for an integrated school. After a lot of searching for a suitable site we ended up with a field with sheep. Remarkably, it was transformed into a sort of playground with several mobile classrooms. NICIE helped us to borrow money. If the school proved viable it could recover that cost. We didn't have personal money in the way that it was with some of the earlier integrated schools where they had to mortgage their houses. Our job was to get the pupils. The other thing was we had to recruit a Principal for a school that didn't exist. Then once we had the Principal, we had to appoint teachers. We appointed teachers every year so I found myself in a lot of interview panels for teachers, something I never thought I'd do. Obviously, we wanted the best quality of teachers that we could get. NICIE helped us with that. We wanted people who were qualified and experienced in education but I personally was looking for teachers who were committed to the integration element. I wasn't interested in teachers who just wanted a job and a career move. I was interested in those who were genuinely committed and I was always interested in the question we asked them about their vision for the integrated element of the school. So that's what I was interested in, their vision and their passion for integration, who seemed creative and innovative and would be prepared to go the extra mile. We were so small and we were just getting started, so we needed teachers who were prepared to really work hard and be committed to it.

On 1st September 1999 we opened the school. It was one of the proudest days of my life. I remember all the children in their wee uniforms and the mobile classrooms. Over the years the school was built and it's still there. Every time I drive past it I feel very proud. Hopefully they will be there long after I'm gone.

Sperrin Integrated College

The college was more difficult because it was a bigger project. We needed to recruit more pupils. We weren't just up against people who didn't want their children to go to an integrated school. We were also up against people who didn't want their children to go to a school that wasn't a grammar school. There were parents who were involved in the integrated primary who didn't get involved in the integrated college because they wanted their children to go to a grammar school.

I think people had got used to the primary school and they could tolerate it. It was a wee primary school for the people who were into that sort of thing, you know, the mixed marriages and the peaceniks like me. But an integrated college, you know, with maybe 500 going to it – now that's a threat to other schools. Also I think people realised if their children were going to go to an integrated college then they might get married. It's okay if they are wee kids at primary school; they will get on and play together; that's nice. But if they go to an integrated college together and are there until they're 17, what if they develop a relationship and decide they are going to marry someone from the other community? It's more serious. They didn't want their kids to deal with that because that's not easy for people here. It was not necessarily a nasty thing, just a want to protect children from what that might mean. Ultimately, I think it's a very sad thing.

We divided the primary schools in the local area up between us to bring the prospectus of the new integrated college. I remember going to one of the local primary schools and meeting the Principal and she asked me not to contact them again. She told me she wouldn't be recommending or letting her children know about the school and she was really quite rude. I took a morning off work to go and meet her and to bring her these prospectuses. I'm pretty sure they went in the bin as soon as I left. I couldn't understand why she wouldn't want to give the children in her school or the parents at that school that option. What was so threatening to her in her local primary school that she didn't want any of her children to go to the integrated college? I couldn't understand this.

The benefits of Integrated Education

That level of sectarianism that was within me – much as I dislike it, I grew up with it. It's not there in my kids at all. It's just completely absent. They've had friends who were Catholics from as young as they can remember. I remember my youngest daughter singing in the choir at her friend's First Holy Communion. And it was the most natural thing in the world for her to go to her friend's church. When I was her age I wouldn't have had a clue what First Holy Communion was and I probably thought it was something bad or something suspicious. I've seen my own children grow up without that whole level of sectarianism; it's just not in them. I also think the integrated schools are really good around personal development. My daughters have grown up to be quite confident and quite rounded. I remember being disappointed in other parents who didn't send their children to the integrated college because they wanted their children to go to a grammar school. When my children went to an integrated college they were middle class kids but they were mixing with working class kids and kids who lived in the estates, and I feel that gave them a much more rounded understanding of life. They were used to dealing with people who were from a different social background from them and making friends with them. That's prepared them for life and for work. It's all very well saying, 'I want my children to go to a nice grammar school where they won't meet any rough kids,' but they're going to have to meet people from a working class background at some stage! My eldest daughter's just got engaged to a Catholic; I don't know whether that would've happened if she hadn't gone to an integrated school.

The most important thing is that your children will have a better, more rounded education and preparation for life. You can't ask for better than that. Your children will benefit hugely from going to an integrated school and I think that's immeasurable.

The future of integration

For me Integrated Education in Northern Ireland is about breaking down the sectarian divide by creating educational institutions that are genuinely integrated and where there's equality and diversity and a really good quality education.

There's a problem when integrated schools are over-subscribed and they've to turn pupils away. I think that's awful. There's no real political commitment to Integrated Education. Northern Ireland is structured in terms of our politics; the power rests with two main political parties who have an ethnic bloc vote that really depends on Northern Ireland continuing to be divided. And you have powerful institutions which include the likes of the Department of Education and the existing schools; people are very loyal to schools and feel very strongly about protecting them as institutions.

I sometimes wish that we had had an equivalent of the Patten Report into education in Northern Ireland. The Patten Report was part of the Good Friday Agreement whereby the Royal Ulster Constabulary (RUC) was seen as one-sided because it was predominantly Protestant. Something had to change politically; the RUC had to change into the Police Service of Northern Ireland (PSNI) and it was a political priority. I'd love to have seen something as radical as that with our education system so that the schools would have to change, not sort of gradually – a wee bit shared and a wee bit more shared education, and not just these baby steps for years and years, actually some major introduction of Integrated Education as the norm in Northern Ireland. That's what needs to happen but I think that's unlikely because our politicians are dependent on it staying divided. Unless there's a major political initiative to transform our education system, I don't see that happening. It might happen very slowly through some of the Shared Education initiatives; that might move gradually in the right direction over 100 years or something!

All you have to do is look at our voting patterns here and you see that we are still a very divided society. It's not as if the community has emerged from conflict and all of a sudden everyone's voting for the Alliance Party. In fact, the opposite is the case. I know all of the surveys for years that NICIE have done have said that over 70% of people would choose Integrated Education if it was available. But the reality is it's not available and if it's not available, it's not gonna be available. You really have to put yourself out; I mean, we had to start two schools! Do you really want to put yourself out that much? You've got your life to get on with, you've got your job, you've got your family. Do you really need to go out and start a school?

People here, we want to live alongside each other peacefully. I think that's where we've got to. That's what the voting patterns would suggest. We want to live alongside each other peacefully but we don't really want to live together. And I think living together means we take down the peace walls, we have integrated housing, and we've Integrated Education. The majority of people in Northern Ireland are comfortable enough, comfortably divided and it's not the Troubles; it's peaceful. There's a lot more cross-community contact than there used to be; it's better than it used to be; there's less trouble. People can get on with their lives and not worry about all of that stuff. People don't want to talk about that stuff. So I think we're quite a comfortably divided society which means there isn't that big thrust for Integrated Education from most parents. I think that's sad but that's the reality. But what I still passionately believe in is that every parent who wants their child to go to an integrated school in Northern Ireland should have that option available to them and I think children being turned away and the Department of Education refusing to allow growth, that needs to be fought. So there's one thing that most people in Northern Ireland are comfortable enough that their children go to separate schools. I think it's another thing to stop the growth of Integrated Education. I think that's deliberate.

Very few ordinary people are anti-Integrated Education. It's more people are against it because they're a politician or they were the Principal of a school who saw the integrated schools as a threat. Most ordinary people I would've talked to thought it was a really good idea but ultimately, they'd rather send their child to the school down the road or to a grammar school, because that's what's more important to them. So it's not that they're against Integrated Education. It's people in powerful positions who are protecting the current system who sort of prevent the growth of Integrated Education, not ordinary people.

I think the future is integrated. But I believe that people will look back at our history and say: what took them so long?

I would definitely do it all over again. I'd still have the school in the same place, still appoint the same Principals as our first Principals. I'd still commit myself to do what I had to do. I'm sure we made mistakes. I might regret that family that we went to visit one night and ultimately they decided not to send their children; maybe it was something that I said that let them down. We chose to be very positive, chose not to criticise other schools. We were saying, 'This is an option that we don't have in this area; we're just extending the options we have as parents.' It's still only 7% of the kids are in an integrated school. I suppose probably if I was doing it now I might be a wee bit more outspoken about the opposition. We just took it; we didn't really fight it. I think some things need said and I would say them now.

Stuart Marriott was involved in setting up two integrated primary schools, Mill Strand IPS in Portrush and Phoenix IPS in Cookstown, and in the governance of another, Windmill IPS in Dungannon.

The beginning: Mill Strand

1986, I think it was, Alan Smith came to me and said was I interested in something called an integrated school. I said, 'Yes,' and my wife said, 'Yes,' and Alan and his wife, me and my wife and a guy called Bill O'Neill who was a colleague of mine and his wife, four or five couples got together and said, 'Can we start a school here?' and that's where it started. After a year of work, in 1987 Mill Strand opened.

Why did I do it? Because my colleague Bill O'Neill had a little girl of the same age as my son. And they played together at nursery school and then when they got to the age of five my son went off to one school and his daughter went off to another, and I thought, 'That's ridiculous.' And so when Alan came to me and said would we get involved, we just said, of course we would. And then when the school started my son and Bill's daughter went to the same school. I taught in London before I came to Northern Ireland. I taught children who were black and yellow and red and brown and white and they came from England, from the West Indies, from Asia, India, Pakistan; some of them were Catholics, some were Muslim, some were Protestant. It didn't matter; they were all just kids!

In London I taught about seven, eight years; my wife taught there as well. The idea of dividing children up simply never crossed our minds. The 11+ had been abolished. The

kids we taught from hugely different backgrounds. All went on to the same comprehensive schools and the idea of dividing children up; Protestants here, Catholics here, grammar schools here, secondary schools there, boys here, girls there, never crossed our minds. When we came here, it was a terrible shock.

At that time, there was no Northern Ireland Council for Integrated Education (NICIE). We had no money, no support, no building, no teachers. We got people with useful skills. We had a guy who worked for the local authority, for the council; we had an accountant, a solicitor, various other people had useful skills. They were all either parents or potential parents. It was a very middle class group with university teachers and so on.

A couple of years later my wife got a job as Principal at Windmill in Dungannon, so we moved down to Cookstown and Lesley worked as the first Principal of the school for seven, eight years. Our kids went there and I was on the Board of Governors. Unfortunately, there was no secondary integrated school in Dungannon at that time, so our kids didn't go to a secondary integrated school, which was a pity. But my younger boy, who's now 30-something, his two best friends are still two boys, one of whom is from a Catholic background, and the other is a Baha'i. Those two are his best friends still. He's got other friends now, of course, and he lives in England.

I would hope that even if they hadn't been to an integrated school they'd still have grown up as tolerant, thoughtful, respectful, well-behaved, people. The fact

Phoenix IPS.

that they went to an integrated school supported that and helped that. But I would've hoped that that would be the case anyway. But it was important for them, even though, unfortunately, they didn't go to the secondary school because there wasn't one. It's a good example of the way Integrated Education isn't just about reading and writing, as important as those are, but it's also about the kind of relationships that you are able to make as you grow up. Obviously, if you grew up in a Protestant community, Protestant school, Protestant housing estate, Protestant work, Protestant games, everything, you don't get that breadth that you can in an integrated school.

There was a thing called the Belfast Trust for Integrated Education (BELTIE) at the time, and a guy called Joe came once every now and again. He said, 'This is going to work,' because he had been involved with starting Hazelwood. He kept coming and saying, 'This is going to work, you're doing the right thing.' That was hugely reassuring because we didn't know what we were doing. How do you start a school?

By the time Windmill started, which was three, four years later, I'm not sure NICIE existed but I think they had a bit more support. Lesley and I weren't involved in setting the school up. By the time I got there, the school was kind of going. It was all a bit ramshackle at the time. Windmill started in a building which had been a car showroom.

Phoenix

By the time we got to Phoenix, which was 2002, it was relatively easy because we had a lot of support from NICIE who knew what they were doing. Roisin was the Development Officer and Iain came and the guy who organised buildings, Lawrence. We still had a lot of work to do but there was that support which was there and was very powerful.

Mill Strand was a very middle class group: solicitors, accountants, academics. In Phoenix it was completely different. It was all women except me and they were ordinary working women, women who worked in Asda, a woman who worked in a factory, a couple of women with children who had never really worked. They weren't middle class people at all; they were ordinary working people and they had never done anything like this before in their lives. The local radio station in mid-Ulster said would somebody go and talk about what we were doing, and they all looked at me because I was the only one who had ever done anything like that before. I said, 'No! You do it!' And they were shaking with worry about this. Eventually one of them went to do it and she was fine! It was ever so good the amount of learning went on in that group about how to do something like this which they'd never done before. How do you interview for a teacher? They'd never done an interview in their lives! The Mill Strand group were used to that sort of way of working; they knew how to do radio; they did a television programme about Mill Strand.

Windmill IPS early days.

So the two kinds of groups of parents were very different kinds of people. Without that support that we got at Phoenix, that group couldn't have done it. They needed all that support they were getting from NICIE and from other places, whereas the Mill Strand group had that sense of, 'We don't know what we're doing but we're doing it anyway.'

A million things to do

In Mill Strand we were terrified because there was a million things we had to do and we didn't know how to do any of them. The guy who worked for the local council was in the planning department in Coleraine and so he knew a bit about land and buildings. He and Alan Smith looked around for a building and couldn't find one in Coleraine. The only one we could find which was possible was this site where it is now in Portrush. We had a very large loan from Nuffield, I think. The Integrated Education Fund (IEF) didn't exist at that time.

The first stage really was, 'How do you publicise this thing; how do you get people interested?' We had some meetings, some of which went very well; one or two were complete disasters. We wanted to elect a kind of steering group. We elected this group and they were all Protestant. And we thought, 'Oh God! You can't do that!' So we had to co-opt people. It's hard to remember now but at that time, nobody in the community knew what Integrated Education

was. They'd never heard of it. It was not something that had ever happened. Now if you talk to people in a community, even if there isn't a school, they have some idea of what you are talking about. So we had to do a lot of just telling people what we were doing and they were astonished. And some hostile. A local Principal wrote to the local newspaper saying his school was entirely integrated; anybody could go to his school. 'And who are these people in the university who know nothing about anything? Who are they to set up a new school? We're going to fight against this.' A lot of the time we were spending holding meetings, talking on local radio, going to the local paper, trying to explain what this thing was. There was quite a lot of scepticism even by people who understood what we were trying to do. Then later on once we'd got the building and the finances which were the crucial things, I suppose, there was all the stuff about how do you make a building which had been a factory into a school? And what about fire regulations, what about toilets, what about square metres, what about a dining hall, how do you manage school dinners, what about transport, a million little things, and normally a local authority would do that. Not ordinary people like us! We sort of staggered our way through and then in the last month or two it was total panic. My colleague from the university and I were off for the summer from the university; Lesley was off as well. A couple of others took extra leave from their work, and we all went around painting

and decorating and fixing and managing and then appointing teachers, appointing caretakers. It was just endless.

We held interviews and asked two young people who said they would want to be teachers for us and then they both withdrew because they were scared. How could they possibly get back into a real school if they came to us in this strange place? Again that's changed because people know what integrated schools are like and it's not a big deal but at that time for those young people to come to us, that was scary. Even though unemployment in teachers was very high and they needed work, their families, their friends said, 'Don't go there.' So we appointed a guy as Principal who was an experienced Principal from Dungiven or somewhere around there.

We started the school with him and two teachers plus a nursery teacher. We weren't going to get any funding for that but we wanted to start a nursery because that feeds the school. We were worried that the school wouldn't have enough kids. So we started a nursery and financially it was very difficult, but it was a good decision even though it was tough at the time because we didn't know where the money was coming from. At that time you had to prove that you were viable for, I think, three years and then they eventually took over. In the first two or three years it was quite scary because we didn't know whether it was going to work. We thought it would, but we weren't sure because we'd never done it before! And so when it was actually taken over by the

Department we all heaved a sigh of relief because financially we were okay once that had happened.

Nuffield funded the school for a couple of years. I'm not sure whether there was money coming from other trusts and bodies. I didn't deal with that. We had a guy in the group who was an accountant and he did a lot with Alan and Jim. And Bill and I did a lot of work on the curriculum of the school because that's what our skills were. There was a solicitor who was helpful because she was able to look into the legal stuff about how you set up what a school needs. We never did find anybody who could do public relations and so our public relations and our media relations weren't that great.

Fundraising and support

Phoenix was the best fundraising because we had a guy on the Board of Governors who ran a second hand car business. And so he put a prize of a Volkswagen car, new car, and that was the prize of the raffle. The tickets were rather expensive but the car cost nearly £5,000-6,000. We made about £10,000, so we had a profit of about £5,000. It was a terribly good idea, I thought. This brand new Volkswagen car was sitting there in the school playground so all the parents saw it as they came by.

I found Phoenix much easier because I knew it was going to work because I'd done it before. And because NICIE and Roisin and Ian and Lawrence were there supporting. The others in the group didn't know it was going to work; they were scared. They weren't a middle class group; they were very ordinary working women. They simply had never done anything like that. So they were worried. I wasn't worried because I knew it was going to be fine. It's hard to get children for the first year because you haven't got a teacher, you haven't got anything except, 'We're gonna start a school!' Even in Phoenix we had nothing to show them because Lawrence took forever to find a site for us .We eventually scraped together 12 or 14 children; most of them were the children of the group. Once we started we appointed Stephen McKernan, who was very good. Once you go into the next year the parents can see that it exists. You can say, 'There's the building, this guy is the Principal of the school.' It's relatively easy. The first year is hard, because you haven't got anything to show people.

We said to Lawrence we would like something towards the middle of the town. And he said, 'You'll have to take what you can get!' In fact, he did find a site in the centre of the town, a very small site and then two or three years later, it was too small and so we moved out where we are now which is on the edge of the town. The original site was in the yard of a man who's a car repairer and it wasn't a very suitable place, but it was fine for us to start because we only had 10 or 12 children. And then the new school started about three years after, about 2005-6. Then last year and the year before we had a lot of extensions and new nursery.

I'm on the Board of Governors. We're now talking to the Department about replacing all that temporary stuff, even though it's new, with a permanent proper building. And that will probably be on the same site on a field just behind because the land belongs to what was the Southern Education and Library Board; it's not privately owned land. So eventually we'll have a proper built school there. So we're now up to about 200 children. We hope to get a proper building and then we'll think about making it a two class school.

The Principal is a crucial person. At Phoenix Stephen McKernan knew exactly what he was doing; he knew what Integrated Education was. He believed in it. He thought it was terribly important. He came to us committed to this thing, which was a huge relief. He liked the idea of starting to create everything from new and not having to inherit; he liked the idea of appointing the teachers he liked and he wanted to work with. He was a young ambitious man. He was there six years. Parents thought he was wonderful, the teachers thought he was wonderful and it was just what we needed to get the school up and running and lively and vibrant. And then he left, he went to work in England. The year after he left, the Inspectorate came around and they said some of the teaching wasn't that great. But the new Principal and the staff worked very hard to improve that. And when the inspectors came back, it was fine.

Lessons

We made mistakes in all three schools; that's part of the process of doing something that's difficult and complicated. Each of the schools in different ways has had problems over the years. So have other integrated schools; some of them have had terrible difficulties over the years. But I can't think of anything fundamental that we could or should have done differently.

At a time of school closures, it's very difficult to think about starting new schools. The Mill Strand group started on its own; we didn't have any funding. The Cookstown group started because NICIE came and said, 'We want to start a school here.' There was a public meeting organised by NICIE and we all came to that. That was different because Mill Strand was not started by anybody except ourselves. Now whether there are no parents who want to start schools or whether NICIE can't start schools, I don't know. I don't suppose NICIE has the resources to go out and start a school somewhere.

There are three or four schools transforming at the moment with the support of NICIE. And the challenges remain the same, I guess, as they always were, which is to provide a really good quality education. Transformation has its own problems. A school that transforms has a tradition and a history and a staff who are used to doing things in a particular way and suddenly they're being asked to be an integrated school and

Phoenix IPS at
Stormont, 20016.

they don't know what it is. They don't know what it means, so I think there's a lot of work to be done in transformed schools to try and show those teachers and parents what integration actually means. I think a lot of the transformed schools are not really integrated schools at all. A few years ago I did some work when Michael Wardlow was at NICIE. I went around all the primary schools looking at the ways in which the schools were working. I produced a report; the report said, 'The transformed schools don't know what they are doing.' But the schools that are started as integrated schools, some are doing it well, some are doing it badly, but at least all of them know what integration means. Whether that's still true I don't know; that was 10 years ago. But some of the transformed schools we went to see, they were controlled schools. They weren't integrated schools.

I've worked in education all my life. I was a teacher; I worked in education in the university and I've always believed that one of the crucial things that schools do as well as the curriculum stuff - the reading, writing and maths, and all the rest of it which is terribly important - we are creating a next generation of citizens, people who are going to take this country or any country forward. And so all that social stuff is very important and in Northern Ireland it's particularly important because we have this terrible history of shooting each other and throwing bombs at each other and we have to spend a lot of time getting those communities to work together through schools, through housing, through work, through sport, through all sorts of aspects of social life. So, if I've made a very tiny little contribution in one area of that I have to be quite pleased.

Roisin Marshall trained and worked as a teacher and spent time as a Development Officer and Senior Development Officer with the Northern Ireland Council for Integrated Education (NICIE) before returning to NICIE in 2016, where she is currently CEO.

Walking distance

I've had a very interesting life journey to date. I didn't realise until probably I did my second round of A-levels, that I wanted to become a teacher. I started teaching in the Catholic maintained sector in 1991 in primary school and then in post-primary. In the primary school I was the Education for Mutual Understanding (EMU) officer. Our school was St Mary's on the Hill, and there was a little controlled school called Ashgrove Primary School and I was really interested in getting my kids with their kids, I was just really curious. There was walking distance between the two. I and a teacher called Lorna in Ashgrove did the planning.

I don't think they spent enough time together in the EMU project, we were a bit too curriculum focused. It was all about the learning, and actually very little down time for the kids to just play together, be together, eat together. That was maybe a downside of the whole EMU thing. These kids actually didn't live that far from each other, I have no doubt they met each other in the street on a Saturday, with their parents or whatever. I certainly hope that they would remember at least that it was a nice experience, you know? But that was the start of the EMU in the early 90s, it got a lot better. We've developed on from that in terms of bringing kids together a little more thoughtfully. But I learnt a lot from that early experience.

Maybe they're not being rude

But to go right back to where my interest in children being educated together started, or when I noticed a difference in terms of Protestants and Catholics, I guess it was from a very young age. I have a sister with autism and Down syndrome and from a very young age, I knew that I was a little bit different because my sister was a little bit different. She was eight or nine or ten and still used a buggy because of her disability. I noticed, when you were out, that people used to stare, and my friend (she had a brother with autism) and I used to get very offended. She used to get very angry and I remember learning that maybe they're not being rude, they're just interested and they're wondering, 'Gosh, I wonder what that child's challenges are,' and so on.

I joined the Junior Gateway Club. It was called the Peter Pan Club at the time, you know, these are kids who never grow up. Very un-PC today but that was what it was known as. Somebody came to my mum and said they would take Briedge, who was six at this stage, on a Saturday and give you a wee bit of a break. So Saturday morning rolled up and a bus arrived to take Briedge and my mum shoved me onto the bus and said, 'You may go with her' I don't know who those people are, so you may go as well.' So off I went, and I remained in that club for the next 15-20 years. That's where I met my friends who were Protestant for the first time and we

Forge IPS at
Stormont, 2017

genuinely were friends because we all had siblings who had a disability. These people became my best friends, we did so much together and we had so much of a connection. We went on holidays together with the club, we all got our first jobs in Ruby House in Newcastle which was a holiday home for children and adults with special needs. I remember, you know, standing in Kilkeel at Orange marches with a group from Ruby House and thinking to myself, 'I hope to goodness nobody from Castlewellan sees me,' you know? I was with the adults on the bus who all wanted to go to see the Orange parade and I distinctly remember thinking that people are actually really enjoying themselves here, this is actually fun! Whereas, what I'd been told was it was evil and, you know, they are out to get us and all of this stuff. We spent our entire summers, I mean literally, I spent every summer from I was 13 until I got married at 26, working in that area. That's where I met some of my best friends who had special needs and so I count myself being extremely lucky.

I just liked her

When I was 10, I went to America and stayed with a Lutheran family. And there's a funny story: my mum rang the lady who was going to be hosting me and the only thing mum was concerned about was that I would go to Mass on a Sunday. Now they weren't Catholic, but they had a relative who was

Catholic. Every Sunday Judy Bokenhower would come and pick me up. We went to Mass and in American churches they always had tea and buns afterwards, it was a lovely experience. It was only when I got to America that I thought that was rather odd for my mum to really insist on that. My religion was very important to my family and therefore to me, I guess.

As well as that I went to Assumption Grammar School in Ballynahinch and I had great experiences as part of a community relations organisation. Basically, it was organised by the Royal Ulster Constabulary: yeah, I know, sounds a bit strange! We used to go up the mountain every Saturday, you know, for a couple of years and this one camp we went we ended up in the north coast in these massive big army camp tents. I was with girls from Saintfield High School. I would never have met those girls in my entire puff without that experience. One of the girls, Hazel Campbell, I became really friendly with and we wrote to each other and stayed friends for the next 10, 15 years. I just liked her. I would never have had that experience had it not been for our school taking a bit of a risk and being involved in in the community relations camps.

I loved every minute of teaching in St Colm's High School in Twinbrook. But part of the challenge for us as teachers was that the young people rarely stepped out of their own community. For example, I would say, 'You know, we are going to go to the Lyric theatre and see a show,' and the kids would say, 'Where's the Lyric theatre? Where's Stranmillis?!'

They had no concept. Buses don't go across the city like that. You have to go down into the centre of town and then you have to go out. They went down into the centre of town but they never went out. I was a Drama and English teacher and we would have debates and discussions and things like that, but I always felt there was a voice missing. There was never an alternative perspective, if you ever got near anything that was a bit controversial.

What's that, I wonder?

When I was teaching in St Colm's, one of my colleagues got a job in Malone Integrated College. So I was, 'Oh, an integrated college, what's that I wonder?' Then when I had my son and he was about one, we moved house. I remember my husband and me driving through Dunmurry. We couldn't afford to live in Finaghy so we moved further out. I remember we were driving down The Cutts in Derriaghy and seeing this sign for Oakwood Integrated Primary School and me saying to my husband, 'Aww, I want to live near that school, there's a school here that Adam could go to.' The school had just opened up and by the time that he was four and I was filling out the little form for which school he would go to, I just put down Oakwood Integrated Primary School. I didn't put any other choice I was so confident, that that's where he was going, and guess what? He didn't get a place.

I had not read the criteria. I'll never forget that, ever since then I say to people, 'Read the criteria!' So the criteria was probably eldest child, I don't know what, but even in those early days, it was so over-subscribed. Another reason was we were Catholic and it was over-subscribed with Catholics. I was totally unaware of any of that, so the thing was we got this letter and my husband said to me, 'Awk, don't worry, you know, it'll be fine,' and I went, 'Wake up and smell the coffee, James! If he doesn't get in he will never be able to go to an integrated school!' We had American visitors sitting in our living room at the time, having tea and sandwiches. And I was in floods of tears. I'm actually emotional now thinking about it. I knew that I may not be able to replicate the things, the great things that I had in my life with him so I really wanted him to be with Protestants and people with different outlooks and it was as simple as that. Because I knew our society was in such a mess.

So that was May and I remember ringing Olwen Frost who was the Principal at the time and saying, 'Olwen I'm devastated.' She was so nice so that made me worse. But by the end of the summer time, guess what? Adam was second on the reserve list and other people had pulled out. So he got in. I was so pleased, it was like somebody had given me a million pounds because I knew if I got him into that school that his experience would be different forever. Now Adam is 21 and just finished final year at university. In Oakwood

Roisin Marshall and
pupils at Stormont, 2016.

Integrated Primary School I joined the Governors. It was always the crèche that picked Adam up so I wanted just to get a little bit closer and so I thought by being a parent governor I'd be able to achieve that and it was brilliant! The governors I worked with and the Principal, Olwen Frost, was just amazing. I learnt so much: I learnt about governance, recruitment, HR issues. I didn't know any of that stuff and when I look back, part of why I'm here is all of those experiences that I was able to talk about in an interview situation.

Olwen tells the story of arriving at the 'munchies' factory which became Oakwood Integrated Primary School and her and her husband peering through the gate and him saying to her, and he was a Principal of a school at the time, 'Olwen, there is no way on earth that that is ever going to be a school,' and she said, 'Robert? It will be, we have to believe it will be,' and by the 1st September the school was open and she was the Principal. And you know, I don't know how they paid her wages, I'm sure she didn't get paid what she was supposed to be paid. All of this was about people having a dream. This notion that if we actually have Protestant and Catholic children and other beliefs, cultures and communities together that actually that will change how people are in the future.

It took me a year and a half to breathe normally!

So, I'm still teaching St Colm's and I love it, passionately love the kids. Most of what I know about teaching I learnt in that school. It had a great leader and we learnt so much because the school was improving every year. We went from something like 9% A* to C pass at GCSE to 48% by the time I left after 10 years. I'm not saying that was down to me, it was a collective effort by the teachers.

I said to myself, 'Do I really want to be in the same place for the next 30 years?' I'd never been out of the classroom. I went to school, to teacher training college. So I started looking to find something different. I applied twice to Malone College but I didn't get the job, I was completely devastated. Then one day I saw this advertisement for NICIE. I didn't know much about Integrated Education, but I knew that I was curious. I knew I wanted my children to have an integrated experience and I wanted to find out more so I applied for the job. Don't even think I got an interview! Anyway, two years later the job came up again and I thought, 'Right, I'm going to go again,' and I didn't tell anybody and I got the job! I guess my child was at an integrated school, I was the governor of an integrated school so going into that interview that second time, I was a whole lot more aware of what Integrated Education was. That was in 2002. I was sad to leave the school but I was excited. I took a £10,000 cut in salary. At that stage work was a passion to me and a thing I did. Yes, it paid the bills but I was more interested in the journey that I was on. I had so much to learn, I had no idea, it took me about a year to a year and a half just to breathe normally again! I had never been anywhere but school, that's just the way life was.

It's only now I'm looking back and I'm thinking, 'Why did you go there, why did you leave a professional teaching job with two management points to go to a job that wasn't even a permanent job?' But you know, I think within one year I was made permanent and that was amazing. But it was scary, I mean I was out working with groups of parents, I'd never done group work in my life. I'd never set up a new school, I was learning with them on the job. What was great about it was there were three Development Officers: myself, Cliodhna Scott-Wills, who is still here, and Elaine McKeown. The three of us worked really closely, we were in the one room, we talked constantly. We were doing the same thing but with different groups so we were able to learn from each other and we learnt from Lorna and Frances who were our Senior Development Officers at the time and from Michael Wardlow who was the Chief Executive Officer at the time.

I joined 2002 and in 2004 we opened six schools. Six in one year! The two I was working on were Phoenix Integrated Primary and Armagh Integrated College so they were my projects. And then I went on to work on Moira Integrated Primary School which later became Rowandale. Also working with the Association of Principals of Integrated Schools (APTIS), the teachers' committee and the anti-bias curriculum.

Life changing

The training that I received at that stage in NICIE was intensive. It was about handling life's conflicts and diversity and for the first time actually talking. I used to sort of pretend that I wasn't really Catholic and that I wasn't really Irish because I felt that that ingratiated me to other people. That's the way I had to do it because I didn't know what else to do. When I joined NICIE for the five years I was there that first time, I became more connected with my own identity than I'd ever been.

My transition from school into NICIE was life changing, I didn't realise it at the time. I would say for the first time I started to talk about me, you know? I'm a woman, I'm Catholic, I'm Irish and being really proud of who I was. Because that's what this is all about. It's not about becoming something different, it's not about losing bits of your identity, it's about being me and nobody looking at me sideways and going, 'Hmm,' you know? But liking me, accepting me for who I was, not somebody I was trying to be. That freed me of so many issues. A lot of people say, 'Oh, you're just trying to make everybody the same by putting them all in together,' and I go, 'No!' I really fight against that. This is about being who you are, who you want to be and being accepted for who you are and not because of the labels that other people put on you. And I will be forever in debt to NICIE for giving me that opportunity.

Not 'if'… 'when'!

I never forget I was working with the Cookstown group, they were mostly parents but there were other people like Stuart Marriot, whose children had been through school so he was a grandparent, but he was interested in starting the Cookstown group. Stuart and I go right back to 2002. He gave me so much energy and drive. I remember Anne, who owned a crèche in Cookstown. She was a fabulous woman. These were a group of people who I went down to, say, every fortnight, and we met in a women's centre. It was a pretty sparse looking room that we met in, but they just had this dream. What they needed me to do was to tell them that it was possible. Not only that it was possible, but that it was easy!

We know it was far from easy but you get this, I'm a new Development Officer, with very little experience of working with parents' groups to open a new school. Who does that, even? I feel privileged that I even had the opportunity to do that. The outcome was a school that is still there.

I remember one night something had happened and it had a very negative impact on the group and everyone was exhausted and they were just, 'What's the point?' I remember Anne said to me, 'Roisin; see if we ever get this school off the ground,' and I went, 'No, Anne, not if, when!' And she goes, 'Okay!' and I says, 'See from now on? We're not gonna talk about if, we're gonna talk about when.' Anne always recalls that story and Stuart remembers that moment too, when it was like, 'We have to stop thinking that this isn't going to happen, we have to start believing that it is.' Once we started believing that it was actually going to happen, nothing was going to stand in our way. We'll get knocked back but we'll get up and we'll keep going. It was the most powerful experience and we're not talking about a lot of people here, we're talking about five or six.

Working with the parents' groups was one thing and that was really exciting but once it actually became a school and the children came. I remember seeing children walking about this mobile or this building for the first time, and thinking, 'Ahh! Now it's real! Okay, are we sure about this?!' When I look back, I describe it as magical because I don't know how that all happened to be perfectly honest. I've got GANT charts and I've got lists of things we did and I've got folders that tell me we had this meeting and then this happened and then we got the admissions criteria. I mean, expecting parents to sign up their children for a school that doesn't exist.

All ability

Primary schools are all ability, as we know. It always strikes me as being odd because nobody makes an issue of it. It's when it comes to post-primary school we have this weird notion that we need to keep all our children who are academic together and we need to separate them out from children who aren't so academic. It's always struck me as being bizarre beyond comprehension. My own son didn't do the transfer exam, we were very lucky because 22 out of 28 of his class just went straight to Malone Integrated College. We wanted them to

have a full integrated education the whole way through so that was perfect. Unfortunately, for whatever reason, selection does exist here, it seems like something that parents want.

I was lucky to have the opportunity to train with an organisation called Playback in Scotland, inspired by a woman who had a son who had a lot of different disabilities. She spent the rest of her life, using whatever sort of ways she could, to try to have our education more inclusive of children with physical and special needs. I learnt an awful lot from her. We brought it over here to the integrated schools and ran a series of training sessions. There was a teacher at Oakwood Primary, and we videoed her. It went something like this: she said, 'We had different toys, like maybe the doll somebody had pulled the arm off, or it had one eye missing or something. I would've thrown that out because it was kind of damaged. I'm gonna keep those from now on and have conversations with the children about the doll.' And I thought, 'Oh my goodness, that's it exactly, you know?' People are not disposable. It was a really powerful message. That school has always been, and still to this day, is over-subscribed, because people, parents, know and understand that regardless of my child's ability, regardless of my child's background or religion or no religion or different philosophy, regardless of the colour of my child, regardless of the race, I'm guaranteed that they're going to be fully included within the life of the school. That's mega. I don't know how you bottle that and sell it but I know that the integrated schools have been doing that for many years and because they've had to pay attention to the difference of religion they've become really good at whatever the difference is.

The integrated factor

I used to joke with my son about waiting for the integrated factor to kick in. I didn't really know what I meant by that, but I see it in my son all the time. He's extremely tolerant, he's got a very broad view of the world. Where we live, basically, if you walk in one direction you're in a very Protestant area, if you walk in another direction you're in a very Catholic area. We

Tea lady at NICIE AGM, 2006.

were always nervous about them walking about. One thing that was interesting was the kids tended to come us, maybe it's because we live in a bit of a mixed area?

My daughter Emily has very fond memories of integrated primary school. She notices that the Catholic grammar school she's at now is very Catholic. She knows, apart from maybe one Hindu in her year, that most people are from a similar perceived background. I don't think her friends are as aware that there isn't the diversity in the school that is in the rest of the world. It's a very single identity school with a Catholic ethos and not that there's anything wrong with that at all but I think Emily's experience had made her aware of the fact that that is the case.

As a mum maybe I've taken opportunities when they've presented themselves, by becoming involved in things. I never underestimate the impact of children and young people being involved in anything that's cross-community. My wee nieces go to a dance school. Like, you realise there's feis dancing and there's festival dancing, basically one community or another historically attended those. But just by default they happened to go to one that was festival dancing and they've made great friends outside of school so I would never underestimate encouraging our kids to get involved in cross-community projects, or through Shared Education, or whatever. We need to give children opportunities to be together.

I've never met anybody who doesn't think Integrated Education is a good idea, you're just not quite sure how we get from here to there. I think it's both interesting and sad, that Integrated Education thrived when we were killing each other on the streets. Because we're not killing each other on the streets, we're having polite encounters and not even, if we look at the state of our political situation. I worry about the apathy that there is with people so it's kind of like, 'We're grand, we don't need to do anything really, we're fine.'

I've just noticed recently, I don't know if it's because it's the 20th anniversary of the 1998 agreement, but I've noticed recently there's a lot of people telling their stories about things that happened, on TV. I worry about particularly in our young don't know what the history is. Some people say that's a good thing but I think they've got to be aware at least of where we've come from in our relatively recent past. The majority of young people will have experienced one community or the other education. Not all of them, and I accept there are schools that are mixed and they are doing a great job but you know we aren't at the stage where it is normal practice for a school to deliberately and intentionally invite people from the minority community into their school. It's just not something that is usual. I think it needs to be usual.

The future

I think we've got to really pay attention to the integrated schools who are there and ensure that they are best possible integrated schools that they can be and whatever we can do to help that is really important. They are the people that have taken the biggest risks. They have put their heads above the parapet within their own communities, encouraged people to go on this journey and it is an ongoing journey. Every time you have a new member of staff, every time you have a new year-group of pupils, every time you have a new leader, every time you have new governors. You are constantly refining, reviewing how you 'do' Integrated Education and it's not an easy journey. This is far more difficult than pretending or imagining that everybody in front of you is from an homogenous group. That's much easier because you can decide what events, sports, literature you're going to study, what holidays, what events to celebrate and there will be very few dissenting voices and everybody will go along with it, in general. Whereas in an integrated school you are constantly thinking, 'Well, how's that gonna land with one community or another if I'm going to do that then I need to be seen to be doing it on an equal basis.' And so it is the harder journey but it is definitely the most rewarding journey, there is no doubt in my mind about that.

We have to support the schools that already exist. We may be doing that for the next five, 10, 15, 30 years. And so be it because we have got to ensure that the little fires that were lit all over Northern Ireland with those 65 schools are kept burning and lighting the way for others. We have fantastic schools in Northern Ireland: a range of different management types, different leaders, all of that. There are a lot of those schools that I know with encouragement from the right places, from ourselves, from the Department of Education, from the Education Authority, from the Council for Catholic Maintained Schools, from the Controlled Schools Support Council, from the grammar school body, and with the right support, could become schools for the whole community. And they aren't at the minute. They've got to do something proactive and it can't be small things, it's got to be big. Both traditions and other traditions are equally celebrated within this school, they've got to have those big things.

We've got to think about what we are trying to achieve in the long term

Regardless of whether they're at a grammar school, a Catholic maintained school, a controlled school, every child in Northern Ireland should have the opportunity to meet a range of people from a range of different backgrounds. Anything other than that, we are doing a disservice to our children. If the first time they're meeting and having meaningful relationships with people from the other community is at 18 or beyond then we've really got to think about what we're trying to achieve here in the long term. That hasn't anything to do with politics; that is just giving people opportunity to get to know each other from a young age. They will have their own religion, their own identity. That is something private and personal to each individual and each individual's family. But it's got to be acknowledged in the school. I often say to people if a child arrived at your door, as a teacher, and they had cerebral palsy, you wouldn't say, 'Now I'm just going to ignore the fact that you've cerebral palsy, for the next year and I'm just gonna teach you as if you didn't have that condition.' You wouldn't do that with a child with a special need so you wouldn't ignore someone's religion if it meant a lot to them. You wouldn't ignore something you know about their cultural background. You wouldn't ignore the fact that somebody has come from a different country. Why would you ignore the fact that somebody is from a different religion? It just doesn't make any sense.

Integrated Education for me is an opportunity. It is a planned opportunity to get to know, understand and become friends with, if that's something you desire, with people that you would not meet through your educational experience in other sectors. Sometimes in a mixed school you will have that opportunity to meet but there may be no acknowledgement of that person's cultural identity and tradition within that school. And that doesn't give people an equal opportunity.

Roisin Marshall at Stormont, 2016.

The experience that my children had was different than mine, in that they had an opportunity from a very young age to meet and be taught by and have classroom assistants who were from different backgrounds. All of that has made them the people they are today and I hope that all of the children who are experiencing Integrated Education are having the best possible opportunity in that way. As CEO of NICIE I feel that it's really important that we are there and the Integrated Education Fund, as an opportunity to give those schools support. They'll get curriculum support, they'll get government support, they'll get various things from other places but the integrated ethos constantly needs to be worked on. You need to be alive to it within your school. Moving forward, NICIE as an organisation have got to be listening to how they can promote Integrated Education to others who may or have not been able to hear the message. We need to encourage schools to be able to think about and find a way for themselves to ensure that the children in their school are having an integrated experience. If we continue with what we have at the minute, with parents making choices because we're not giving them other choices, we will continue to have people who, through no fault of their own, don't understand that a different perspective is as equally viable and valuable as your own.

Jason Milligan was the Principal of Killyleagh Primary School. In this role, he had oversight of its transformation to become Killyleagh Integrated Primary School in 2016.

The impetus to transform

I had heard of Integrated Education but hadn't really considered it as an option. The idea for transforming Killyleagh Primary School came from an Integrated Education Fund (IEF) leaflet, the one that comes out every year about transformation. I brought it to the governors and the governors then wanted to find out more. From a strategic point of view, when you are transforming, you have extra support for advertising and marketing from the IEF.

I contacted the Northern Ireland Council for Integrated Education (NICIE) and Frances came out to talk to us. The governors were very interested and knew that the next stage would be to inform the parents. For this second stage they invited Frances to come back and speak to the parents. I had been Principal for a year, and the school had a large number of pupils from mixed relationships, so religion wasn't really a major issue for those parents. Some of them didn't even know what religion they were. Plus, we were in a situation where the school needed to make big improvements and as part of that I wanted to rebrand. By transforming, we would have a fresh start with a new uniform and a new ethos and a new culture. When I shared that vision with the governors they were keen for it to happen.

Addressing the parents

Our parents' meeting was also attended by the governors. Some parents seemed to be opposed to transformation, but the majority were supportive, so the governors decided to go to the next stage, which was the parent ballot. Between that meeting and the parent ballot, there was a further parent meeting. Not many parents had turned up to the first meeting, and some had gone to a local councillor who came along to the second meeting. The councillor had some questions and we were able to address the concerns he raised.

One issue was that Killyleagh PS was the Protestant school in the town and if it transformed there would be no Protestant school. By the end of the meeting the councillor was on board and expressed his support for the school's transformation. Since then he has been very supportive. He was a key figure because he is a DUP councillor and very vocal in the local community.

Getting whipped up by social media

We then went to parent ballot which was a huge success with 84% of parents who voted, voting in favour of transformation. That was at Christmas 2014. The most challenging thing for me in getting people involved was the culture of rumours and misinformation. Although no one was coming into the school

to ask for clarification, there were Chinese whispers going round the town through social media to the point where some parents were extremely whipped up.

Our next meeting started off quite intense, but by the end of the evening, the parents who had been whipped up had actually changed their opinion of transformation and were in support of it. The people who were doing their best to oppose the idea actually ended up alienating themselves from the parents they had approached, so their efforts backfired. I am only talking about three or four families. Having said that, throughout the whole process, we didn't lose a single family. Nobody left the school because it was transforming.

Not just accepting, but recognising and celebrating difference

I think it was fear of losing the Protestant school. I explained that Killyleagh PS wasn't a Protestant school. I could actually speak about this issue because I had been the Principal of one of the last Protestant Church primary school in Northern Ireland, which had closed in 2007. I explained that Killyleagh PS was a controlled school, and that it would become a controlled integrated school, which was basically the same thing, but instead of just accepting children from all different religions, we would now be recognising and celebrating the differences. There would be a cultural change in ethos. When

it came to running the school, nobody's identity was going to be lost. I know that there are parents watching carefully to make sure this is the case.

Impact on the community

The next practical step was selling the idea to the local community, which was a big thing. We had our media launch, where we had quite a lot of things going out in the local newspapers. We had community days where we opened the whole school up for the whole community, invited people in and had activities. Those events were very successful. There were also quite a few wee individual stories, like when one of the pupils came along to say that now that we were an integrated school that she was going to be a Catholic and do the sacraments, because before she wasn't sure what she was.

It is important to keep professional, cordial relationships with other schools in the area. I spoke to St Mary's and I said from the beginning that my target hasn't been Catholic children in the town; my target is children who leave the town to go to other schools including other integrated schools.

At the start of this year, the pupils were designing wee name tags for their coat hangers and some of them made Union Jacks because that was what they identified with. One actually made a Union Jack in the colours of green white and orange. That started a conversation, and those are the type of opportunities you look out for arising naturally and then debate the ideas. I think that we are working towards creating an environment where ideas can come out without anybody feeling they are being offensive or being offended.

Governor response to transformation

Every governor bar one was 100% for transformation. The one governor was against change rather than anything else and they stepped down. Having said that, when we had our official opening, they came along to support it. When we transformed, the structure of the Board of Governors changed. What was really good was that members from the steering group came on as governors because of their commitment to the school for the previous year and a half. When we had our first sacrament service down in the chapel last year, governors were there to show their support for what the school was trying to do.

Staff response to transformation

We have been lucky with our teachers in that there is natural integration. We have teachers here who have done the anti-bias training with NICIE. We went on a residential last February for a team building exercise, looking at integration, developing an ethos and so on. I did the anti-bias training myself and found it very interesting, examining your own prejudices. Every school is different and I understand that, but if you come away from training with a skeleton that is a starting point, then you can add your own ideas to bring back to your school. Discussions on ethos and culture and what we're trying to develop are fine, but you also need something practical that you can implement. You need to make sure you have references to integration in your policies and develop the ideas.

Impact of transforming a school

From a management point of view, three years into the process, I am looking at the impact in the classroom. We've got our ethos, everybody's committed to the integrated ethos and culture. I want to see how that now filters down into our policies and into the classrooms and I want to see that connection next. This doesn't just include Religious Education, it includes everything we do in the classroom. How do we enhance the integrated ethos? That's a big thing, and it's not something that is going to happen overnight. It's going to be happening at different levels and in different classes.

Now that we are integrated, we need to challenge our recruitment process for teachers. We have brought in two teachers. I wanted a Catholic teacher, but ended up, I think, employing the only Catholic teacher in Northern Ireland who doesn't have the Catholic Certificate of Education! Our special needs teacher, who is Protestant, has the Catholic Certificate, and so she delivers preparation for the sacraments.

The whole school context

We have to be realistic: Killyleagh is a small school of just 105 pupils. What we can do is limited and so we need to concentrate on the most pressing issues. We are committed to integration, but also committed to dealing with deprivation, getting parents on board with the values of education and developing aspirations. We have brought in Home Start to work with families and as many of our parents had their children as teenagers themselves, addressing social need is urgent. Integration can be worked on step by step. There are child protection and safeguarding issues, practical issues for parents in getting their children to school.

Looking back, Killyleagh has unique challenges but the positive support of the parents was key. The parents all chipped in when we had our fun day. We have a good core of very committed parents as well as the parents who find it very difficult to engage with us. The speed of our process was break-neck, so we probably couldn't have involved the parents who find it hard to engage with school on any issues.

Transformation should probably be done over three years, because that is the natural cycle of a development plan.

We ran our transformation action plan in parallel with the three year development plan we had already written. What should happen is that transformation is central to the development plan itself. So that when you are looking at literacy, for example, you are tying it in with transformation.

Recommendations

If NICIE were to ask me now how a school should proceed, I would say engage with your parents. Obviously you can't do anything until you have the support of a parent ballot. Then make the first year of your transformation plan also Year 1 of your school development plan. The Education Authority (EA) and the Inspectorate would need to know this was happening. The core of the development plan for the first three years should be transformation. This is where NICIE can help with signposts as to the training, etc. you should build in for each year. It is also important that the EA officers also have training in the process of transformation because the experience isn't there at present. More coordination between NICIE, the EA and the Department of Education on transformation would be good.

A training and support package that provides guidance for Principals would maybe encourage those who might be daunted by the steps that need to be taken to transform a school. Principals need signposts and a timeframe and guidance as to how to do each task. I think it would be very useful for Principals considering transformation to have this guidance for the three years of transformation in the development plan. It isn't difficult, it's common sense, but principals already have a heavy workload. From what I see, the people who work for NICIE and the IEF are very committed and want to see transformation developed. Support is also needed from the EA and the Inspectorate.

Teachers also need training from the early stages or there won't be any impact in the classroom. I think more could be done to involve pupils: they were involved in our case in designing the uniform and badge, but more needs to happen earlier for them in the classroom. One idea would be to have a programme for P6/7 pupils in the first year of transformation, perhaps led by NICIE staff because teachers won't yet have the skills or confidence. This could then be providing a model for teachers to build on.

Planning to develop transformation

For us in Killyleagh, this year is about transforming RE, and next year we need something that suits us and promotes to the children that we are all different and we can celebrate difference. In terms of future work in the classroom, time is needed to develop lessons and units of work on, for example, some of the videos from the anti-bias training. It takes time.

I think it has been successful so far. The children have been more open to discussion in the classroom. Some of the parent governors say that their children and their friends value the school more and are more proud of their school. We've raised standards, we've raised expectations and we're all on a positive cycle.

Denise Morgan has been involved in integrated education for over 25 years, first as a founder parent of Cedar Integrated Primary School, then as a school governor. She currently works at the Northern Ireland Council for Integrated Education (NICIE) as a Senior Development Officer.

My first child was born in 1990 and probably about '93, I remember seeing a wee ad in the paper about a public meeting for an integrated school in Crossgar. From Crossgar originally, I had been living in Kilkenny, Castlewellan, then Belfast and had moved back up to Crossgar area again at the end of 1992. I was starting to think as every parent would about where their child might go to school. When you become a parent yourself and you'd maybe been away living elsewhere, your perspective can be altered, my thinking had moved to wanting things to be a bit different for my child. So I started to keep an eye on developments and then eventually took the step to look into this integrated school that was being planned for Crossgar. The school eventually opened in 1995 but at that stage my daughter had already gone through P1, she started school in 1994. So she had gone to another very good school in the area and I had the dilemma of, 'Do I take her out of that school because I want to move her to a school that is different, a school that is integrated?' Whenever I started thinking about this and people were saying, 'Oh yes, there is going to be a school and it's going to open on 1st September,' and I was saying, 'But where will it be?' They were replying, 'We'll be down the Kilmore Road.' I would go down the Kilmore Road and look over this wall into a green field with cows in it and thinking, 'I can't get my head around a school being here in four months' time.' I was kind of toying with the idea and my husband and I were talking about it and we were

sort of thinking, 'Will we, won't we? What will we do?' Then we thought, 'We'll go along to a couple of meetings, we'll see how it goes, we'll take our daughter.'

The parents who came up with the idea of an integrated school in the area

The parents at the meetings were all living in the area or around the area, probably within a ten mile radius. I believe the thinking was that Crossgar would be a good place for an integrated school. They were also looking at feeder towns of Saintfield, Ballynahinch, Killyleagh, Downpatrick, so it was a good central place to have a school and would likely be able to draw enough pupils to make the school sustainable.

NICIE would have been involved in the process of opening the school, they had a Development Officer who was facilitating meetings with the parents and setting up a steering group. NICIE and these parents were really driving the school forward. At that time NICIE had a very small staff and if you look back at the mid-1990s, there was a great growth spurt of integrated schools, so I can only imagine NICIE Officers running around the country, trying to help all these parents' steering groups. You know, if they were anything like the parent group who opened Cedar, they would have been very passionate, very engaged, very forward thinking, very, you know, 'Nothing's going to stop us. We're going to do this!'

The first group of P1 and P2 pupils at Cedar IPS, 1995.

There was a real belief in the integrated ethos, the parents that I met in the early days of Cedar were a very mixed group of people from a lot of mixed backgrounds with a real passion, drive and enthusiasm for opening this school. There were a few parents in particular who really inspired and enthused us. A lovely couple from Killyleagh really supported us in making the decision to give this school a chance. Linda was the lady who initiated the very first meeting and Ultan was the local GP in Killyleagh at the time. I was just blown away by their enthusiasm, their dedication to this project and the hard work that they were putting in to get this school opened. There was nothing too big for them and there was nothing that was going to get in their way. But they had a lovely way of being, they were very warm and welcoming, you could feel the ethos almost. There were a lot of other parents in that group who were the same, people were very warm and welcoming and they really wanted to work together to develop this school.

There was a good mix of Catholics and Protestant parents and that was talked about quite a lot. When you went along to those meetings, people would have been explaining what an integrated school would be about and the NICIE Statement of Principles was highlighted. Even at that stage there were explanations about why it was important for people to be comfortable with talking about their religious or community backgrounds, so that the school would be able to ensure that it could maintain the balance to make sure that we would have a really, truly integrated school. Back

then, you needed 25 pupils on the 1st September for P1 in order to have met the criteria set down by the Department of Education. So all of that was explained to us and to be honest I was probably number 25 teetering on the line! Because as I said, my daughter had already gone through P1 in a good school, she was quite settled, but she was thoroughly enjoying meeting all the new children in this group at Cedar. I honestly kept going down every week and looking over the wall and seeing a green field and thinking, 'where is this school? Am I really going to do this? Am I going to take this risk with my child?' And then again, as I said, those parents were just so inspirational, the belief that they had in what they were doing. Anyway, we went to a few events and we decided we were going to sign up to it. We did and I will never forget the feeling of having made this decision after much soul searching. I remember being quite inspired and thinking back, these parents are pretty amazing to have all those other people on board to get them this far, to open this school.

The day when the mobiles arrive to the site of the school

I remember the day the mobiles arrived, I think it was two weeks before the school was due to open and I'm pretty sure it was my dad who actually rang me to tell me. He had driven up the road and rang to say the mobiles were on the site.

Cedar IPS
early class, 1999.

We decided to go with it and do whatever was needed to get Emma ready for this change and all the rest that goes with it. Two nights before they were due to start school, the parents had a wee event with all the children who were going to be starting so that they could meet the new Principal and the P1 /P2 teacher. This was really a landmark and we were really beginning to feel like this is going to be a school that will work. I remember that first day in September, getting Emma dressed and ready, then getting her into the car and taking her down for this new journey. I had my other daughter, Roisin, at that stage, she was six months old at the time. I clearly remember driving up to the school, there was so much excitement, two mobiles were in place, one a very small one that was the Principal's office, a disabled toilet and a very tiny office for the photocopier and any sort of secretarial work that would be going on. The other was a two classroom mobile and that was it, that was the school. I just remember that feeling of, you know, let's give this a go. We've got this far, these people were right, they said it would open, they've opened, let's go with it. I recall my thinking of, 'right, well, you know, it's a place where, if the kids are going and there's twenty-five pupils, they've turned up, we've got to grow this school to keep it open, I've got to help out.'

Becoming more involved in the school as a parent

I joined the Parents' Council. The Governor who was setting up the first Parents' Council at the school was very explicit in highlighting the integrated nature of the school. I remember him explaining that the school was integrated and this meant that the Board of Governors would be integrated and the staff in the school would also reflect the integration. The committees would all be integrated too so it was essential that the Parents' Council reflected the religious balance as well as gender balance, where possible. The Parents' Council would have been involved in helping out, planning and setting up events, doing some fund raising and helping the school to market and grow. In those early days, you were raising money to maybe buy some library books or very small things that made a big difference. The school had started from scratch with 25 pupils from P1 to P5 and had very limited resources.

My daughter's class, the first group of P2s, I think was seven. I can remember all their wee faces. I think there was 12 P1s, seven P2s and maybe a few P3s, the same for P4 and 5. The P3, P4 and P5 were all in one classroom and the P1 and P2 were in the other. My child was very happy there and loved it. She thrived in the environment, couldn't wait to get there and was a different child really.

I then went on to become a governor in the school eventually. I was a parent governor and I was still doing a lot

Cedar IPS at Stormont, 1999.

of work with the Parents' Council. I was the link person on the Board of Governors, reporting back on the valuable work that the Parents' Council was doing. We were all trying to work together to promote Cedar, market Cedar, to grow Cedar and work with the school staff. There was a lot of giving up your evenings and your Saturdays to do fun days, maintaining the school playground and grounds as well as Governors' meetings, running discos and baking cakes.

A strong sense of community

One of the memories I have was that this was very much a community. I really remember the community feeling about the school. The school community placed a very big focus on the environment and environmental elements of the school. Part of the school grounds is along the river bank of the Glasswater River which runs very close to the school. There was a lot of thinking about how the school site would be developed to be a nice, educational and fun outdoor space. Some of the plans included planting a willow walk and building a straw bale house. I remember Saturday mornings being spent down at the school planting willows to create the willow walk and going down then throughout the years as the willows grew to start weaving them to develop the walkway. As a keen gardener myself, I was hoping to make sure it was going to grow right so that it would be a nice willow tunnel

for the kids to play in. The straw bale house was built and that was all done over weekends. So there was lots of coming together and things like planting flower beds, we didn't have that much money so it was about just making the best of what we had.

I remember planting flower beds while my sister-in-law, she's quite artistic, came down and chalked out some designs in the playground. We had gathered up paints through the Parents' Council. She painted designs on the playground for the kids to play on: hopscotch, snakes, spiders' webs, numbers and so on to make the playground more attractive for the kids.

Supporting other integrated schools

My two daughters went through Cedar, so I was involved in Cedar for at least fourteen years. I had a background in early years and one of Cedar's aims was to develop wraparound provision which included a playgroup, a breakfast and after school club. In 1998 I met Lorna McAlpine who was the Senior Development Officer at NICIE. Lorna was looking after all Pre-School in NICIE, she managed the Early Years Committee and was supporting Integrated schools in good practice and achieving funding that was coming in through Peace funding streams. The governors at Cedar managed to get some money to develop a children's centre. I volunteered to help out in setting the playgroup up. My term as Governor had run out and I eventually then actually ran that Pre-School as Leader as time went on. I worked alongside NICIE and the school to draft and lodge the development proposal and worked with them to get approval for a nursery unit which Cedar now has well established.

While I was that playgroup leader at Cedar I also was involved with NICIE on the Early Years Committee and I went on to become a NICIE Director, serving for nearly six years. It would have been around '97/'98 whenever I started working with the Early Years Committee in NICIE on a volunteering basis. The NICIE Early Years Committee supported playgroups because integrated schools couldn't open a new school with a nursery unit, this meant that a brand new school couldn't establish a nursery unit when opening. So the only route for integrated schools to have pre-school was if they opened a playgroup themselves. This was often independently funded by parents but run with high quality teaching staff. In 1998 the money came along for the Government funded places. Lorna McAlpine worked tirelessly with integrated schools to help them to achieve pre-school funded places for their playgroups. In 1997, new pre-school policy emerged. This was swiftly followed by new curricular guidance. NICIE Early Years Committee was vital as a forum for sharing good practice and supporting one another. NICIE were working to support us to make sure that if we were opening and operating playgroups that they were good ones. It was very much about good practice, about the integrated ethos and developing a support network across integrated schools. Those meetings were busy, we were all very eager to work together to be the best that we could be and support one another. It was the NICIE Early Years Committee who developed the very first anti-bias approaches booklet, I think it was '97 when we started developing it. That was the one thing we were finding as early years practitioners, when we were reflecting on the integrated nature of the school, we felt that there wasn't many appropriate resources around to support us in engaging in reflective practice which further developed our confidence in putting that into practice, develop approaches and think about the appropriate language to use with the children. At that time we were still in the very, very early days of the Peace Process here.

Then there was a parent group set up for Millennium in Carryduff, hoping to develop an integrated primary school and I did get involved with them for a short time as a Governor, I think it was about two years. I was still working with Cedar and I would have been working with Millennium as a NICIE Trust Governor and it was really just to help and support them in getting their project off the ground. In my opinion, I think it was probably a very different experience and the challenges were different than some of those faced by Cedar.

I remember leafleting around Carryduff and you would have had different responses, it wouldn't have been as welcoming with regard to the integrated nature of the school. I suppose by that stage I was completely bitten by the integrated bug. I really loved seeing these schools progress and I just was amazed by the people who were involved. The more I engaged in supporting the growth and development of Integrated Education and the more stories I heard about the different experiences people had, the things that they had gone through and achieved opening these schools, just blew me away.

Again, in Drumlins, NICIE officers contacted anyone who would help them to come along to speak to a public meeting about your experience as a parent who had made the choice for Integrated Education for your child or if you'd been involved in developing an integrated school. So I offered my support and actually spoke at the first public meeting for what became Drumlins IPS in Ballynahinch. I also was the parent who spoke at the first public meeting for the school that became Rowandale IPS in Moira. Those are the two that I remember the most. It was exciting to be part of their journey and I still feel really pleased at how far these two schools have come. I had so much admiration for the NICIE Officers because being on the Board of Directors and doing the work that I had done with the Early Years Committee, I got a real sense of the huge level of commitment from the staff in NICIE to the work they were doing. The real belief in what they were doing, they just gave their all and I thought I could give a little bit back by sharing my experience and doing a little bit to support Integrated Education. Always as a volunteer, during my time as a Governor, on Parents' Council, at any of those meetings and the Early Years Committee, I didn't mind, I enjoyed it.

I learned a lot and especially enjoyed the Early Years Committee gatherings. I felt we benefited a lot in really enhancing our integrated ethos. Looking back, you've been a part of that development of Early Years in the integrated sector but also you've lived through all the policy changes and the introduction of funded places. You've been part of something and seen something grow and evolve, which has been really quite interesting and exciting.

The challenges of bringing on board the whole community

At the beginning I don't think the local community was keen on the idea of opening an Integrated school. I mean, there were hurdles, there were people who would have said, 'Well, why are you sending your child there?' The churches, well, that would have been quite difficult. I suppose it's a bit of a journey, and it's about your perspective on the journey you're on. At that time as a parent, I didn't realise how much work and effort the school was having to put in, in the background, to facilitate involvement with local community events. The staff in the school were also building relationships with the church and doing a lot of work on building relationships and engagement. My daughter was one of the first children at Cedar to make her First Holy Communion. It was a very different experience for us compared to the Cedar whole school celebration when my second daughter received her sacrament.

With my first daughter there was only a small number of the children making their Communion and it was with the local Catholic school and we didn't feel terribly welcomed by the church. We didn't feel as much a part of it, even though the children had been prepared very well by a teacher with a Catholic RE certificate. As a Catholic parent, if my child hadn't had the opportunity to make First Holy Communion and Confirmation I wouldn't have sent her to an integrated school. It was very important for me knowing that was possible. I also

wanted her to have a truly integrated experience so that she would know and be friends with children from many walks of life. I just thought there was a richness to the possibility of kids being able to go to one school but coming from lots of different faith backgrounds to learn with, from and about each other. I remember thinking at the time that that experience was probably tougher for me than anybody else because probably I noticed it more than anybody else. I was thinking, this is not how my Holy Communion had been. I was part of a bigger school. Now, the local Catholic school were very welcoming and invited us for tea and everything but I didn't know at that time, the Principal from Cedar hadn't been invited. I was sad about that when I learned of it.

After that experience one of the roles I took on the Parents' Council was to work to ensure that when other children would experience First Holy Communion, Harvest or other celebrations in the future, that I would like to help generate our thinking into action to do something to mark special occasions for everyone as a whole school community in the future. The first step was to arrange a tea party for families with children making Communion at Cedar, so that we could come together as a school to mark the occasion. As the school grew the children came from so many different parishes and the priest wanted them to make the Communion in their own parish. So you could have had kids making Communion in five different parishes on different days. What we did was we tried to pick a day when as many of them as possible were making it and then the other ones would get dressed up again and we'd have our own school celebration for that. I felt that was very important because that was about our integrated ethos. Now the school staff did amazing things and I'm not even sure if they realised how amazing they were, because they're probably just doing it as their job and maybe not thinking about as much. There was lovely gestures of the Cedar community engaging in services as a school across a number of churches. The staff really worked hard to develop this area of work within the wider community.

When I look back I see how far Cedar has come with regard to all of that because when my second daughter

Cedar IPS performing at the Ulster Museum, 2017.

came along to receive her sacrament, there's five years age difference between my two daughters, the school was making it as a whole class. So, it was Cedar's own First Communion and it was absolutely lovely. And what was really nice about that was the way the school managed it. The whole class had the opportunity to take part in that service, to play a part so the children who were maybe from different faith backgrounds were forming part of the choir or were involved in other ways and their parents were happy for them to do this. This grew during my time with Cedar to having Harvest and Christmas services in other churches with the whole school engaging. The way the school handled it at that time, was really, really lovely. I suppose I was lucky to have those two experiences and to see something that wasn't the best experience moving towards something that was really good and heartwarming.

Other things that really stand out for me was attending the Harvest Festival that the school did as a whole school in the local Presbyterian Church, or maybe a carol service. It was very much about taking opportunities to do those things within your own community as a whole school, celebrating different faiths and backgrounds in one another's places of worship. I thought that was a really, really enriching and nice thing. I think the school always did it really well and it was always well supported. I do wonder if that was partly down to that really strong foundation established in the early days of the NICIE Statement of Principles being highlighted and communicated to the parents.

The parents were very aware of how important it was to support the school in that ethos. When we went to the different churches, making sure that you were supporting the school, because that was the type of school you had signed up to have your child educated in. The early '90s were a very different time. I was in a parent group because there was so much going on around you in Northern Ireland that wasn't good. The Troubles were still ongoing, there was still things happening and you were a bit afraid of doing something that was maybe too out there. But then there was something about your belief that things have got to be better. We've got to do something to make things better, I want to play a role in driving something good and positive forward. On reflection, I think that was the thing that really pushed me to keep working at this.

During my time working with NICIE as a member of the Development Team, I have worked closely with some of the parent groups who went on to establish schools or who were involved in expanding their school's provision. I have been with NICIE for 13 years now and when I first came I managed two very dynamic parent groups. Again, really inspirational, determined people who really, really wanted this opportunity for their children. Actually two groups in my first year working to establish new integrated provision and lots of other schools since working on supporting schools to increase enrolment and also to establish nursery provision. Just seeing that journey of very inspired parents who were determined to just keep going and get their school opened and see what they've gone on to achieve is a pretty amazing thing to be part of.

The impact of Integrated Education

I think one of the best things my children have got out of this experience is the way they deal with difference as well as their perspectives on things and outlook. I also think they have developed a real sense of justice, rights and equality. I think I would get a sense of that from them in discussions they would have with you. Because they're grown women now. They're very comfortable talking about difference and being with people from lots of different backgrounds.

I think if I was looking back and I could have done something differently, I probably would have got involved with Cedar sooner. It's quite something to see an ad in the paper, then attend a public meeting to learn more about this idea and then 20-odd years later to look down the line and see this fabulous school with all these children in Cedar uniforms. You see them around the town in that uniform and sometimes I wonder if people realise the sheer hard work and dedication from parents that went into setting it up and making it into a successful school. I still remember that first day of driving in and a real, warm fuzzy feeling that it evoked.

I would hope that at some stage, Integrated Education really comes into its own. It finds its own time if you like. I would like to see more political support and motivation for thinking about an integrated solution as a school for a village where children can grow, learn and build friendships together in a shared space. I remember, when I was at primary school, knowing people in the village who were the same age as me but I knew they were from a different church background and I never played with them. I just think that it's not really natural, in my opinion, for children not to be given the opportunities of growing up and learning with the children who live around them.

I would like to think that the future for Integrated Education will be much brighter than it's been, I would like to see there being much more growth. In the last two years we have seen a lot of growth and that gives me a lot of hope. Moreso with existing schools but equally we have parents who are interested, who have expressed interest in seeing provision develop in their own areas. I do feel there is a bit more momentum coming back. I think maybe for a wee while there was a bit of a lull because people here just hadn't been used to living in a more peaceful time. I think more recently with the failure of the Executive to keep running and all the different things that have been going on politically, maybe people are starting to realise this is actually still a very divided society. I feel there's still a lot we need to do here in relation to working towards greater understanding of one another and creating spaces to establish new ways of working together. I feel that people on the ground are beginning to think we need to do something if we want things to happen here. A bit like we did back in the early days of Integrated Education. You know, if you don't play your part then you can't expect things to change. I have found great inspiration from many people involved in Integrated Education over the years. However in particular, I have been very inspired by Cecil Linehan. Cecil's energy and enthusiasm has never waned since the early 70s, when she wrote the letter to the newspaper that created space for a dedicated group of parents from Protestant and Catholic backgrounds, to come together to establish the first integrated school in Northern Ireland. I have found Cecil's energy and zest for growing Integrated Education truly infectious and uplifting.

I think as a whole we really did succeed with Cedar and I really would like to pay tribute to those unsung heroes: people, the very first people who drove that school forward. They were amazing. They were good at marketing, they were very good at making sure they were always in the local paper. So, if you were maybe on the sidelines as a parent, like me, you were watching this development but you hadn't quite decided if you were going to be a part of it, you were able to see how they had progressed their plans to deliver their dream.

For me, being involved in the Integrated Education movement has been one of the most enriching experiences of my life. I've had opportunities to meet people from such a broad range of backgrounds, religions, communities. I've just learned so much about people and situations and, you know, things people have been through in the Troubles maybe or people's desire and reasons for becoming involved. Some like me, thought it was a good idea, others may have very different reasons, very poignant reasons. But for everybody it is a very positive and optimistic outcome and I just think that for me, probably the most important thing has been a really enriching experience for me and my family. I can see my children loved their school. I think that deeply embedded integrated ethos in the primary really helped my daughters in life and their perspective and their outlook. And I get wee glimpses every now and again, of wee things they say. I kind of think, 'Mmm, I remember similar conversations when they were young,' and I can often link it to early experiences. Sometimes they would even quote some of their teachers still. I think that's testament to the work the staff, led by Mary Laverty, did on the ethos in the early days of Cedar. The experience of that ethos has been really important.

Anne Odling-Smee CBE has been, among other positions, Chair of Belfast Education and Library Board and a lecturer at Queen's University. She was also centrally involved in the formation of Lagan College and was a founding governor of the Integrated Education Fund.

Beginnings

In 1970 we came with our family to Northern Ireland. It was a time when things were beginning to become very difficult on the streets because the actions of the IRA and the counter actions were just beginning to boil up. My husband is an Anglican and I'm a Roman Catholic and we were bringing our children up in both traditions. When we got here, we discovered that life was very segregated. Schools were segregated, the areas where people lived were segregated. We sent our children to the nearest primary school and that was a school which prided itself on being very open, but in fact it was largely Protestant with a Protestant culture and this was quite difficult because there was sectarianism in the school, there was bigotry and there were things said about the children. We had to do a good deal of engaging with the staff to explain where we were coming from and they were very good and very helpful, but it was just the nature of the thing. I did not want them to go to a Catholic school, because that would've been too much the other way. In England you could just have sent them to the local school.

There was also academic selection at 11 which we had just left behind in Tyneside. We campaigned to get rid of it and so we had comprehensive schools.

Nobody can believe how segregated Northern Ireland is. And it's quite deliberate. You have Christian traditions that believe they are the one and only church and the other ones have nothing good about them. I can remember coming home from school in Lancashire and saying to my mother, 'Only Catholics go to heaven, don't they, mummy?' 'And what about your grandma?' because my mother had been an Anglican and she had become a Catholic. She wasn't going to have any ideas like that floating around.

About 1974/5 we met Tony Spencer, who also had just come over here at the same time with his family and he was putting them into school. He was a Catholic with a Catholic family and he was finding it very difficult as well. Tony Spencer introduced me to Cecil Linehan, Betty Benton, Margaret Kennedy and Bill Brown and all the people who had begun a group in Bangor so their children could go to the state school but receive their instruction in the Catholic tradition outside of school. That's where All Children Together (ACT) began. We had a lot of meetings with the people in Dublin who are Educate Together and they gave us a lot of support. They came to our conferences and we went to their conferences and we discussed the whole idea of how we would create schools which could be open and welcoming for everybody. I was also involved with the Association for Comprehensive Education and in the N.I. Mixed Marriage Association.

My husband was a surgeon so he was very busy in the Royal, and later at the Mater and the City, and eventually I became a lecturer in Queen's as a colleague of Tony Spencer in

Lagan College, 2007.

the Social Studies Department. I was training social workers and teaching Social Policy. The students taught me a lot about what it was like for them having grown up here, how they felt about segregation and how they would like society to be.

In 1981 they changed the quota for the grammar schools and the non-selection schools and there weren't many places in the grammar school. It was really quite a mess with how you made the jump from being in P7 to the first year in your post-primary school. We met in the Quaker Meeting House in March and we decided that we would set up a post-primary school in September.

Basil McIvor was of great assistance because he had been the Minister for Education in the power-sharing Executive in 1974 and he was bringing forward the idea of integrated schools. He was privy councillor, so that helped. John Carson who was the Lord Mayor, was very helpful. We had to raise money; we had jumble sales and friends of ours in England would send us the odd cheque.

We had this extremely good principal, Sheila Greenfield. She had taught in a comprehensive school in England so she knew how you ran a comprehensive school. The whole thing was done on behalf of the children and they all had their learning pathway and you put them into whatever exams were seen to be right for them and what they felt they could do.

Hugh, our youngest child, had been born in Belfast in 1973 and he would join when he was 11. A number of people said that to me, 'He ought to be going to a grammar school,' and I said, 'That's just where I don't want him to go!' He said on the first day one of the children said to him, because it was known if you were English you're supposed to be Protestant, there were more of them than there are of us. Hugh said, 'No, we're 50/50.' Because he was in a family which was mixed, we were Catholic and Protestant.

People put their names down and eventually we had 27/28 children, including Tony Spencer's daughter and Cecil's son. We called it an all-ability school because some are wary about the name comprehensive and terrible stories told about the comprehensives in England. We wanted it to be socially mixed and we wanted it to be open and welcoming to Protestants, Catholics and others so that they could learn from each other. The teachers and staff would be involved in this. It could be quite a big step for teachers who had grown up in one community or another and taught in either a Catholic school or a Protestant school.

Basically, it was to bring Protestants and Catholics together in school so that they could be educated together and they could learn about each other and that through them the teachers would also learn and exchange, and the parents and the cousins and the sisters and their aunts. But it was also about academic selection. We were talking to the Secretary of State, Michael Ancram. Grammar schools were being allowed open enrolment, which meant that we had a number of people who could have got a grammar school place but wanted to come to Lagan College, but they were worried, because we were over-subscribed, whether they would find a place. Then where would they go? Could they then get into grammar school? The grammar schools would look at them and say, 'Why do you want to come to us? You didn't want to come to us. You put Lagan College first.' Eventually we were allowed to take what we call a banded entry; we would take a third of pupils who had got the 11+ and were coming to us and not going to a grammar school. They preferred to come to a comprehensive even though they could've gone to a grammar school. Michael Ancram was a very helpful Secretary of State. He was keen that we should be able to proceed with our comprehensive intake and the banded entry is quite a reasonable way of doing it.

Finances

We had to ask people to make a subscription because we had no money at all! We had no money except what we were raising. People who could afford to pay, paid but we had a special fund set up so those people who couldn't would not be hindered from coming. We had an awful lot of little jumble sales; we had appeals; we got money from the Nuffield Foundation and the Rowntree Foundation and Europe eventually. But it was a matter of writing constant letters to people asking for money. We did make it but it was quite difficult making ends meet. Some people would say, 'I love what you're doing; let me give you this,' and £2000 would appear. Anybody who had a mortgage on their house offered to re-mortgage it.

It was worrying for the teachers because they were giving up posts which had got an increment. When we were interviewing somebody who was coming from a post which had got this extra with it, one of our staff said, 'He can have some of my salary because he's got a big family. Until we can sort the money out I'm prepared to give up some of mine.'

Nuffield and Rowntree felt that they had to rationalise the way in which we were raising money for integrated schools. They and people within the Department felt we could set up what became the Integrated Education Fund (IEF). This would be an independent body that would have money which it could distribute to schools which were setting up because no school got any capital funding until they had been accepted and proved to be viable. We had to find the capital for the first three years and the IEF was there to provide the capital. It was Brian Mawhinney really who pushed this, that they would set up a body to promote and support integrated schools and that became the Northern Ireland Council for Integrated Education (NICIE). Then the IEF was established in '92 to provide the capital funding independently.

I was on the Board of Governors of Lagan College and I was asked to go onto the IEF in 1992. Jonathan Bardon was also appointed and Fionnuala Cook, whose son had gone to Brownlow when it transformed to integrated status in Craigavon and Alan Smith a Mill Strand Integrated Primary founder.

Lagan College

The idea was that some of the existing schools would transform to integrated status; that was Tony Spencer's idea. We'd got a dip in the population. Populations in Belfast were changing all the time. The idea was that there would be schools which were closing or reducing in number that we would then have as an integrated school and attract people who wanted to go to school together. There was one attempt at the Throne School which is fairly near Hazelwood Primary. But the Belfast Education and Library Board (BELB) wouldn't support it. Tony Spencer was on the Board, but he couldn't get them to. That was fairly tough going. By the time I was on the Education and Library Board things had settled a bit. I was nominated by ACT to go on and so I was on it for 12 years. By that time the integrated schools had begun to get going. There was opposition and you had to take things very carefully. In 1981 it was triggered because there was a crisis at 11+. We needed to start a school because it was never going to start if we didn't do this, so we did.

You sat around in a room planning how you would do this and what you wanted to do and what you wanted your aim to be. And then we decided at that meeting that we would go ahead and so the people who were the key people in ACT then began raising money and finding somewhere to start. It was hopefully to be in South Belfast. You had got these 27 kids signed up for it. The Scouts offered to rent the Scout Centre. Then the South Eastern Education and Library Board, upon which Cecil Linehan and Betty Benton sat, said that they had got this little school that had been a special school in Church Road in Castlereagh. That was agreed and so at Christmas they moved to the Castlereagh building. When the next year came that school couldn't accommodate them. They went to the Ulster Folk Museum for a term until the Castlereagh Council allowed them to have permission to put mobiles on the site.

By '85 Forge Integrated Primary School had started up where Malone Primary School had been. That belonged to the BELB. Tony Spencer arranged to use some space in the primary school for the first term. After the first term Castlereagh Council allowed us to have another mobile and then they went up there. My son was very annoyed because he had been at Malone Primary School, it had closed, then he went to Lagan College and found he was still in Malone Primary School which had by that time become Forge!

It was pretty difficult running that school because mobiles are cold. It was difficult to keep the toilets in decent order and we were always shifting things around. We wanted to employ more teachers; we had to do the interviews in the little small mobile that was the music hut!

We had 27, then the next year I think the total came up to about 60. After that we were accommodating about 60 a year. When other schools were closing, half the staff room would be applying to come to Lagan College! Catholic priests were saying rude things from the pulpit and still Catholic teachers came; we never had any problem. We had the representative number.

In those days it was very much in the heart of the country. Martha my grand-daughter is now at Loughview which is in the building in which her father went to Lagan College; it's the old Lagan College building! She thinks it's very funny.

Ending the silence

The fear is very deep so what you do if you mix is you don't say anything. I was appointed to the chair of the Education and Library Board; I was nominated by the Unionist Party. Then in 1999 Margo Harkin from Derry made a programme called 'A Plague on Both Your Houses'. My husband and I figure as one of the mixed marriage couples. When I went in the Board next time, one of the Unionist councillors, came to me and said, 'Anne, I saw that programme. My wife's a Catholic, you know.' I'd go into the chemist and they'd say, 'We're a mixed marriage but we just don't talk about it.' Why shouldn't you be able to talk about the fact that you're married to a Catholic or your children are Catholics? And because people didn't talk about religion they were totally ignorant. I would go to a coffee morning and I'd be told that old one, 'They're told to breed, have big families so that they can out-vote us.' So I said, 'I am a Catholic and I'd never heard that.' And that was the sort of thing you got at a very middle class coffee morning. They didn't know because I was English and they knew my husband going to the Church of Ireland.

I think we got it right. It's been tough; you had to argue with people, you had to convince people. And you will still have people who think we are much better off kept separate. It's safer that way. But there are other people who have joined in and said, 'Yes, it is much better that we be together.' For instance, we had a Methodist minister on the Board of Governors at Lagan College; they observe Ash Wednesday. A Catholic said, 'Didn't know the Methodists observed it.' They didn't know about each other. There have been a lot of people in Northern Ireland who actually wanted to mix. They wanted to go to school together, they wanted to work together. There was no way until we got this going that they had a chance. We've got an opportunity for people to be together in a way which they can talk about each other and talk to each other and they're safe.

I had four went through the ordinary way because they were older. They found it very difficult; there was a lot of sectarianism, a lot of bigotry. They went to Malone Primary and to Friends' School, Lisburn. At Friends' School things went nicer than most but only one or two teachers were really able to know how to teach across the whole community. Everybody's being too careful or too polite. There was one teacher who said he'd never spoken to my daughter because he'd never spoken to a Catholic so he didn't know what to say. The whole time he taught her in class she couldn't understand why he wouldn't talk to her.

There were difficulties and some things didn't work that well but on the whole you are meeting so many people right across Belfast. I know that there are a proportion of Catholics in all of the schools but unless they're acknowledged and used as a resource and they're allowed to speak about themselves, what's the point?

Successes and problems

It is the ordinary people who don't want this to go on anymore and they're determined and very brave people.

We cannot underestimate what they call the ancestral voices that are about in this divided community. What we have got to do is give the space to be together and live together and work together and know about each other in so far as we possibly can. And as far as I'm concerned the best way is for them to go to school together. I think that the integrated schools have given this. I'm very regretful that so many people haven't been able to get in. I'm sorry other people put the barriers in the way; I think they should think about that very hard. Since 1981 thousands of children have been able to go to school together, to get to know each other, to still be friends when they've left school, to have a great range of contacts and friendships now when they're out in the world. That's all to the good. They can think for themselves, they know about each other, they learn their history together and they understand what the religions are all about.

We cannot go on being ignorant of each other. I actually find it very difficult to be in a group that's all Protestant or all Catholic. I just cannot stand it!

In 1999 I was awarded the CBE for services to education. It implied that integrated schools had taken their place in NI Education and vindicated everything that we had been doing. It really was awarded to everybody!

Mary Roulston came to Northern Ireland from England in 1977. She was involved in community work and taught in the Ards Peninsula before becoming the first principal of Millennium Integrated Primary School between Carryduff and Saintfield.

Every stage of my career led me to Integrated Education

I'm from England and I've been in Northern Ireland since 1977. Not being from here is at times an advantage and at times a disadvantage. I didn't realise it at the time, but every stage of my career has led me into Integrated Education. If we go right back to when I was at university, I did a lot of work with children during the summer holidays. I was in France for three consecutive summers working with children from institutions from all over France who came for a holiday but they were blind, deaf, dumb and autistic. It was incredible training because we were blindfolded and had to actually manage ourselves for a couple of days before the children arrived. There is no better training for understanding how much disability can affect day to day living. I worked in the international school, outside Paris, that allowed me to see diversity in its widest sense in terms of different cultures because there were all the different sections of all the different nationalities. It was a school of privilege but there were also the workers within that school who did the lesser jobs who I got friendly with equally as much as with the ambassadors and diplomats. So, I've always had friends right across every possible divide. I think that I've always wanted to just meet the person. I'm not interested really particularly in labels whether it's any sort of label. I think in all aspects of life that relationships are the crux of the matter. It's well worth investing in relationships whether it's with organisations or staff within organisations, with your parent body, the staff or the children. I think that's the most important aspect of life you see, whether it's with your partner, your children, or your work colleagues.

I worked in the Steiner school in Holywood for a couple of years and that also was where I really developed the whole aspect of real child centeredness. It was very empowering to work there as I was there in the early stages of their history as well. My first introduction into Integrated Education happened when I worked there. I remember the All Children Together (ACT) group coming to meet with the teachers. I feel every school I worked in has contributed to the development of Millennium. I worked in a school in a very loyalist village and that also shaped me. It was almost like I was on a journey that was going to end up in Integrated Education. Once I came here, it was like this is what I was meant to do all along. This was where I should've been - in the integrated sector right from the very beginning in some respects, but maybe I wouldn't have been able to do it earlier in my career. Maybe I would've done it very badly had I not had all of that beforehand.

Last day in
Breda Park, 2002.

Community work

In the late 80s, early 90s, I became very involved in a parent and toddler group and that was the beginning of my cross-community work. The village was very badly off for general services and we knew that we would never get the provision that we felt our children deserved without a community association. I went from being chair of the parent and toddler group to being chair of the community association! I was involved in getting peace money for the village and other money to develop a neutral venue, a community hall with health facilities. I also helped with a cross-community youth group in the new venue as well as the parent and toddler group. At this point I'd taken a break from teaching because my family were young. I was developing all the necessary skills of working with both sides of the community: mediation and organising big community events, making sure that both sides of the community were involved. We even managed to get the two local bands to lead a community day parade which was unheard of at that time. There were so many things that I was doing that led me to believe that with everything that was happening in Northern Ireland, our children should be together, young people should be together. It's the norm in most countries.

This community work wasn't without its problems. We had some open meetings where we were heckled and threatened. We were mainly a group of women, and we were told by the local council that we had to get some men on the committee to be taken seriously. We didn't like this suggestion at all, but we went ahead and got some men involved. But I have to say the bulk of the work was still with the females! We carried on and we delivered all that we set out to do including a cross-community nursery school. I'm still Chair of Governors of that nursery school. As parents of young children, we didn't want our children being educated separately and we also didn't want the maintained school or the controlled school at the time, to get the European funding which was available for nursery provision. We wanted a stand-alone cross-community nursery. We had to have high profile mediators in at times to sort out problems. For example, at the time we got our neutral venue, the council was insistent that at the end of every single event in that neutral hall we had to play the National Anthem. That would take away its neutrality straight away. I had to work with local councillors and I've worked with all the extremes of politicians and with the community. So I understood the fears and the tensions which could so easily arise.

When I went back into a permanent teaching post I was taking on more responsibilities within the school and people kept saying to me that I really should be thinking about going for a Principal post and I kept saying, 'Well, I don't really want to be a Principal! I want to stay in the classroom.' I enjoy being with the children and that's really my passion in life. At the same time, the open meetings were happening in Carryduff

Nativity in Breda Park.

for Millennium and I was reading about it all in the local paper and I mean it was amazing what was happening. There was so much adversity towards an integrated school in the Carryduff area. There were newspaper reports about people not wanting an integrated school, about what was happening at the open meetings. I never thought I would ever aim for Principal. It was not on the radar at all. Then I saw the job advert and I looked at the criteria and I thought, 'Well, this post really is right up my street!' I was totally into cross-community work, having seen the difficulties and having seen the kind of attitudes that could be changed over time and also having seen the success of it and what it means for a community when they're working well together. And this was a post that would allow me to carry on teaching. This was really important for me and I also thought that it was an amazing opportunity to start a school from scratch. I went to the interview not believing that I had any chance of getting the post. I thought, 'It'll be good experience, but I'm not likely to get it.'

Belief

I think the reason I really wanted to go into Integrated Education was because I just believed in it. I had seen how well it worked when children played together and did things together and when parents, you know mothers, particularly, were together, I think that was part of it. I didn't know very much about Integrated Education when I applied. I really didn't know about all the things that you needed to think about when setting up an integrated school and if you take into account the fact that I really didn't think I was going to get the job, there was a certain naivety. For example, I didn't even fully realise that there wasn't going to be any funding in that first year. I took an enormous risk without really fully realising in the initial stages how big a risk it was! But it didn't matter once I started. I suppose if I feel there's an injustice then I always throw myself into it. I felt it was wrong to be denying children Integrated Education. I often think that if I was around in the suffragette days I would have been one of the suffragettes, I tend to feel very passionately about things being done.

Early memories of Millennium IPS

One of the first memories was when the phone call came to say I had the post, bearing in mind that I was absolutely convinced that I had no chance. I left the classroom and I said to my classroom assistant, 'If they think I'm going for a second round of interviews after what they put me through in the first round, they've no chance. I'm not going!' When I went to the phone and they said that they were offering me the post I came back into the classroom. My classroom assistant was a girl called Jennifer Slane, a fabulous classroom assistant, and I said to her, 'I've got the job Jennifer. I can't believe it!' She

Mary at the launch of the new school uniform.

threw her arms around me and all the P1 class were saying, 'Mrs Roulston's kissing Jennifer!' I said to Jennifer, 'We're going to be the talk of this village if they go home and say we were kissing in the classroom!'

Another memory was Lorna McAlpine from the Northern Ireland Council for Integrated Education (NICIE) explaining the difficulties that were coming up and the fact that it looked like Millennium wasn't going to open. I had handed in my notice and it was a shock being told at the last minute that we weren't going to be able to come on site. The plans were for a mobile to be on site for the P1 class, and we were going to use the house that was on the site for my office and a staffroom. And all of a sudden, they wouldn't allow us on site. That was the politics of the time. There was a farm, a furniture showroom and a car showroom on the site. There were all those things and so there was traffic coming in and out and yet they couldn't allow a teacher, an assistant and 10 children to come on site. So that was a real eye opener, to be homeless days before school was about to open. I've always had a good relationship with NICIE and with the Integrated Education Fund (IEF) and with the Belfast Charitable Trust for Integrated Education (BELTIE) and with everybody that I needed to work with. I'm certainly not saying it was easy all the way but I think relationships are very important. I remember scouring the countryside with the governors and Lorna to try and find new premises. Somebody in the Health

Trust helped us to get a temporary lease on a Trust owned building and another pivotal memory was going down to see it and the shocking state it was in because it hadn't been used for a long period of time. It was vandalised and dirty and one of my governors, Barnie Thompson, who was with the project right from the beginning, started to cry and said, 'I can't bring my daughter Rachel to this! They can't expect me to bring her into this!' And I was trying to reassure and said to Barnie, 'It won't be like this. I promise you it won't be like this. We will work really hard to turn this around and NICIE and other people and you will help me do it. We'll have a lovely place for the children to come to.' In the build up from being appointed and to the school opening, I was managing two jobs. I was still working in my previous school but I was having meetings in the evening with the steering group and NICIE and working to plan and prepare for the incoming term. It was quite a challenge to do that with a young family.

The first parents

That original steering committee knocked on a lot of doors. I was absolutely amazed, and the more I went through the journey, the more amazed I was by these 10 parents who passionately wanted Integrated Education. They signed up when there was no building and the school had no reputation. They didn't know me as a person, what I was like or how I was going to teach their children. I think they had a good idea that the funding was going to be very limited and yet they wanted Integrated Education that much that they were prepared to send their children into all that unknown. So many times I was just amazed.

We had a family who were considering sending their child to Millennium but they probably had the biggest decision of all to make as Lucy had a disability. For them to commit to us meant that that she would have no assistant. Neither the Health Trust nor the Department of Education would give an assistant even though she fully deserved an assistant. Lucy was in a wheelchair and we had no disabled access or facilities. But they were so committed, they really wanted Integrated Education. I met them in their home and they decided to send Lucy to us, which was an amazing thing for them to do. I must say, very sadly, Lucy passed away. She was with us for the first year and then they moved away. They were great parents and very supportive of Millennium. I found it very shocking that neither the Health Trust nor the Department of Education would make an exception. If Lucy had gone to a mainstream school, not an unfunded, integrated school, as they talked about it, then she could've had all the support but because she was in an unfunded, integrated school they wouldn't give it.

Many of our early families were mixed marriages and had their roots in East and West Belfast. They had grown up in areas and had personal experience of what it was like and they wanted something different for their children. Many of them had incredible aspirations for their children and they did not want their children to have the same experience that they had had themselves. They had to come out of their communities and came to Carryduff because it is probably one of the most mixed areas in terms of mixed marriages. It was a safer place for them to be and, of course, they and their children were going back and forwards to the extended family in East Belfast and West Belfast. They wanted their children to understand the cultures that they came from and to have respect for both. There was also an element of keeping the grandparents happy. Catholic grandparents weren't going to be happy if their grandchild was at a controlled school and vice versa, so

the integrated school helped some of the family tensions at that level.

Seven out of the 10 children in the first class came from mixed marriages. However, because of our geographical location we have never really had difficulty getting balance. We haven't had to do the hard work that some schools have had to do. Within the mixed marriages, some of the children have been brought up Catholic, some children have been brought up Protestant, and some children are actually brought up within both and attending both churches every weekend. Some children had parents or families that moved out of all of that and it was 'Other' that they designated themselves to. They weren't aligning themselves to anything. But then we also were an equal distance from Saintfield and Ballygowan which are predominantly Protestant. With those two smaller villages and then Carryduff with its mixed marriage and its large Catholic community, it has meant that the balance has always been easy.

One was phoning New York, the other was phoning Westminster

When we were in our temporary accommodation in Breda Park, we couldn't even put up a sign to say what we were because there was a fear that we would probably have been put out of the building by politicians who had premises nearby. The rooms were very small, trying to teach a class of 19 children in an L-shaped living room is quite something! We were a hidden school, we had no choice for a period of time. So much so that I would meet colleagues who would say to me, 'I'm so sorry to hear that your school never opened, Mary.' People really thought the school had never opened because we were quiet.

Once we moved on to our present site, the major issue we dealt with was politicians who couldn't close the school but wanted to close the school. They had the power to close the road and threatened to close the main road from Downpatrick to Carryduff so the school would have to close! There were all sorts of things that happened along the way that were very difficult and challenging. It was the way they happened. I received a phone call asking me if I was aware that the children weren't safe, and I asked the person what they meant. Put this into the context of all that was going on at Holy Cross and the rest of the Troubles, I was nervous that somebody was going to attack us and the children. The person said to me that she was a reporter but there was an embargo on it. I phoned Michael Wardlow at NICIE and said, 'I've had the strangest phone call. I don't know whether it's a hoax. Can you have a look into it and see if you can find anything out?' And he told me wait in school and that he would make some enquiries. He phoned me back and said that there didn't seem to be anything to worry about and that I should go home.

I picked up everything and I was ready to go out the door and the phone rang again and it was Michael to tell me that I needed to have an emergency Board of Governors' meeting. I was going to be served with an Enforcement Order the following morning and I was going to have to decide whether to bring the children into school or not. We had two governors at the emergency meeting, one was phoning New York, to try and find out what was going on with a very high-profile politician at the time. And another governor was phoning Westminster to another high-profile politician, both from different sides of the community, which reflected our situation. The end result was that we decided to open the school but we had to walk the children in while the whole of the opposite side of the road was full of TV cameras. The Enforcement Order was served but the actual procedure hadn't been followed. NICIE committed to put in a filter lane in the Saintfield direction immediately and so it all fizzled out. We were main news, basically. It was quite something to deal with diplomatically. We had hurdles like that all the time. The planning went backwards and forwards to Castlereagh Borough Councill and every excuse that could be found, was found, to delay the building of the school, in the hope that that would affect future enrolments, that parents would say that this school's never going to happen. It did affect enrolments, particularly in the third year.

Teachers

The most important thing for me in a teacher is being child centred, valuing and welcoming to every single child no matter what that child brings with them. No matter if that child is going to be a difficult child to have in the classroom. I passionately believe that every single child, no matter what their needs are, should be given every opportunity to succeed and that schools should be doing their absolute utmost to make a difference. I would have always been very conscious of the need to have a good ratio of male teachers because I'm always looking at balance. At every level I think it's absolutely crucial that children are being educated in a school that reflects all aspects of life. Yes, it's about the religious balance in an integrated school but it's also about having a male/female balance as well. We have always aspired to this and once the school started to grow, we've always had two, three, four, five male members of staff in the school. We always appointed the best candidate and we were very fortunate that some incredible male teachers came along because, you know, applications at primary school are very weighted in terms of female applications. A commitment to Integrated Education would be absolutely vital.

I think particularly as I grew in confidence and as the governors grew in confidence alongside me we started to change our interview process. We've conducted interviews where, yes, they've had their questions but they've also had to teach in front of the governors or teach the governors themselves. They may well have had to do a role play, which would be teasing out personal qualities in terms of how they relate when they're put under pressure. You can skill people up with how to teach, how the school runs or what you want to do in a school, but what is very hard to change is their personality, personal beliefs, temperaments and attitudes towards parents or children. Those are the bits that tend to be quite fixed in people because they come from maybe years of thinking in a certain way or behaving in a certain way and that's harder to change.

Building Millennium IPS.

I think one of the things that's very important for the work we do in this school is that we have an incredible Integrated Education Co-ordinator. He is not afraid to be very direct and he has done some amazing assemblies. You know, he did an assembly here where he had a real hot air balloon and he had the children in it and each child was representing a different denomination, a different background, a different world faith. He went to the heart of the kind of things that people say about each faith. He did quizzes such as 'Spot the Catholic', 'Spot the Protestant', and puts in all the really ridiculous perceptions there are and then explores them. We often questioned whether we should let the little ones come. We decided to let the P2 class come and we couldn't believe the impact. For example, one of the P2 classes went back and wrote an amazing story where they re-adapted the story of Billy Goats Gruff to represent Integrated Education. It is amazing if you have the visuals and talk about things in a very direct manner, how much can be done.

He has done some amazing training with the staff, even to the point you know that they had a member of staff sitting facing the rest of the staff with a sash on and getting them to talk about, 'What's the first thought that comes into your head, what do you feel about the person in the sash?' And then something very much representing the other tradition and what that meant and then teasing out all that – the perceptions and bias that we all carry. He has really

at times, really challenged the staff. And really challenged the children and the parents. We've done a lot of fairly controversial stuff here in this school and the staffroom is where there are many interesting conversations as well.

Reflections

The experience that the early children had in comparison to what the children at the end of my principalship have was very different. Those first ten children had an amazing experience in some ways because it was such a small class and they were like our family with myself and the P1 assistant, Marie. It was a very warm, small environment and it met the needs very well of all of those children and, in fact, those children have done very well academically. Those early classes have done amazingly, academically. You know, the majority of them are at university and doing very, very well. So that was a plus, but the provision that they had, say, maybe for music or for sports was very limited. Millennium children receive a much wider experience now with this great big staff team coaching sports, drama, art and music. We've lost obviously the kind of extreme family feel we had in the early days. We've always tried to hold on to the positives of that stage in our development as much as we can. But it's a different experience for a child that's in a class of 10 children or a class of 31, or 32 or 34 children. The school has constantly evolved and moved forward and the whole staff team have been brilliant at helping me to realise the community that we have here today.

Spend the time talking to parents

One of the challenges is helping parents to understand why you are doing certain things. The children embrace whatever you provide for them basically, especially when you're talking about the nursery children and the P1 children, but the parents are more likely to be carrying baggage. We developed a reputation for managing the needs of children with very difficult needs, particularly children with ASD. We had a lot of parents who never saw themselves in Integrated Education. They moved their children here or chose this school because of its developing reputation for actually helping children to be happy in school first and foremost, because that is what underpins everything we do here. In the early years you're making sure that you're reflecting what's important to those from Protestant, Catholic and Other traditions. I was challenged many times and had to explain what we were doing and why we were doing it, why it was important. There would have been a knock on the door and parents would've come in complaining about something I was about to do or had done. They felt we shouldn't be doing it because it was too Protestant, or too Catholic. It was very interesting in the early years because that would've happened fairly regularly. I think the reason

they don't come in anymore or haven't come in for so many years is because they trust what we do here, they trust me as a person and the staff. Most of the staff have been here a long time. There is that trust and I think that has allowed us to tackle some of the very thorny issues. We did work on the recent anniversaries of the Ulster Covenant and the 1916 Rising without any kind of challenge from parents.

I realised fairly quickly how important it was at open days to really spend time talking to prospective parents about what you were signing up to when you chose Integrated Education. I showed them the clip and the newspaper article about the children being brought into Lagan College under armed guard and the fact that there still is resistance. The fact that you know if you come to an integrated school it is not about ignoring the backgrounds of children, it's actually about celebrating and it's about diversity and it's about valuing every single member of the school community. This is what we will be doing and going through it all so that they couldn't come and say, 'When we came here we didn't realise what we were signing up to,' and that has become really important because I want parents to want Integrated Education and to understand what it means.

I tell parents very clearly that they've a great choice. This area has incredible schools, across all sectors, really good schools, and they've a great choice. We are one of the very good schools in the area but what they'll get different here is

Lawrence Rowan joined the Northern Ireland Council for Integrated Education (NICIE) in January 1995 as a Clerk of Works.

I was looking for work and there was an advert in the paper for a Clerk of Works for NICIE and I thought, 'Okay, it's only a year contract but I'll go for it,' and lucky enough I got it. Lagan College had been in the news lots of times over the previous years, so I knew Integrated Education existed. I didn't know anything about the size of it or how it was developing, I had to read up on that before I went for the interview.

I was Clerk of Works to oversee the construction of two colleges, Shimna College in Newcastle and Erne College in Enniskillen. What it meant was I spent two days a week in Newcastle and two days a week in Enniskillen and one day a week in the office. There was a fair lot of driving to be done over the period!

The year passed quickly and the two colleges were completed and the schools moved from temporary accommodation to the new buildings. Now those two schools were actually special examples of the school development programme that we were going to adopt into NICIE in the years ahead. After the first year was over I sat down with the then Chief Executive, Michael Wardlow, and we talked about the future because officially after one year my contract was over.

I want to buy your site

In 1996/97 another seven or eight schools came on line but they were brand new schools. They didn't have a Principal, they didn't have a steering group, they didn't have pupils, they didn't have a site, didn't have anything. Basically, Lorna and Frances who were Senior Development Officers would have brought me in and said, 'We have an application here from half a dozen interested parents in Crossgar and they want to set up a new school.' The Development Officers would take that on board and increase the steering group to a reasonable size, find out what the views in the local area were, who would send their children to this. Is it viable? And they had a viability process to go through with the Department of Education before they would get initial approval to set up a school in a temporary building.

The Department of Education wouldn't pay for a permanent structure on day one, it had to be a mobile building so I would look at the possibilities of where this would be. I would head off in my car to Crossgar and drive around in circles looking at plots of land. I have to be looking inside this circle in the development area. Some of the sites we looked at might have had a 'for sale' sign on them. It could have been an old factory building, a disused railway station, anything. We looked at everything and I evaluated everything for the feasibility of building a school. Then you approach the owners of the land and say, 'I want to buy your site.'

Barry McGuigan with some of the Rowandale governors.

15 schools in 15 years

I was in constant touch with all the Planning Services in Northern Ireland and I started at the top of the Planning Service by meeting the Chief Planner and discussing what we were attempting to do over the next 10-15 years. We're talking here about 15 schools in 15 years and 15 sites. He in turn put me in touch with his boss in Belfast, in Londonderry, in the Enniskillen area so we then had people to contact. So if you were looking for a school in that particular area, I would contact and meet him and have a chat with him. What's the feasibility of this? What's the possibilities? We would have problems right here because of traffic or whatever it may be. I continued driving around all these areas which covered the whole of Northern Ireland. I mean, you could have been in Crossgar this morning and in Ballymena this afternoon and back to the office before tea time. I was always driving.

There's Crossgar, Omagh, Dungannon, Coleraine, Belfast, Ballymena, Malone, Carrowdore, Ulidia, Magherafelt, Carryduff, Randalstown, Ballynahinch, Cookstown, Limavady, Moira and Downpatrick, so it's the whole of Northern Ireland.

Building schools by stages

The Department of Education would only give approval to build a certain size of school dependent on your projected enrolments. They're not going to build a school for 700 people when you've only got 20 enrolled. So you would design a school then add this bit on and then this bit and it's now a 700 pupil school. That would be done over maybe four or five years.

For example, a standard primary classroom is 28m^2, it doesn't matter where it is, it's 28m^2 in size. A standard classroom in the post-primary college is 35m^2 because the children need more room. They had a schedule of accommodation and in a general classroom you had to have A, B, C, D & E. Now the Principal or steering group might have said, 'I want F as well.' You're not entitled to it at this point so we would try and maybe you'll get it next year. The design of a school would depend on the site, it could be an 'L' shape, or a block shape. You had to look at the site and say where the entrance is going to be, which road and what part of the road. Then we would check with the planners; could we put an entrance there?

I would have been meeting with the parents probably within the first couple of months of them approaching NICIE. We had no site, we just talked about what the school might look like. I showed them photographs of previous schools. It's

Drumlins IPS
opening, 2004.

amazing some of the things that did happen in schools over the period, you know? We could get the approval in January to develop a school and they would allow you cloakrooms, toilets, an office, staff room, two classrooms and an assembly hall type thing. That was your first allowance. Then I got my pencil out and I drew a plan of what I thought it should look like in line with the Department's rules. I had to think not just what this first bit was like but what the second bit and the third bit was like, because it might be two years before they get approval for a permanent building.

Next year, you're entitled to more classrooms, because they have another intake and then you start to bring in specialised stuff like an area for computers. You're designing in your head and when you're driving along the road, you're thinking about all these things and then you put them on paper. When we got Department approval we had to employ architects and engineers to design the thing.

My remit for each school was the same in that I would work with the initial steering group and the development team to ascertain where would be the best location for the school. Then basically I followed a set strategy for the school development as follows: initial site search, school development with the Department of Education, procurement of the site, appointing a design team, school design, Department of Education approval, contract selection and approval for a contractor, overseeing the construction on the site, liaison with school governors and Principal, hand over and occupation by the school.

From a derelict hospital to an integrated school

I remember that Omagh was a difficult place to find a site. We found warehouses and a green field site but they weren't suitable. What turned up in Omagh was the old mental hospital, which was a five storey building. I did a survey of the building, spoke to the hospital people and they had a section of the building that was derelict and had been for some years. We wanted the ground floor and first floor which was a self-contained unit. Basically, I did a quick evaluation of the site, took the architect with me and we talked about it, how we could do it. Some of the classrooms were 60m² because they were a hospital ward at one time, so they had big rooms. We had to make a big room maybe do two things, a general classroom at this end and a music classroom at this end. We didn't get started 'till the 1st June and so we had only three months, but we knew what the enrolment was going to be and what accommodation they needed. We had to work flat out. Within a day or two of the school opening, another 10 children signed up, so we had 135. I don't remember the exact dates but I think it was about a week before the school actually opened the door that they were able to bring desks and chairs and all the other bits and pieces in. The teachers had to unpack them and get them all set out with their books and everything.

With Integrated College Dungannon, we had an awful job finding a site. Eventually we found a site which was owned by the local Gaelic Athletic Association (GAA) Club, and there were two or three tennis courts on it which they never used. We did a deal with the GAA to rent the tennis courts for a temporary school in mobiles. And we had a big problem with access. We had to make it bigger. When I say bigger, I mean bigger! There was a narrow lane up through a bank on the top. We had to take this lane, open it way out and there was a very tight schedule to get that done.

In Integrated College Dungannon we had to move from the GAA to another part of the town where we got a very good site. At that time they had had four years in temporary accommodation so we moved them out and cleared it.

The six day wonder

For New-Bridge College, we bought a site outside Loughbrickland. We got a site outside it that belonged to a farmer. We had a lot of problems because he wanted to sell the land for housing development which means the land is worth more. We had to meet him half way and eventually we got him to agree to it. We got on site about the 15th July and it was only when we got the levels sorted out that we could tell the mobile contractor what size and shape the buildings were and where they were going to sit. He had four weeks to finish the development of the site.

The Principal of the school went off on holiday and he said, 'I look forward to seeing my school when I come back.' I said, 'Dead on, Peter, have a great holiday!' He came back on the 10th August and there were no buildings on the site. He blew his top. I said, 'Peter, don't worry, your school will be here.' In a short time. He came from Belfast and drove past every night: no change, because the mobile man was making the building. The school was scheduled to open on the Tuesday. He drove past the site the previous Tuesday and what was on site? Nothing. He rang me and he said, 'Lawrence, I am not happy, my Board of Governors, our steering group aren't happy and the Chair is talking to Michael Wardlow.' I said, 'I told you, you'll have a school. That's all you need to know, you'll have a school.' So on the Friday night he drove past the school and there was nothing on site. On Saturday morning at 6am, 10 lorries and three cranes arrived and he came on to the site on Monday morning at 8 o'clock to see what was happening. His buildings were ready. The power was on, we were finishing painting bits and pieces. 'You can move in, Peter, you've two days to open,' and the school opened. The six day wonder, I called it! This happened quite a lot!

The schools building development programme

At the same time as you're thinking about the new schools at Integrated College Dungannon and Newbridge you already know in August of '95 that somebody from North Coast in Coleraine, somebody from Oakwood and somebody from Slemish, want schools next year. As well as that, the three schools that you did in '95 need more buildings in '96. So that then becomes six schools in one year you're trying to develop. In August of '96 we knew that Malone College, Strangford College and Ulidia College had groups and wanted new schools the following year. So now you've nine groups floating about in your head. By the time you get to 1999, it's stacking up.

Every year it just kept going, I was known as the magician! What I found was that steering groups got to hear about this fella Lawrence Rowan and when he says he'll do something, he'll do it. I always pointed out to them; 'You might get your school at 12 o'clock midnight and you're opening at 8 o'clock in the morning but that's your problem, I've delivered!'

There's no point saying that if you're going to open a new school with 25 kids in P1 that you'll have it the 1st August and have a month to sort it out. Dream on, dear! It doesn't work that way all the time. You could have a month, you could have a day, but you will have a school. There's no doubt about that.

A different journey: Blackwater Integrated College

In about 2007 Blackwater College, which is now based in Downpatrick, took over the old Down Academy building. When I first went for approval for that school we couldn't find a site. Eventually we did find one, a big derelict hospital at Purdysburn. I made a few calls to the Hospital Services, got the right person; met him; he showed me the site; he didn't want the buildings; too much trouble; massive car park (football pitch size); perfect for us. We did all the development and all the stuff went through the Department for approval and in mid-August, the Department of Education said, 'No.'

There were various issues. The number of pupils they reckoned wasn't high enough, they were drawing pupils away from different areas, too far away. The steering group didn't know what to do. The IEF, after lots of discussions, said, 'We will fund this for the first year. Tell us, Lawrence how much it will be?' I can't remember but I think it was probably coming up £½ million, the development of the site. Time was so short we didn't know what we could do. We took an existing admin building and moved into it with a fortnight to go until the school opened. It was like 20, 23 hour working for about seven or eight days to get this into shape. Then the second year came along and they went back to the Department of Education with new proposals, new enrolment figures, much higher than the first year. All was looking positive and the Department said, 'No. We want you to show us three years before we'll approve the school.'

We thought the school was going to close and they were trying all avenues of private finance, everything they could think of. At the end of July the IEF said, 'Right, we will fund it but we're only giving you half a million. Nothing more, nothing less.' So we had to create a school for around 100 pupils literally within two to three weeks. I had a meeting onsite and I drew up my own plan in my head of what I wanted. I could have put it anywhere, it doesn't matter. I needed so many classrooms, an office, a store room, a toilet block which had to be specially made because there were no other toilets available. I think about the 8th August, I had the builder, the architect and the engineers there and I said, 'Right, you need to cut tracks at the back of the building, run the services down, electric, water and waste. The toilet block at the very end, the manhole is there. Just run it all into it, it's acceptable.' They started getting their plans very quickly drawn to do that. I told the mobile contractor, 'I need those buildings and I want them here in a week.' And he said, 'No hope. You've no hope.' I said, 'Well, I know another contractor who will do it.' His next comment was, 'We'll be here on Monday week with the buildings.' They had to go and find good quality second hand buildings, I wouldn't take anything less. The buildings arrived onsite on a Thursday, the school moved in Saturday, Sunday and Monday and school opened on Tuesday.

Later on they got approval to move into the old Down High School, or Down Academy in Downpatrick which was an existing secondary level school. We only had minimal work to do to it and it's still here today.

The red peg

The Principal of Blackwater was Olwen Griffith and she was appointed Vice Principal at Ulidia Integrated College down in Carrickfergus in their second year. The first year Ulidia got four mobiles, the second year they got another six. The Principal, Eugene Martin, was away on holiday and Olwen was onsite every day pestering, 'Where's the building? Where's this? Where's that?' I said, 'Olwen, it's coming, you know.' Another six day wonder happened. The school opened the second phase and hunky dory. I was then nicknamed Lawrence of Arabia!

Ulidia College was a three-year phased development. Now this is a true story. Eugene Martin loves the sea. When he first looked at the site and we were putting temporaries in, we walked up onto the main site and he said, 'I would love to look out at that view there, out to where the sea is.' I said, 'Would you?' I says, 'Well, tell me where you want to sit.' And he had a good look and he says, 'I fancy my desk here, I can see straight through the window.' I got a timber peg and I put the timber peg in the ground and I told the fella to paint it

Ulidia Integrated College.

red and he did. I said, 'Nobody moves that peg.' The day he moved into his office, the peg was in the floor. We took it out and filled the floor.

From mobiles to permanent buildings

Spires Integrated College had two years in mobiles and then we moved them into the first phase of the new building. Most schools wouldn't have had their permanent building until their fourth year, sometimes fifth, but that would be rare. For Millennium I drove up and down the Saintfield Road for a month. I sent the solicitor a map and I mark on it an 'X' there. I say, 'Who owns that?' And he goes through Land Registry and says, 'That belongs to Joe who lives next door.' So I went next door and said, 'I am interested in buying your site, would you interested in selling it?' 'What for?' I said, 'A school, an integrated school.' He says, 'Aye.' So I put the solicitors in touch, let them talk about it. He had gates across the road he wanted fitted and access sorted out for him, which we did. There was £300,000 for breaking out rock, so his £100 or £200 didn't matter, you know. The school is built on the side of a hill of solid rock so that was a big job to excavate. Millennium was two years in a temporary house down in Newtownbreda and then they had two years in that temporary building while we built first phase up on this rocky hill.

Really it was a miracle that some of these schools actually happened. The momentum was at fever pitch for 10 years and we went from having 22 schools in 1995 to having 65 now.

I enjoyed my 15 years working in NICIE, the staff were great, the boss was great, and basically 99% of the schools were first class. Whenever I first started in NICIE, there only were, I think, six staff and one of the early conversations I had with Michael was over a long coffee. Michael's job, from the point of view of the Board of Directors was to restructure NICIE for what was going to happen in the future. They knew we were going to grow dramatically over 15 years, the organisation was going to go bang! At the height of my career, there were 36 staff and that included communications and all the different teams, you know. Everybody worked well together, young, middle aged and old, it didn't matter whether you were a Chief Executive or whoever you were.

Alan Smith is a founder parent of Mill Strand Integrated Primary School and has been involved in Integrated Education for over 30 years.

My name is Alan Smith, I'm a university professor at Ulster University. Since 1999, I've held the UNESCO Chair at the University. I grew up in East Belfast and didn't really know many Catholics, maybe one or two other Catholics in our street. That would have been the late '50s and early '60s. I was brought up to think of Catholics and Protestants as antagonistic towards each other.

It was really by going to a school outside my neighbourhood that my world began to expand a little bit. It brought me into contact with people from other communities but also different levels of society in terms of socio-economic background. It was all to do with the 11+. Because of that I went to a grammar school in Holywood. I was brought up on the Newtownards Road and the nearest grammar schools were either in the city centre or in Holywood. That began to expand my world a little bit and later when I went to the University of Ulster in Coleraine, that was taking me further away from home and meeting other people. That's where I met my wife to be, Elaine, who was studying French and Spanish there and ended up teaching French and Spanish for most of her career.

We met at university, we went out for a long time, probably six or seven years, and I would say one of the reasons that we went out for a long time and didn't get married, was anxiety of how our parents might react because she was from a Catholic family in North Belfast. I think part of people's biography is that if you get into that kind of a relationship then you start to think about the type of education you want to have for your own family.

Far from home

Our initial reaction, whenever we graduated from University in the late '70s, when the conflict was still quite bleak here, was not to move back to Belfast. We applied for jobs and ended up teaching in Zimbabwe for three years. We went there in 1981 and we ended up helping set up a new school there, shortly after independence. Robert Mugabe had just come into power, there was great optimism. He was making the right noises in terms of not nationalising all the businesses and there was a big commitment to expand education. Particularly for black Zimbabweans because up until then, a few years schooling was what most black Zimbabweans would have had.

Elaine and I worked in a school which had 1,500 pupils, but there were only 16 classrooms. We taught in a shift system, so-called 'hot seating' where half the school would go in the morning, half the school would go in the afternoon. That was a very formative experience for us, I think. We were far away from home, we were on our own in a society which had actually just come through a bloody war. We had a mix of international teachers who were there along with local teachers and Mugabe welcomed us all to help with the expansion of the education system and announced that he was very committed

North Coast
Integrated College.

to reconciliation between the black and white population. I'd never really heard the term reconciliation before.

Over those few years, we were in a strange position in that society, we were neither part of the former white Rhodesian population who socialised around the country club nor were we really part of the black Zimbabwean population living in very dense housing close to the school that we worked in. We would go to the beer hall and have a few drinks but, you know, we didn't have a common past so there was only so much we could share. So we were kind of in the middle of these two communities and treated with suspicion, certainly by the white Rhodesian community as why we would come and work in this new Zimbabwe. We worked there for a few years but a couple of things happened; one, our eldest daughter Christine was born there in 1984 and she was the only white baby born in the hospital. I remember the nurses coming and asking me, 'Do you think she has a little bit of jaundice?' And I said, 'I don't know, eh, this is our first child, I don't know what colour she's supposed to be,' and they said, 'Well, we don't know what colour she's supposed to be either, because we're used to delivering black babies.' So they said, 'Well, we'll put her out in the sun for a while and see if that works.'

I think once our first child was born then we began to feel a bit a bit more of a pull back towards home and, you know, proud to show her off to grandparents, but also we did have concerns about healthcare there, having to take medicines to prevent malaria and this kind of thing.

Coming back to Northern Ireland

So we eventually came back to Northern Ireland in 1984 and again, rather than come back to Belfast, we moved to Portstewart which is where we had been to university together. I managed to get a job eventually in the university as a researcher in a what for then was quite an unusual multi-disciplinary research centre called the Centre for the Study of Conflict. Interestingly, the job that I had when I was first appointed was to carry out research into education programmes that were bringing schools together, an inter-school links type programme, a bit like what some people would now call Shared Education. But this was 35 years ago. But the research job also gave me an opportunity to find out more about this new phenomenon that was happening in Belfast around the idea of integrated schooling.

We were away when Lagan College opened in 1981, and we came back in 1985 whenever Hazelwood College had just opened. I made a contact with Tony Spencer who was an academic, a sociologist based at Queen's University at that time. He had set up the Belfast Trust for Integrated Education (BELTIE) and I was very much convinced by Tony's analysis, that it's not just about bringing children together, it's about actually creating new institutions that people have joint responsibility for, there's an integrated workforce, it's about teachers as well as children and ancillary staff. It's also about the governance

Mill Strand IPS
'The Voyage' 20th Anniversary
celebration.

and having joint management of schools. I think that's where sometimes in these debates about Shared and Integrated Education things get lost a little bit. It's great having children mixing but it's also something more than that. It's about collective ownership of schools and us taking on this shared responsibility for children's education.

Our second daughter was born in 1986, and by that stage we had begun to think about where will they go to school? Like most couples from different backgrounds it's a difficult choice. Our fears at the time, our anxieties were, that if we sent our child to a state school then Elaine's parents might be offended, because they were committed Catholics. At the same time, my family might not understand if I were sending our child to a Catholic school. So it seemed like an attractive option to explore the possibility of setting up an integrated school ourselves.

I remember at the time also going down and meeting someone called Belinda Loftus and interviewing her about her motivations for getting involved in setting up an integrated school. Well, it seemed to me that her motivation was the fact that she came from outside this society, she wasn't from Northern Ireland. I've often thought about what are people's motivations for getting involved in Integrated Education and obviously people who are of different denominations or those from outside who see our separate school system for the strange system it is. The people that I didn't understand fully

and I've great admiration, are those who didn't need to make this choice. People like my colleagues, Derek and Dot Wilson. They're very committed, but they come from Presbyterian backgrounds, both from the same sort of background. They didn't need to stick their head above the parapet at all and yet they did.

So in many respects I have a lot more admiration for those people because they didn't need to do it, they could have just conformed, shall we say. And also those who are very strong in their Catholic faith, again could have just sent their children to the local Catholic school and follow that sort of line of least resistance for them. I think many of them are the unsung heroes in terms of taking that risk or making that commitment whereas people like Elaine and I, in a sense, our motivation was very pragmatic. It was about finding a shared space for our children where they could be educated with people from all backgrounds.

The first meeting

The initial steps for us were to try and draw up short list of people we knew who might be interested in an integrated school. The first meeting we had was in our house in early 1986 and essentially it was to test the water. It was a mixture, there were probably about three couples that were the same as ourselves, and we obviously tried to think of people with

Mill Strand IPS
'The Voyage' 20th Anniversary
celebration.

children the same age and therefore were having to make choices soon. But there were some other people who were not necessarily in that category, but they seemed the sort of people that might be open to exploring ideas such as this.

We just met sitting on cushions on the floor in our front room. We didn't live in a big house, and it was more or less me saying, 'Look, I've been finding out about integrated schools being set up and I am just sharing what information I have about the process.' Asking how many people would be interested in exploring this further, explaining that maybe we would need to expand the group a little bit and think about the kind of skills or experience we might need, but also then the idea of going to a public meeting in the area and trying to gauge the level of support, and also trying to think about where we could get a little bit of seed funding.

It was at the second or third meeting when I invited Joe Mulvenna who was the Development Officer for the Belfast Trust for Integrated Education (BELTIE). He said, 'Have the public meeting and I'll help if you need someone to come and talk in a bit more detail about how the Hazelwood Schools were set up, or what process the others are going through.' And that's what happened and to be honest, that was the start of a fairly intense relationship because I was a kind of co-ordinator for the development of Mill Strand and Joe was supporting Hazelwood Schools, but also trying to support the expansion of other schools in other areas.

That was the beginning probably of about nine or 10 years of my life. I became completely absorbed and overtaken by Integrated Education and the development of Integrated Education in many forms. I think for me, I learned more, I got more out of the involvement in Integrated Education than all that amount of time and commitment I put in it. It helped me develop as a person.

The challenges of getting support from all sections of the community

The old thorny issue about how you deal with religious education always came up but I think the fact that Dot and Derek worked in an ecumenical environment in Corrymeela, they were able to reassure about that. We weren't starting completely from scratch because some of these things had been thought through. We did realise that it would be very difficult to get support from the Catholic Church. Tony Farquhar was the chaplain in the university and he married us in the Catholic Church in Portstewart, which I was happy to do and he was happy to do the service and I thought Elaine's parents would be pleased. He was older than me but he was still a fairly youngish university chaplain, and seemed to have quite progressive ideas. Elaine and I, after having been away, we wrote a letter explaining we had been away to Zimbabwe, had a child, and came back, and we reminded him about the

Mill Strand IPS
Class of '87.

wedding, the reception, all the rest but that we were now exploring this idea of creating an integrated school. He just never replied to it, you know. I don't know if we were hurt or angry or what, but we were probably naïve in thinking that because we'd known him on a personal level or because he had married us that he might feel some responsibility to support us in how we wanted to educate our children. But at that time, I don't think the Catholic Church was very open at all to the idea of Integrated Education.

I remember one other person who was in the group, he worked in a local Catholic secondary school and again was very open to this idea and progressive and said this is the way forward and all the rest of it. But as we got closer to the idea of a public meeting and he spoke with his colleagues in the school, he realised he had to withdraw from the group. He just didn't feel that he could cope with the pressure.

Jim Cavalleros was a quite senior person in town planning, so in terms of identifying potential sites for the school and subsequently helping with negotiations over purchase and all that kind of thing, Jim was great. There was Kieran Mullan who was an architect and there was Eavan White, a dentist from a well-known and respected Catholic family in the neighbourhood, and to have people with that sort of credibility was important.

It was a nerve-wracking time. I think this is where Joe Mulvenna's support was extremely important, because we were putting our heads above the parapet in the community that we were living in. We needed the support of someone like Joe coming from Belfast, to support us and say, 'You know, have you thought how you would respond to these kind of questions that you might get from the audience? They will ask what are you going to do about religious education, they will ask where's the money coming from, they will ask when is this going to open, they will ask will it have a school uniform, how are you going to prepare children for the 11+, all these things.'

Joe was great at preparing us for the public meeting, but it was still a nerve-wracking thing to rent out the leisure centre in Coleraine and put a notice in the local paper saying there will be a meeting in Coleraine Leisure Centre on such and such a date and time. It was winter and we were wondering if anyone would turn up. I remember Joe had little tricks, one of these was just to put out 30 chairs and then as more people come in we'd have to get more chairs and then that will generate the sensation, 'Oh, there's not enough chairs for everybody here, so interest is high.' Rather than putting out 100 chairs and only 30 people come and see it half empty, you know, a small detail. We ended up with around 200 people turned up that night and not as aggressive as we expected. There were some who put the view that community relations are fine here, why do you think we need an integrated school? The schools here are great, we all co-operate very well, we get on great, this is an insult, you're insulting us by saying that you can't get on, this kind of thing. But we came away from that meeting on quite a high because there was a lot of nervous energy leading up to it and then you are speaking to people who you know from the community. It was more positive than negative, the feeling of people saying, 'Yes, this is good, go for this,' and we had sheets, on Joe's advice, to get people's details, a contact number and if they have any children. Then you start producing a newsletter, making sure people are kept informed, keep the momentum going, have another meeting in a month's time, elect people onto an interim steering group, that would potentially become the Board of Governors of the school when it started to get formal.

It was certainly less than a year, I think, going from nothing, from one meeting of 10 people to opening the school with a building and staff appointed. As I said, the skills I learned along the way, not just in terms of interpersonal skills but what I learned about people's fears and anxieties. I learned an awful lot about people's expectations for the education of their children, in faith terms as well. I don't think I was quite as secularly minded as I probably would be now. This Christian ethos debate was also a central point right from the start and also through the public meetings. Is it a Christian school or not? The debate continued through into the Northern Ireland Council for Integrated Education (NICIE) Charter, you know that integrated schools are Christian schools or broadly Christian schools welcoming all. There

certainly were people who turned up to public meetings who were very committed to more secular community type schools, but I don't think it was the majority view.

I suppose from an early stage I realised that my compromise was that even though I would have preferred something more secular, that for most people, that was still an important dimension, and particularly for the Catholic parents because they were already stepping away from the expectations of their family and community. I came to the view that for them it was a big step even to become associated with an integrated school. I think it was the same for many of the Protestant parents who still wanted their Religious Education, and would there be Bible study or if they will learn prayers? I think probably there were misconceptions in Protestant parents' minds that there would be a lot of Catholic religious ritual going on in the school, because of the need to meet Catholic parents' expectations. I think gradually as the school got established, they worked their way through these things. They negotiated with the local parish priest to have a First Communion for some of the first children, this was a big breakthrough and as in many other schools, a lot of the Protestants, the whole school community went to support.

I think the occasion of First Communion is obviously a happy event for the children in those families but I think the fact that the church had a separate ceremony was, again, disappointing in that it was saying, 'Well, yes, these children can be confirmed but we're not confirming them with the other Catholic children in the parish.' I felt for the Catholic parents on those occasions.

Sharing the learning, spreading the word

At one point, through my involvement with Mill Strand, I used to go and speak at meetings, public meetings in other places, in Enniskillen and when they opened a school in Omagh. This kind of handing the baton, where a parent who had gone through setting up a school would then go to the next and speak at the public meetings. I think we did that as well, we had someone from Hazelwood, who had already gone through the process and was able to say this can all be worked out. I think there was what these days we would call co-produced knowledge and there was an accumulation of knowledge which was passed on from school to school: you'll see a similarity even in the format of documentation, the legal documents that were used were very often templates from the previous ones or the newsletters or, you know, many of these things. The communication of that knowledge through open meetings where people could say, 'It's not just hypothetical, here's someone who has just done this in such and such a place and they'll talk about how they dealt with that.'

Other things I learned and helped me greatly in my career and professionally was certainly the fundraising side of things. What I'd found out was that we had an open door with the Rowntree Foundation and the Nuffield Foundation who were the initial supporters and there was personal contact there with the Assistant Director. We had to write a proposal but it wasn't a bureaucratic process. These were bodies that have trustees who make decisions at their meetings based on a proposal that they receive to complete a piece of work or support a piece of development. The time involved in actually developing relationships and talking people through the story of why we're doing and what we're trying to achieve, was very important, I think. Not just for the people who were the employees of these trusts and foundations but also the trustees themselves.

Then there was the need to begin co-ordinating. The trusts and foundations were beginning to get many different applications from different groups and new schools that were emerging. So this is where the idea of a more co-ordinated approach came from. So rather than schools competing with each other to put applications into these mainly English foundations, what we were being encouraged to do was to come together, identify our overall need and come to some discussion and agreement between ourselves about what we would ask for and what our orders of priority would be.

Then once we began having those meetings, a treasurers' working group (as it was called then) was established, which was essentially the precursor to the formation of NICIE. Anthony Tomei from the Nuffield Foundation said, 'Well, now that you've identified your needs, what I'll do is go around all the various foundations, Halley Stewart, Sainsburys, the Wates Foundation etc., and ask if they would be interested in a meeting to hear about Integrated Education and to hear about what you're trying to achieve and what the financial needs are.'

Myself and Joe Mulvenna then went over to the Nuffield Foundation. Anthony set up meetings for us to meet about 10 foundations over the course of two days. That was tremendous training for someone like me who ended up going into research, where part of my whole career has been built on raising external funding for research. You need to demonstrate that you understand what your needs are, that you're going through various numbers of processes; legal, financial, in terms of governance, all these things are in place but very often the thing that made the difference or seemed to make more of an impact were the personal stories that we would be able to tell. I mean, about why people are involved in Integrated Education, what is it about these schools where parents have decided to come together, the humanity of it. It was about making the case and convincing people that it's worth spending money on this, and if we got enough critical mass that would eventually force the system to change.

Although that hasn't happened to the degree that we would have hoped, within a decade, during the '80s it went from Lagan College, one school, the two Hazelwood Schools and Forge, so that was two primary and two post-primary schools in Belfast and then the Newcastle school outside Belfast, Mill Strand and Banbridge opened in '87, within the first 10 years.

The political context and the Education Reform Order

By the end of the 1980s, the idea of the Education Reform Order wasn't particular to Northern Ireland, but there was a new category of school, which would make schools more independent of local education authority control, because in England, local education authorities had always been quite politically on the left. Now, whenever you had a Conservative government, and particularly one with Margaret Thatcher in charge, they wanted to break that control that Labour had on the governance of schools. So they introduced a new category of school called Grant Maintained Integrated (GMI) Schools which would mean that schools could be autonomous. They would get their money directly from the Department of Education. They didn't have to go through a local education authority.

This could have been potentially damaging, I suppose, for the development of integrated schools, because in Northern Ireland, GMI status was a kind of variation of that. Funding came straight from the Department to create these new schools, independent of local education authorities.

This is one of the frustrations about the way Integrated Education has developed for me in that it has been contained in a way, compartmentalised as a sector and contained, rather than seen as a catalyst for change to the whole system. I mean, you can't anticipate these things from the outset and, obviously, whenever you're just growing and you've only a handful of schools, the idea of being a sector is maybe even quite attractive because it gives you more representational rights, it gives you a sense that you've arrived and you're recognised and that sort of thing. But I think ultimately what it has done is further fragment the education system and allowed what I would call a segregationist view of society to kind of define you.

I'd always felt that was never the purpose; the purpose was to demonstrate that schools could operate on an all-inclusive basis and that it was a possibility for all schools in the society to move in that direction. The Minister of Education at the time was Brian Mawhinney. He was quite an outspoken person, and I think he was quite sympathetic to grammar schools. I think he liked the Lagan College model, which in a sense was all ability but it has a different demographic than the Hazelwood School in North Belfast. There's a complex kind of political dynamic at play there but in essence the 1989 Education Reform Order, partly because of Brian Mawhinney and the personality he was and maybe his own biography, he wanted to make a change, he wanted to say that we could fund these schools from the outset, that we would encourage them. We all knew there was a limit to the number of new schools you can build in a system where the population is declining. But there was direct rule at the time. I doubt whether the 1989 Reform Order that introduced support for Integrated Education would never have happened if there had been a local devolved assembly here.

The beginnings of a support body for Integrated Education

I think what happened then was the consultation on the 1989 Education Reform Order. We did get prior drafts of what would be in the Order. In those drafts there were some good news and there was also this clause which people were trying to make sense of which said that the Department of Education would be empowered to provide funding for a body to support the development of Integrated Education or something like that. Now that did spark off a debate within what you might call the broad movement, if there is such a thing. All Children Together (ACT) very much saw this, I think, as finally a sort of recognition. Basil McIvor was still alive at the time, he's a former Minister of Education from Northern Ireland, from the Unionist Party and I think they were probably seeing this as a possibility for ACT to become a sort of support body for the development of new integrated schools.

I don't think BELTIE were making the argument that they should be such a body, but what they were arguing was what actually happened, the formation of a more representative body of the current schools, and that's very much the line that Joe Mulvenna was encouraging the treasurers to take. He was facilitating the meeting of those treasurers to make their joint bids to the foundations.

Eventually, in the Order it was left that the government could have the statutory power to fund a body to support the development of Integrated Education. Meanwhile through the discussions in the treasurers' group, we eventually realised that we just go ahead and form this more democratically representative body. So that's how there was agreement amongst the treasurers, let's just form the body and make it a council for Integrated Education. I don't think we had any assurances that it would get funded by government. NICIE was created and we were trying to force government's hand in a sense by saying, 'Look we've created this body and you have a clause in your new legislation.' We formalised NICIE and created it with broadly democratic representation. It was quite cumbersome because of all the schools that were around at the time and everybody wanted to be on the Council. We moved quite quickly and as part of that process, it was Tony Spencer who wanted us to create a Statement of Principles. So that meant bringing all the schools together to try and create a common Statement of Principles that would represent the values of Integrated Education.

Well, because of this, the same debates again emerged that everybody had gone through in their own school context. Is this a Christian school? What do we mean by a Christian school? What about people of other faiths, what about people of none? There was a whole debate about child centred commitment and academic selection. Those would be the three things that would all come up through debates in Integrated Education and everybody had worked through them and realised, 'Well, you can't resolve these things on paper and legislation.' At the end of the day, you go through very long discussions into the night and you end up kind of compromising, everybody compromises in some way. I also think that people realise that the important thing is how it works in practice, in the classroom, in the schools and through the people you appoint. Working out these issues in practice is a difficult challenge for Principals but that was because people were passionate about what they felt about how their children were to be educated.

So there was a person called Andrew Phillips, who was the solicitor for the Nuffield Foundation and later became appointed to the House of Lords. He flew over for a weekend and we went on a residential to the Ulster People's College in Belfast. We had people from all the different schools and we talked through the Statement of Principles, which I think is still the same. Eventually we all signed up, named our representatives and elected the first Chair. I was an interim Chair before that and we secured funding to employ staff. Kevin Lambe who is now the Principal of the integrated school in Newcastle was one of the first Development Officers.

A life committed to Integrated Education

A good part of life has been dedicated to the development of Integrated Education, running around getting furniture, finding offices with cheap rents to set up new organisations and securing funding for the staff to move things forward. Perhaps the biggest disappointment is the way in which Integrated Education has been contained as a sector. If there had been strategies or ways to have avoided that I think I would have followed them. At times I've even said, 'Look, would it not be far better just to stop calling these integrated schools, to do something unexpected or unconventional to try and get away from this mind set?' But I think the point is, once people have invested time and energy in creating a school in their own community, that's what they want to see grow and flourish, and that's rightly where their preoccupation is and why they can become defensive.

The legacy of Integrated Education

My children have grown up with a value for education. Obviously if you see your parents setting up a school, you'd probably get the impression that education is important. I must admit I haven't talked to them a lot about what they feel. I've always thought, 'Well, if they want to tell me what they think their education was like or what it did for them then they will tell me.' It wasn't all plain sailing. I mean, they did sometimes have teachers that they didn't gel with. I do think it gave them a freedom both in terms of their own identity development. I don't think that has necessarily come from Elaine and myself. I think part of it has been seeing the way in which their schools have had to create space for people to discover what they want to be. I think it has made them comfortable with their friendships and their relationships, I think they're quite inclusive in their outlook. They've both done well in terms of their careers and academically.

Probably some of the legacies were that whenever my eldest daughter was in the Religious Education class, I remember her saying, 'I've been asked to do a project on the church. We were all told to go off and find out information about a church.' This was quite a religious RE teacher who assumed everybody went to church. And our daughter said, 'Well, I don't go to a church, I don't have a church, what am I going to do?' And I said, 'Well, have you talked to the teacher and explained that?' And she said, 'Yes,' she had and her teacher said, 'Well, sure, you must have been, where were you baptised?' And Christine said, 'I wasn't baptised, I was born in Africa and my parents didn't do it there.' She had this kind of conversation and at the end the teacher had said to her, 'Well, sure, just pick a church, any church,' and Christine says, 'But I don't want to just pick a church.' I said, 'Well, do you know what the alternative is? Have you ever heard of Humanism as a belief system? Why don't you go back to your teacher and say that you want to find out more about that sort of belief system?' So that was her way of dealing with that.

I'm not an aggressive secularist. Faith clearly matters to people, but I do like there being space for people of no faith to be able to say what they believe. I think there were benefits for my children in that they obviously had some freedom that perhaps I did not have, that I wouldn't have remembered from schooling, where not joining in prayers or singing hymns or some of these religious practices in school, it just wasn't an option you know.

A tremendously exciting and exhausting journey

It's been a journey of growth, tremendously exciting and exhausting. For me personally, as a family I think it just became part and parcel of our life, as you would expect. If you think about it, I don't know what anxieties people might have about marrying between denominations or faiths or whatever, but certainly the fact that we were involved in such a committed way in Integrated Education has probably brought us much closer together. Our relationship has benefitted, my personal experience has developed, I have learned an awful lot. But I think, in an unexpected way, it just helped me in my career as well because so many of the things I learned are things then that have subsequently applied in my professional life.

I've good memories and we still have good friends and you go through these journeys in life with people in different times, different places and, you know, they always kind of bond you together. I've always argued, 'Why should parents be expected, particularly if they're not very privileged backgrounds, don't have much time or money or space or whatever, why would you expect them to start a school for their child on top of all that?' I've always berated the government for not being more proactive in providing leadership in promoting greater provision for Integrated Education. But on the other hand, I must say that once you've gone through a process of self-help for the benefit of your own children, the level of commitment and the satisfaction you get out of it is life changing.

Jane Stewart is a former pupil at Mill Strand Integrated Primary School, Portrush.

I've worked for 10 years or so within Higher Education and having gone to university myself, I have a particular interest in education and an awareness of the importance of education and the difference that a good education can make, not just academically but socially.

I went to an integrated school because it was a new school in our area. It was a very exciting project. I was educated in a school in the next town because I have a physical disability and that was seen to be the best school to meet my needs at that time. But my mother wanted me to move to a school in the local community and when Mill Strand Integrated School was developing and was going to open, she saw that as a great opportunity for me to grow up with children from our local town. My mum is a teacher and a trained nurse and I came from a mixed marriage as well, so the idea of an integrated school both from a religious point of view and from a disability point of view appealed to her. I moved to Mill Strand Integrated School into P3 in September 1987 and I stayed at Mill Strand until the end of my primary education.

Early memories

My very earliest memory was the meeting that my mum and I had with the first headmaster. It must have been the summer before the school opened and I can remember us going up to the building, which was an old house. We went into the headmaster's office and had a discussion about my possible transition to the school that September. I can remember being very excited that I was moving schools and there was a really positive vibe. I also remember being really excited about not having to wear a uniform. I think around that time, I got to meet my teacher and I got to see the classrooms and so on. My first teacher was Mrs Grace Doone, she taught me for the first two years at Mill Strand.

I was part of the first intake of children when the school opened in September 1987. There was only a handful of pupils and the classes were amalgamated to accommodate us all within what was a very small building. The school numbers increased rapidly and there was a new build and an extension on to the school and I can remember all of that happening. I can remember us all having our photograph taken at the front of the school. There was a new sign and we were all sat on the green on the hill, all of us and the teachers, and we had our photograph taken.

I was very aware that it was an integrated school and that was something that I think we were all very aware of. Although I was only six coming seven, we as children must have absorbed the conversations and the discussions that were happening around us. We were obviously told about how special and unique the school was, what it was about and the movement that it was a part of. I remember that we knew that Mill Strand was different. We knew it was an integrated school,

Mill Strand IPS
'The Voyage' 20th Anniversary
celebration

we knew it was about bringing people together, it was about religion and it was about bringing people from all different backgrounds together. We knew that from the outset.

Many of the friends that I made at Mill Strand are still my friends today, many of us have gone off to university in different places and worked elsewhere. It's strange because so many people have come back to the local area and their children are now at Mill Strand, our children are at Mill Strand. My friends that went on to secondary school with me, one of my friends at university, even, we all started out Mill Strand School.

Slightly different challenges

The challenges that I faced when I went to Mill Strand were probably slightly different to the majority of the children that were at the school because I have a physical disability. I came from a mixed marriage and although our town was divided along the lines of religion in terms of the local schools and churches and so on, I probably was not as aware of that as I would have been of divisions, segregation and exclusion along the lines of disability. I was very aware that I went to school outside of our local town because I had a disability and that's where I should go. Although it was a mainstream school, it had provision for children with various disabilities built within it.

So the barriers that I faced would have been more likely to do with my disability and the physical challenges of being included and accessing normal social opportunities. That said, I had a mum who was very passionate and very good at making sure that I was included. She brought me along to all kinds of things, whether I wanted to go or not! To make sure that I had the same opportunities to socialise and make friends as other children. I went to Bunnies and Brownies and different youth groups and just anything that was on at that time. I was very aware of my own difference and how that impacted on my inclusion, not just within schools and education, but in relation to social opportunities within the community.

I do remember Mill Strand trying to adjust what was essentially an old house to make it inclusive of my needs. It was far from accessible for most children, never mind one with a physical disability but I was educated at a time when there was no legislation that protected the rights of disabled children. So any adjustments that were made were based on the goodwill of the school. And in Mill Strand, I can never remember it being a problem. I can remember the adjustments that they made. The caretaker made me a step within the toilets so that I was able to access the toilet and the bathroom and sinks and so on. The teachers lifted me and carried me up and down the stairs. As far as I remember, I had a normal desk and chair and I think probably the approach was that we will cross each bridge as we come to it.

The ethos of integration was the backdrop to everything in Mill Strand

There are so many stories that stand out in my memory of being educated at Mill Strand but probably towards the end we had a teacher for our Primary 6 and Primary 7 year who was very enthused by nature and creative writing. He had come from a school in England which we all thought was amazing, he had lots of stories to tell us and we loved hearing them! He was an incredible teacher and had so much wisdom and knowledge that he tried to pass on to us. He took us to the cliff tops, along the cliff path walks and taught us about all kinds of things to do with nature and plants and wildlife and sea life. He incorporated that as well into lessons about creative writing, particularly poetry. He was passionate about poetry and we would have written poems literally while sitting on the edge of the cliff!

This teacher just brought me along with the rest of the class. There were no differences made. By that stage in my journey I had a wheelchair that I used for these trips outside of school. My friends would have pushed me in my chair and when we got to the cliff tops if the chair couldn't go I would have got out of the chair. I would have walked along the path or whatever and joined in with the rest of my friends. The disability didn't come into it for this teacher: he treated me the same as other children.

We loved it. We were educated at a time when there was probably much more freedom for the school to diversify the learning experience for us, if you want to put it that way. But Mill Strand School even now, do have an outside classroom tradition, so that has been embedded within the culture of the school.

The impact of Integrated Education

The incorporation of the ethos of integration into the day to day life of the school was something that I feel was always there. We were very much aware of integration and what it meant for us, what it meant for the wider community and society as a whole. It was the backdrop to everything that happened within the school. I can remember visiting different churches, we celebrated different religious days, we as a school. Integration was always on the agenda, always discussed. It was always something that was celebrated and we were very proud of it.

I cannot underestimate the influence that attending an integrated school, specifically Mill Strand School, has had on my personal development. I think education is fundamental to every child's personal development and their long-term outcomes as an adult. I believe I had first class quality education, not just academically but socially and emotionally and in every way. They took an holistic approach to education.

It was about making Northern Ireland a better place

My friends and I are very proud to say that we went to Mill Strand School. We knew we were part of something different. Some of my friends' parents actually founded the school. So it's not surprising that we were very acutely aware of integration and what it meant. It was along the lines of religion in the early days. It was about Catholics and Protestants coming together, it was about making Northern Ireland a better place.

I suppose for me now, as an adult looking back, for me personally the disability element of my identity at Mill Strand was really important for me and how I viewed myself then and also in the future. At Mill Strand, I was just allowed to be me.

My son has a physical disability as well and he's a part-time wheelchair user too. Saul had very complex health needs when he was born and we weren't sure what his long term outcome might be in terms of his health, his ability, but I was always sure that he would be educated at Mill Strand. That was very important to me and to us. I believe that the Integrated Education movement provides an excellent framework for facilitating disabled childrens' inclusion within mainstream settings, because that ethos is there of equality, tolerance and acceptance.

My son has a Statement of Special Educational Needs and he has been born in an era where the language that we use to talk about disabled children has very much changed from the language that we would have used when I was going to school. How we do things subsequently has changed, however there is still very much an embedded special or segregated education system for disabled children within Northern Ireland.

So Saul is also now at Mill Strand in Year 5 and this year his teacher is Mrs Doone who first taught me back in 1987. He has a Statement of Special Educational Needs which protects his right for reasonable adjustments to be made to enable him to access the curriculum. We were kind of 'winging it' back in 1987 and hoping for the best! Saul had his transition to primary school very much managed and has had a proliferation of professionals involved in that process, making sure that his needs are best met. The upshot of that is that the school is inclusive of his needs and indeed those of other disabled children in the future.

Children of difference

I think the greatest gift that Mill Strand gave me was the opportunity to build resilience. They gave me so many opportunities just to get on with it and to do it my way, to problem solve and to overcome the challenges myself, with help from the teachers and my friends.

Saul knows he is in an integrated school and I have taught him that this means that everybody be educated together, and that is probably the disability dimension coming into things again. He's very aware that at Mill Strand children come from all backgrounds, religions, abilities and cultures and that would be something that I would talk about and make a point of talking about with him. I do that to give him perspective about his own situation; so that he knows that he's not the only child who is different, there are other children who are different in other ways. We have lots of those conversations. He is attracted to children who are different and he attracts children who are different. They feel comfortable with him and likewise him with them. So, that ethos of difference and diversity is something that he lives. Saul has broken down many barriers by just being who he is, which I hope will help pave the way for other disabled children.

Experiencing a mix of schools

I've been through Integrated Education myself and then I went to a secondary school that wasn't integrated. That was a huge contrast for me coming from Mill Strand. There wasn't an integrated college at that stage so many of us went to a local Catholic grammar school and whilst it was a fantastic school, I remember being acutely aware of the religious dimension.

Starting off in what would have been a Protestant state primary school, then moving to an integrated school,

Mill Strand IPS
with their ECO flag.

then a Catholic grammar school, I kind of experienced a mix of school settings. I think Integrated Education is the only way forward in Northern Ireland. As long as we have a system that's segregated along the lines of religion, disability, cultural difference, we are going to produce a segregated wider society. Education is more than an academic experience, it's a social experience producing the adults that are going to function and carry forward society. So for me, Integrated Education is the only way forward.

The future of Integrated Education

I think the integrated school movement and Integrated Education movement is going to be very much influenced by the wider political and social landscape within Northern Ireland and what happens there. It's going to take real fundamental and radical change to the education system to bring about integration for every single child within Northern Ireland anytime soon. There needs to be a mindset that is open and willing to change, that understands the social and cultural dynamics and role that education has to play in our society within Northern Ireland.

Integrated Education was essential to the core of who I am and how I view the world around me. It has provided me with a moral and social backdrop for everything else that has come after that experience. It provided a vehicle for me to be included through my education, right through to university and into an adult life. Teaching me valuable lessons in tolerance, acceptance and equality.

Michael Wardlow joined the Northern Ireland Council for Integrated Education (NICIE) as CEO in February 1995 and left in 2009. He is presently the Chief Commissioner of the Equality Commission for Northern Ireland.

Personal beginnings

I had just come back to Northern Ireland from Uganda in 1981 when Lagan had set up. I encountered the hunger strikes and Lagan emerging. There were really no integrated primary schools close to me so when my first child was born, although there was some talk of an integrated primary school around, I didn't know anything about it and it was only really when I started to research for the job in NICIE that I discovered more. I hadn't realised there were a few thousand people involved in Integrated Education. I thought this was a great idea so I applied for the position. That was really my journey. I believe that when you bring people together, and they journey together and you make that a safe place which challenges prejudice and stereotypes, they can ask questions. And I saw it work. This wasn't as if there was a worked out educational theory at that stage. I've always believed that if faith means anything it has to get its hands dirty. When I saw that integrated schools were essentially Christian in character, I felt that that's interesting. It is clear that Northern Ireland is a society that has a strong Christian basis in the sense that most people here have come through some church involvement, and that it is only in more recent years that we're having people from new communities coming into this place. When I started with NICIE in 1995 the number of people we had from other communities was very small and the conflict was still

going on. When I took over there were 23 schools, and when I left there were 62. We had a huge growth in Grant Maintained Integrated (GMI) schools. That was a period of huge growth and something like 18 of the 30 schools which opened in my time were grant maintained. So almost half the schools were parent driven and about half the schools were existing schools that transformed to integrated status. My experience over those 15 years was probably a fairly unique one because we had a building programme that probably spent £90 million in building new schools.

Identities and balance

In the 60s and 70s discrimination happened and it tended to revolve around people's perceived religion and culture, and in this place, ticking a box which indicates you are a Protestant or a Catholic is a proxy. It doesn't necessarily mean you go to church, it's a proxy for politics, it's a proxy for culture. We all know that if, for example, I tick a box marked Protestant, it doesn't mean I've ever attended a church. It means that my perceived community background is Protestant. Therefore, when people began to get the opportunity to say Protestant, Catholic or Other, some were saying Other because they actually genuinely did not have any faith whatsoever. Some people reacted against having to classify themselves at all. Some genuinely are in what we would call mixed marriages, probably about 5%, and yet 19% of people in the 2011 census stated that they were Other. And that's growing. It seems clear that many people don't want to be put in boxes any more but if we still want to know whether or not discrimination still takes place for Protestants and Catholics, then it's necessary to collect data. It's the same if you wanted to open a new integrated school; it was necessary to demonstrate that the integrated school had 30% of the minority tradition, Catholic or Protestant. The legislation doesn't actually state 30% minority, the legislation says roughly equal numbers of the two traditions. So the 1989 Education Order doesn't give us an actual percentage. It's the enabling letters that have come from the Department of Education that designated 30%. The percentage can be changed as they are not in primary legislation.

A theory of balance

Contact theory is the basis on which sharing in schools takes place. Such theory says that when two groups come together in regular contact in a safe environment that negative views towards the out-group can be moderated. Below about 30% of a minority, the group tends to be less robust and less vocal and it is for that minority I think that the figure of 30% was drawn. It wasn't just pulled out of the air. Research and contact theory says that this is a number at which people feel safe to express their difference to the out-group. The bigger question is why does the 30% have to be orange or green? The 30% could be other than the majority. This is something I started arguing probably in the year 2000. Why could the minority simply be 30% of everybody else? Once the majority gets more than 70% whatever your minority is they tend to be quieter. As long as you cap the majority at 70%, I don't see any reason why that shouldn't happen. Even in my time we had some schools which were approaching 30% Other. We were told those pupils were excluded, not even taken into consideration in working out whether you've got a minority of 30%. Now that never made sense to me. That meant the numbers were the more important thing than what was going on in the school, in other words it was just statistics. I welcome the fact we are now saying we are no longer simply a binary community, there is now a third community which is made up of a whole host of other communities. Integrated schools were established to allow Protestants and Catholics to be brought together in one school. If that's still the issue, our integrated schools should still be primarily concerned about orange and green. I think it has moved beyond that however, and that's an issue I raised in my doctorate, the question that if they're looking at integration in a broader sense, then you've got to look at the balance within a school beyond orange and green, and you've got to look at the curriculum. I think that's changed since my time.

Founding Parents
of Malone IC at their
10th Anniversary, 2007.

Grant Maintained Integrated openings

When I came in in 1995 there were already Erne and Shimna Colleges, which were the first time that two schools were coming forward in one year driven by parents saying they needed new schools. This caused the Department of Education a particular problem, because this was reactive, it wasn't planned. NICIE has never had a direct role in actively planning for integrated schools. NICIE always has responded to parental demand. That seems crazy and it has always been my view that this should never be the case. When I came in we had Erne and Shimna emerging. We had two sets of architects and two sets of builders about to build two separate schools and the Department declared that these schools should be erected as a core plus mobiles and that the Department would not be building permanent schools. It is my view that this was primarily a finance issue where DE felt that you can't just simply get a group of parents demanding a new school that would be very expensive, and the whole policy idea was that the growth for integration should come through controlled or transforming schools. When Brian Mawhinney became Minister of Education in 1989, it is clear what he expected would be that existing schools would transform, Protestant and Catholic. He never anticipated that there would be a majority of growth coming through parental demand and new builds. When Erne and Shimna came along, it caused problems for the

Department. They said all new builds from that point would be a core plus mobiles.

Grant Maintained Integrated expansion

Erne and Shimna were viable once the founding groups had proof of 60 students for the first year of the new school, and could show similar numbers for the following three years through consent forms signed by parents. I haven't seen anything that says that somehow in 1994 the spirit of Northern Ireland changed and everybody said, 'Lets live together and be happy.' I think that if that was the case for integrated schools, you would have seen the same demand for shared housing and shared stuff in other schools and that demand wasn't there. I think that what happened then was that until 1994 there had been a few new schools, about one a year, and suddenly two parent groups, one in Enniskillen and one in Newcastle, emerged. NICIE was beginning to become more vocal. I have no doubt about this, partly it was the ceasefires. In other words, people began to think maybe we can actually take this risk, maybe we can move forward. Partly it was the fact that we still had some money and drive within the Department of Education. Integrated Education was still something that could be actively promoted and I don't think anybody genuinely anticipated the growth we would have during this period. What happened the next

Slemish College.

year was that five schools came forward. Erne and Shimna began to be built, there was a lot of publicity around this, the ceasefire had its first year and NICIE began to have a serious outreach programme to say we've got to make a change, we can develop integrated schools. What happened then was as these parent groups came forward and we had Development Officers who went out and were brilliant. The Development Officers supported the parents through the development proposals. NICIE employed a Clerk of Works, Lawrence Rowan. We were able then to work through a process where I was able to get three banks to come together and allow us to borrow money if the school had conditional approval from the Department of Education.

For example, Dungannon Integrated College. A group of parents said they'd like an integrated school, and there were no schools in Dungannon that wanted to become integrated. So this group of parents said they would go out and get forms signed to demonstrate an interest in a new school and NICIE Development Officers worked with them. They got all the necessary forms signed up, showing a need for the next three years. People said, 'I want my child to go to that school.' It was necessary that the group made sure that 30% were from the minority community, in that case it was the Protestant tradition. The parents and NICIE filled in the development proposal, it was published and then went to the Department of Education and they then looked at it. They said this looked like a case which could go forward and gave it conditional approval.

How the finance worked

Once the parents had conditional approval, I could go to the bank and show the letter from the Department showing that the school would receive recurrent financial support for the next three years, and in three years' time, if the school was viable, the Department would take it over. The letter was effectively a letter of comfort for the banks. Based on that letter the bank then allowed me to go out and begin to build a temporary school. I was able to borrow money from the bank and pay builders to build it. The way it worked was a bit complex, NICIE borrowed the money and built a school. NICIE charged the school rent, which was exactly the same amount as the interest on the money NICIE had borrowed. NICIE used the rental income to pay the interest to the bank. The Department of Education paid the school rent, so they didn't pay NICIE and didn't pay the bank. So it was all perfectly legitimate. Therefore, I was building a school and the school cost a quarter of a million for the mobiles. The bank said, 'We'll lend you a quarter of a million and that will cost you £X in interest.' The school went to the Department and the Department paid them the same amount in rent, NICIE got the money and everybody was happy.

18 schools went through this system, through the 'club bank'. It was the first time this had ever happened. At one time I had on NICIE's account borrowings of £18million, where NICIE carried the entire risk. The Department had no risk at all. As the Accounting Officer acting on behalf of a charity that was a limited company with charitable status NICIE's board were taking so many risks. Consider that at one time there were five schools, and any one of them could've gone down in which case we would've been looking at being closed down as a charity because we were not liquid. The banks allowed me to have the money on the grounds that the Department of Education said on paper this school looks good and viable. The first time a school ever failed was Armagh College. It ran for three years, but it ran into a series of unfortunate events which caused the school to close, leaving the debt with NICIE and just after I left there was an agreement made with the three banks to address the deficit in order to ensure that NICIE didn't have to go into liquidation. All the other 18 new build schools proved that they were viable and in three years the Department then paid the capital back. The bank got its money, and the school was transferred to the Board of Governors and NICIE was no longer responsible. So there was a three year rolling programme, and each of the schools in their three or sometimes four years showed that they achieved the numbers that the Department required.

Parental passion

I can tell you this was parental involvement and passion. Some Lagan College parents mortgaged their houses to get Lagan College off the ground. When it came to these newer schools, parents were out three, four, five nights a week. Some parents were taking abuse. Some of the schools we opened, for example, Drumragh College and Omagh opened in an old mental hospital and the children got abuse because of the school they went to. When Rowallane, which became Blackwater, was created, we used the old hospital site at Belvoir. We put mobiles on top of hockey pitches down in Dungannon while we were building a new primary school. I can remember one case where basically I bought a site by putting a bid in an envelope and handing it in without having an access road. Eventually we had to pay three quarters of a million for an access road. That was at Malone College. I remember putting the bid in on the day not knowing who else I was going up against. Putting a sealed bid in to get the site and if we didn't have the site we wouldn't have a school. Lawrence can tell about the number of times we came into the office and said we had a problem, the planners were saying this. We had Millenium IPS closed down for a weekend because a minister was going along and his car got held up when parents' cars were turning in right across the road. He was told by his civil servants that the delay was caused by a new integrated school and he went and checked the planning permission. NICIE had an agreement with the planners to open without official approval for a few weeks until the required roadworks were completed to allow us to access the school. Because the formal planning wasn't through, the Minister requested that the school be closed. I got a phone call from the BBC saying, 'What do you think about the school being closed?' I knew nothing about it. So we had to go and see the Chief Planning Officer and say, 'What's going on here? How do we get this sorted?' and we had the school open on Monday again.

Parent involvement

There were really, really difficult times. But the parents put so much trust in NICIE, because they just said, 'You've done it before.' During this period the growth was iterative in that the parents said, 'This can be done and we'll do it.' And some of those parents then were able to come along and talk to the new parent groups. The NICIE Development Officers were out helping in the snow and the rain, saying, 'This can be done.' They were out helping parents set up the limited company, they were filling the forms in, they were showing them how to hold governor meetings, doing the training for people who had never been on a board before. This was a huge task, you think of the number of people, 39 new schools during my time and every one of those schools had 16 on their Board of Governors. You multiply that by 39 and think how many people were then being responsible for the governance of shared projects. That's not talked about anywhere in peace-building.

Parental motivation

The parents were involved for different reasons, because there isn't one reason. I would love to tell you it was because everybody wanted love to break out. For some people it was they genuinely believed in integration and for others it was because they didn't like the grammar system and they wanted an all ability choice. For some it was they wanted a really strong Christian ethos to a school. For others they felt that they wanted to be involved in really delivering something for their local community and there wasn't a community school, but all of them I don't think realised how much hassle they would get to do this. Yet the fall off rate was very small. Some of these people had never worked with another tradition before and then they had to sit and think about the name of their school, or what their school badge was going to be.

Some of these decisions were highly contentious, because what do you call it? Is it orange or green? Are you going to have a crown on it or are you not? What are the entry criteria to the school? First child in the family? A lot of the parents had never had any experience of this before. For the first time they got involved in a project where they managed something. They had to interview for head teachers. They were running budgets in schools and they'd never done it before. The thing that bound them together, I think, was they thought they were part of a something that was making a real difference and a real change. I have no doubt of that, but whether that was what drove them, I don't know. I know for some it did, but I can't tell you that's what kept them at it once they were there.

GMI schools and transformed schools

The literature seems to say that it's easier to develop a new school than change an existing school. Certainly, my experience would be that it's easier to develop a new ethos than change an existing one. Transformation is much harder. Parents would rather set up a new school. I think it's easier in terms of the long term plan. Rather than change something that's been going for a long time with all the inbuilt perceptions. If you take the GMI schools, when they came to NICIE there was training done initially and the training included addressing integration in theory as well as practice. I am sure that All Children Together (ACT) never had a developed idea of pedagogy. They implicitly felt that if children are together for most of the school day something positive in terms of relationships was going to happen. They never had a concept of what we would now talk about as an integrated, shared ethos. ACT wanted it to be based on a Christian principle and the reasons for that were very simple. First, they never thought the Catholic church would accept any integrated school which wasn't faith based. And secondly, they also themselves came from a faith based background and felt that when you had faith within the centre of a school, not an attempt at evangelism, but if faith was within the centre of the school, as it's been forever in Northern Ireland, that that was the type of school that they wanted. In short, they didn't want secular schools. So there was a personal commitment to a Christian ethos and a clear view that they didn't want a secular system.

Ethos issues

The all ability issue was clear in the early days because it was core to the creation of both Lagan and Hazelwood. Primary schools are all ability, so it was never an issue for the primary but for the post-primary it was. But Hazelwood and Lagan wanted to get the schools established as clearly all ability in the early days, and although that was important, the most important thing if you talk to those people was the Protestant and Catholic sharing classes. The pedagogy and how you develop curriculum and how the school operates was something that happened as the school grew. When NICIE then began to grow, when a new school came in, you could say, 'Well, all integrated schools sign up to the NICIE Statement of Principles, which are essentially Christian in character.' They promote a Christian rather than a secular view of education and when a school signed up that was its working premise. My research, which just finished a few years ago, was actually saying there isn't one all defining ethos, there are 65 because every school is different. I think my experience and theirs was you'd have a Board of Governors, who were setting up a new school and they had this vision of Protestants and Catholics and an all ability context and there was faith in the school. I don't think anybody ever sat down to say, 'I wonder what that will look like.' They agreed on the overall presentation or look of the school because part of the ethos is in the feel when you walk in. For example, you see 'Welcome'

in 25 languages, or Irish signage or even the fact that there's a cross and a crucifix or a statue of Mary. A lot of schools give a lot of thought to the visual image of the school. There's no doubt that they also thought about how the school does extra-curricular activities. All that was part of the ethos, if you like, there was a visible ethos. There were certain things that the head teacher and governors would've said that they would do on certain days they might mark. They might get certain people in from the outside. Some schools, for example, chose not to bring Protestant ministers in because the Catholic priests wouldn't come into the schools. Others decided, 'Well, it's the Catholic Church's loss,' and they would have brought Protestant ministers in to do assembly. So there was a pick and mix approach. Most of it was down to the Principal. Most people tend to think that the Board of Governors drives the ethos. Maybe in the early days, but my experience has been it was the Principal. If the Principal was in good standing with the Chair of the Board of Governors, and he or she brought reports to the Board of Governors, they were content. The ethos then developed in classrooms with teachers. In other words, it was this mediated, waterfall type of effect and I'm sure a lot of Principals didn't really know how teachers did what they did in the classroom.

Ethos issues in transformation

Terry McMackin was brought into Brownlow as a Catholic teacher when Brownlow transformed to integrated status. Terry later joined NICIE and took on the responsibility of being an Ethos Officer. So there was active involvement on NICIE's part and then this developed later when Roisin came in 2005 to do the Integrating Education Programme funded by the International Fund for Ireland (IFI). Part of the programme was definitely around the question of, 'What does an integrated ethos look like?' I think this debate around ethos has been a long standing one. My own experience was that all the schools have probably shared values and they would be about being child centred. They would be about parental choice, they would be about parental involvement. They would be around democracy. They would be around encouraging difference, challenging prejudice. They were value-led and then those values were embedded in the school. Some schools like Hazelwood had the teachers on first name terms. Others didn't. In some schools like Parkhall the teachers wore robes at prize giving and some didn't. Since then, some schools have started to do partial selection. Lagan and Slemish now select a certain amount of their children through academic ability which sets aside the all ability issue and that in my time caused an issue. A lot of people from the early integrated schools said this isn't what integration was about. The argument made for partial selection was that we'd no control over the ability intake unless we select a certain percentage based on academic ability. I believe some of this was driven by local competition. Slemish, for example, as Ballymena is a hugely grammar influenced catchment. I think part of why Slemish chose to go down the partial selection route was to compete with the grammar schools. This is about autonomy.

Governance and transformation

In the controlled integrated schools there was a big issue about how the school changes. The governing body was reduced in the number of people from churches from four to two, and that was a big issue for the churches. But a lot were happier for a controlled integrated school to happen than a new grant maintained school to jump up. Certainly, the Unionist community and Unionist politicians would have been much happier with transformation than grant maintained schools. In other words, they didn't feel they had 'lost' the school.

Before my time there were schools such as Forge and All Children's which were set up as controlled integrated schools. In my mind they were like grant maintained schools in their ethos. They decided that to draw their money and their support from the Education and Library Board was better. Since my time there were something like 20 controlled schools that transformed. During that time the Department decided to develop a transformation template. They decided to have targets for transformation and to fund transformation,

in other words, fund additional teachers coming in. This was partly because you had so many new grant maintained schools coming. It was costing money and then you had the existing schools going, 'Here's competition. Why do we need this other school in our area?' During the early days when the five came forward in 1995, we didn't really have to go into local schools in any serious way and ask schools in the local community, 'Do you want to change to integrated status?' There was no written or agreed protocol. But once there were another five or six new schools, the Department and ourselves got into a much more formal way of operating. We would then formally have to consult with existing schools and allow them to consider whether they would transform to integrated status before we could come up with a development proposal for a new school. So there was a phased approach for transformation. Brian Mawhinney had thought integration would all happen mostly through transformation. He thought it would happen for Catholic schools as well as state schools and he hoped that through organic transformation Northern Ireland would become an integrated school system. But he allowed grant maintained schools to be set up because in Britain at the time there were grant maintained schools under the Conservative government. He said, 'Well, let's take that model and bring it over to Northern Ireland, just in case.' He never expected that there would be so much growth in grant maintained schools and so little pick up of transformation.

Transformation grows

The question is then why there was the pick-up in transformation? Why did it happen? I have no doubt it was partly because the drive of new integrated schools. It was the awareness that there was money available. There were schools which were afraid that they might close. People have the idea that only failed schools transformed and that's not true. A lot of our transforming schools were vibrant schools like Glengormley or Cave Hill, schools that didn't need to integrate because they were failing. I also think there was the threat that if we don't do it there would be a grant maintained school. I'm sure that was there as well for a lot of them. The fact that the Education Board themselves also felt transformation was a better way. There was a tipping point coming. There was this real drive of grant maintained schools and then suddenly there was this decision from the Department, you need to do this more. You need to be looking more at existing schools because the birth rates had dropped and we began to get a system where there were 20-30,000 spare places. The issue was, here's a new school opening with 60 children and here are two existing schools with hundreds of spare places and that doesn't make sense. Our argument was that those weren't integrated places. And the Board's argument was, 'Well, maybe we should try to integrate.'

Very early on the Catholic Church said, 'If a Catholic school decides to integrate on the model of controlled schools, it can't, because that option doesn't exist.' So for a Catholic school to transform, it must become a grant maintained school. That's the only option. Then Council for Catholic Maintained Schools (CCMS) would go and open a new Catholic school. That's what they said to me and that's what they have on record. They have the duty to provide schools in each parish so that if a Catholic school chooses integration, bless it, but that's no longer a Catholic school, so they have to provide for Catholic education and open another school. So the idea that a Catholic school can't transform isn't true, they can transform.

Before my time there was Stella Maris, a school in North Belfast and the Catholic Church closed it in the end, though there were sufficient parents wanting to transform. Since my time there have been several Catholic schools that have actually said they would like to transform to integrated, but none of them has. They wouldn't have been encouraged by the Catholic Church or CCMS to transform because they would effectively be leaving the fold.

Other Options

From 2001 I argued to consider shared church schools. This isn't a new thing, it's been around for a long time. We took a group from CCMS and from the Transferors' Council to Britain and we looked at a couple of those shared campuses. In the end the Catholic Church said they had schools but the Protestant churches didn't, so there wasn't equivalence. 'We don't have a trade, you don't have a school to come to us to become a joint church school.' We said, 'Why don't you set one up?' but the churches never rose to the challenge. I think this was hugely unfortunate because I think there was an opportunity where you could have said you don't give up your Catholicity. The other option would've been to look at a hybrid model, the same as a controlled integrated school. CCMS just basically said that was like saying you can make a circle a square. The hybrid model doesn't exist but I just think consideration could and should have been given to it. I think always at the back of this was what would be the driving force for Catholic parents to change their existing school when the way ahead was so hard. They got really well supported and then suddenly they might have to leave and become a grant maintained school. That would be a different thing to do than a group of parents within a controlled school, simply changing the name over the door. The school is still there, it's still receiving its funding, the head teacher is still there. The school is still called whatever it's called.

Experiences of transformation

When Glengormley transformed to integrated status, there was a real feeling in that group and in the North Eastern Education and Library Board that this was a school serving a community and that it could attract Catholics because of where it sat. It could serve the local community and really grow a good integrated school. That's been proved correct because they have a fantastic Principal. The school is turning children away. That was through a transformation process where they talked with us at every decision. We worked with them and it was a shared project and co-delivered. Other examples occurred where there wasn't so much thought at the start of the process or we weren't involved as NICIE and the Board decided they'd run with the project. These tended to be less successful. I think when people think it through and plan it and they work through NICIE and the Board and the parents, it is possible. In a planned process parents are brought along. Parents have a vote for transformation but not just dropped out of the air, they are brought through a process. The interesting thing for transformation is that a teachers' vote isn't necessary, which seems to me bizarre. In addition, the children are never consulted. It is suggested that they should be consulted but most schools don't. So it's a parents' vote. But parents are only there for seven years, and that group of parents could say we should transform the school for the next 50. That doesn't sound like democracy to me. So there is something about planning integration which has never happened. We've never been able to plan for integrated schools. It's always been a random thing depending on the Board, depending on parents. NICIE was always in the middle trying to react to things and even when we came forward with proactivity and said we wanted 10% in 10 years and the Integrated Education Fund (IEF) came in with money and we had 35 staff at one time, people working in Westminster. We had real targets. We were driving this. We had advertising campaigns but that didn't create the 10%. I think since I left in 2009 there have only been three new integrated schools.

Motivation

If I think of Glengormley there is no doubt in those early discussions on the Board with the Board of Governors, they looked at the options, so this was really considered and thought through. This was a considered development proposal. For every one of those really planned and worked through there was another one where the Principal decided. We had a couple where it was the Principal's own idea. I don't buy, 'Let's just integrate at any cost.' I am quite happy that people share classrooms absolutely, but if that sharing isn't safe and isn't facilitated, it can be more damaging to peace. I've seen projects that damage people. This notion that somehow all you do is get children in a classroom and magic happens is nonsense, because that sometimes re-enforces stereotypes. If the teachers aren't trained this can be very difficult.

Shared Education

Shared schools was a very big project from IFI and Atlantic Philanthropies that tried to support Shared Education to develop. I saw some of the proposals coming forward and as a board we sent some back and said, 'You've got to think this through.' For example, we wanted to know, 'Where was the teacher training?' Whether or not the Board of Governors was involved, was the project a sensible one and was the contact good and enduring? You know you're saying that your two schools are coming together and going to teach English together. The children are going to be together for 10 classroom hours in three weeks. You need to ask the questions. What are you achieving in this? That's an output, what's the outcome? What is the change? What is the attitudinal change? What does success look like for you? I think that sometimes a badly managed project is worse than no project. I believe that there's something happening when children get together, because children are children, but if their differences aren't explored in a safe way, if a teacher isn't available to try to help that process, if prejudice isn't challenged, if you're not actively encouraging and talking about hard things, children very soon get to understand what the process is. If it is simply something like Education for Mutual Understanding, where they go to a zoo or a museum together, where the teachers stand either side talking to their own, such examples need to be challenged. We've seen this happen so I accept that people sometimes start a journey with less than noble intentions, but somewhere along the way they catch the virus, that's great. I think if people just say, 'Well, wouldn't it be a good idea to integrate the school?' and they don't really consider what that means in terms of training for governors and teachers, how you test it, how you measure it, how you evaluate it, I think it can damage. Therefore, the idea of sharing in schools, just saying, 'We've a school with 10% of the other tradition.' What does that mean?

The future of transformation

I don't disagree that transformation is now the only way to grow integration. But why would people want to transform is the question. What's in it for them ultimately? Well, it's also about money. When I left NICIE I became a freelance consultant and I did quite a lot of evaluations of projects and the number of projects that I did which were pilots that were working and then finished after three years. There is so much good practice out there that's been funded by organisations like Atlantic Philanthropies, the American Ireland Fund, IFI, Community Relations Council and somehow we do it for three years and then it goes. You're thinking, 'How many of these pilots do we have to do before we mainstream?' We actually know good practice. I think there is plenty of evidence of it. And I would've thought, 'Why don't we incentivise it, and dis-incentivise separation?' I've talked about this before. If all of our state schools were shared schools, I would love that, but I don't think it's ever going to happen.

An historical view

A shared school and an integrated school aren't necessarily different. Back in 1921, Lord Londonderry wanted to have shared schools here and the politicians and the churches said,'No.' Lord Londonderry hadn't this grand plan about what it would look like but he thought if people shared the same schools that somehow we might learn how to live together and I think that was a noble aspiration.

In 1974 when we had a power sharing executive Basil McIvor, the Minister for Education, said he wanted shared education and the Executive fell before it could be brought through. It took parents to set up Lagan College, mortgaging their houses to embarrass the government into doing something. There's always been a drive for people who want to be together. 65% of people in surveys said, 'We'd love shared schools.' Why do only 10% do something about it? It's no different when you ask somebody, 'Would you like to have a shared workplace?' and they say, 'Yes,' but how many will actually do something? I've always argued that this 5 or 10% of people who will put their head up and take the decision and really move something in the early stages, those are the pioneers. What happens is, once it's set up and the experiment works, people come and join so people in Northern Ireland like to see and touch something like we are on at the minute. Many people have a real investment in grammar schools because they don't think you get as good an education in a non-grammar.

The Catholic Church about 12 years ago looked at the system and decided to offer, grammar and non-grammar on the same site. Children will move between them and now so many of the grammar schools in the Catholic side are no longer grammar. This is over a 12-15 year project, and they've actually demonstrated that it works. 65 integrated schools' parents can now look and say this stuff works. So the question is, 'Why isn't there a demand?' Because there isn't a proactive government policy to plan for integrated schools. But left to people's own desire, left to parental demand where there's no real pressure, well, there's no monetary benefit for transformation.

Balance

Some schools still struggle with balance and I'm thinking radically in this. The majority community may be Other, rather than Protestant or Catholic and if they're not more than 70%, why not? I think rules are there to be challenged, I mean, we changed rules. We lobbied Martin McGuinness when it used to be you needed 100 children to start a post-primary school and he dropped it to 60 and then 50. Now people argued he did it cynically because of Irish Medium schools. I was with him and I don't think he did. I think he recognised the fact that peace building needed to have a good start, a running start. That drop allowed a number of our schools to get over that benchmark. I think Ulidia had to make five applications before it was agreed by the Department of Education, because they kept saying, 'You're not going to get Catholics.' The IEF funded Ulidia for years. Teachers stepped out of the system where there are pensions, weren't paid to take up posts in Blackwater and Ulidia. They were independent schools, the

Inspectorate had to go in to give them an inspection number and accept them as an independent school in Northern Ireland before the Department approved them. And Dungannon Integrated College, I think, applied three times. That's the drive and energy that these parents said, 'We'll not be put down.' and now Ulidia does take its 30% Catholics in. Despite the accusation that we're bussing Catholics in, that's what I used to get. 'These aren't real community schools, you're bussing children in.' How many grammar schools simply fill up from local communities? This is a nonsense.

The boom years

It surprises me that since I left in 2009 there have only been three new schools. I had probably thought there would be one a year if I'm being honest. When I look back I wonder, 'How on earth did we grow from 23 up to 62, how come?' There was a ceasefire, the Good Friday Agreement, peace broke out but it was also a period when parental demand was challenged by 80,000 spare places in the system. I genuinely didn't think there's commitment from government. So if 60%+ want shared schools and only 8% are in shared schools, there is a mismatch. If there was a demand for a product from 65% of people and their market share was 8% you'd be firing the Chief Executive, right? Now, who is the Chief Executive? It's the Executive in Stormont. It's not Roisin, it's not the heads of the other bodies. It needs to be incentivised. If you're saying that a child brings with it 100% of grant aid, maybe in a shared school a child should have 105%.

Associate integrated status

When the Integrating Education Programme moved to the North Eastern Board, I can remember the first time taking the NICIE Chair of Directors down to Sion Mills Primary School. Sion Mills is an old school that was set up for a community that worked in the mills, and it was a Protestant controlled school. They really wanted to embrace integration but it could never become a controlled integrated school because

there wouldn't have been support for it locally. Sion Mills became the first associate integrated school, because they were integrated but it was only pragmatism that meant they couldn't change their name. I began to develop in my head this notion of Integrated Education as a product. If it's a product that happens in this specific type of school, surely you don't need to have a formally integrated school to take this product on. So what would an existing school need in order to take this product on? With Nichola Lynagh we looked at this in terms of you had a shared curriculum going and you had sharing with other schools going. So, if a school had a shared curriculum and it shared with other schools, you could be moving over to effectively running an integrated curriculum. If they had training from NICIE to develop sharing in the classroom, if they learnt how to deal with hard subjects, if the Boards of Governors were trained. If they actively encouraged sharing and celebrating difference, I think you could effectively help a school steward a shared and integrated ethos and in an integrated curriculum. I think it's eminently possible.

Integrating Education

The transformation process is very tedious, we were saying this from 2005. We were looking at the notion of how we actually let the integrated virus affect people: surely those principles that integrated schools have shown to work could be transferred to another place? If the 'product', in other words, was able to be stewarded in the same environment, in another school. That for me, and I don't care what they call the school, as long as what was happening was those children were having the experience. And I think that's possible.

I think NICIE was getting down that route just before I left in terms of some of the stuff that we were doing and the Integrating Education Programme was absolutely that. Roisin moved up to the North Eastern Board with the project and ran it with 60 or 70 schools, none of which were integrated. She was really working to try to develop an integrated ethos in those schools and there was a very good evaluation of it carried out at the end of the programme. I do think that

Rowandale IPS

there is the potential in the Shared Education programme if they really embrace all the values and the principles and the methodologies. I think that they can make a huge difference. That way you can extend and the fear I have is that some people think there is a gold standard that can only be achieved by integrated schools. And then there's silver and there's bronze. You're bronze but we want you to come to gold. I think that's arrogant and it's a question of form and function. If we're so elevating the form that we're losing the function. I'm more focused on the function. In other words, the stuff that happens. I still think things can happen. I'm convinced things can happen.

Conclusion

I was 15 years director of a movement, as I would always have called it, which brought together people right across Northern Ireland who actually wanted to make a real difference. The thing that I constantly referred to during that time was TS Eliot, a poem called 'Journey of the Magi'. It was the Wise Men and at one point before they moved to follow the star, they said, 'I am no longer at ease in this dispensation.' In other words: it's got to be better than this. I think the thing that drove those parents, and the people that I worked with in that 15 years was that: it's got to be better than this. It was the notion of the journey, and I think the journey's not over yet. I think that on the journey we're with different fellow travellers than maybe we were 10 years ago. That might be a wake-up call because I think that what we're believing in hasn't changed, but how we might deliver it, I think, has.

A history in pictues...

01. Lagan IC (1981)

02. Forge CIPS (1985)

03. Hazelwood IC (1985)

04. Hazelwood IPS (1985)

05. All Children's CIPS (1986)

06. Bridge IPS (1987)

07. Mill Strand IPS (1987)

08. Windmill IPS (1988)

09. Braidside IPS (1989)

10. Enniskillen IPS (1989)

11. Omagh IPS (1990)

12. Portadown IPS (1990)

13. Brownlow CIC (1991)

14. Carhill CIPS (1991)

15. Corran IPS (1991)

16. Oakgrove IPS (1991)

A history in pictues...

17. Acorn IPS (1992)

18. Oakgrove IC (1992)

19. Cranmore IPS (1993)

20. Lough View IPS (1993)

21. Saints and Scholars IPS (1993)

22. Erne IC (1994)

23. Shimna IC (1994)

24. Cedar IPS (1995)

25. Drumragh IC (1995)

26. IC Dungannon (1995)

27. New-Bridge IC (1995)

28. Portaferry CIPS (1995)

29. North Coast IC (1996)

30. Oakwood IPS (1996)

31. Six Mile CIPS (1996)

32. Slemish IC (1996)

A history in pictues...

33. Annsborough CIPS (1997)

34. Malone IC (1997)

35. Strangford IC (1997)

36. Ulidia IC (1997)

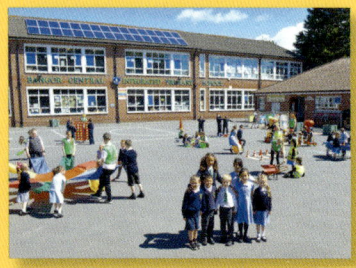

37. Bangor Central CIPS (1998)

38. Fort Hill CIC (1998)

39. Kilbroney CIPS (1998)

40. Kircubbin CIPS (1998)

41. Priory CIC (1998)

42. Spires IPS (1999)

43. Millennium IPS (2000)

44. Carnlough CIPS (2001)

45. Sperrin IC (2002)

46. Glengormley CIPS (2003)

47. Maine IPS (2003)

48. Round Tower CIPS (2003)

A history in pictues...

49. Drumlins IPS (2004)

50. Glencraig CIPS (2004)

51. Phoenix IPS (2004)

52. Roe Valley IPS (2004)

53. Groarty CIPS (2005)

54. Ballycastle CIPS (2006)

55. Crumlin CIC (2006)

56. Rowandale IPS (2007)

57. Blackwater IC (2008)

58. Cliftonville CIPS (2008)

59. Ballymoney CIPS (2009)

60. Crumlin IPS (2009)

61. Fort Hill CIPS (2009)

62. Parkhall CIC (2009)

63. Mallusk IPS (2016)

64. Loughries IPS (2016)

65. Killyleagh IPS (2016)